More praise for *The Sweater Letter:*

"This one has it all. It's just a great story!" **Bill Flood, Producer, Court TV's *Forensic Files***

"*The Sweater Letter* is a solid, suspenseful true-crime chronicle that shows not only sensitivity toward the survivors of a cruel, cynical murder but also deep affection for the brave and stubborn people who hang on to the wild beauty of the Upper Peninsula of Michigan." **Henry Kisor, author of *Season's Revenge***

"Reporter unravels compelling tale in *Sweater Letter*! Hard to put aside!" ***Oakland Press***

"Great book! Riveting! You're not going to believe some of the twists and turns!" **Natalie Hurst, News Anchor, WFRV-TV, Green Bay, Wisconsin**

"The story unfolds with one bizarre twist after another. Dave and Lynn Distel have done a thorough job of researching the story and a fine job of following the torturous trail." ***Traverse City Record-Eagle***

"For those of you who find reading nonfiction to be dull, you may change your mind after reading *The Sweater Letter*. It was a book I simply could not put down." **Joe Carlson, Ironwood Carnegie Library**

"*The Sweater Letter* has sure caused many people to get reacquainted with their bookmarkers and reading lamps. For someone who can barely find time to read a stop sign, let alone a book, I found it totally fascinating and intriguing. I too could not put the book down." **Sandra Baker,** *Lake Superior Voice*

"Great reading, great writing! You captured the town and people perfectly. A must for murder mystery fans of all stripe" **Dr. Bruce Nelson Stratton, Quality Broadcasting, Corpus Christi, Texas**

"This book is going to be in my library forever!" **Joe Scheibinger, KFIZ, Fond du Lac, Wisconsin**

The Sweater Letter

The Sweater Letter

By DAVE DISTEL
With Lynn Distel

Writers Club Press
New York Lincoln Shanghai

The Sweater Letter

Writers Club Press
an imprint of iUniverse, Inc.

For information address:
iUniverse, Inc.
2021 Pine Lake Road, Suite 100
Lincoln, NE 68512
www.iuniverse.com

ISBN: 0-595-25933-2 (pbk)
ISBN: 0-595-65446-0 (cloth)

Printed in the United States of America

Contents

Acknowledgements

Many thanks to Bob Ball, whose memory was as meticulous as his investigation, and Beth Paczesny, whose enthusiasm for the book project matched the energy she exuded in prosecuting the case. Thanks to David Blake and Lee Anne Wysocki for their insightful and empathetic recollections of Judy Blake Moilanen as well as their equally insightful though far less empathetic recollections of Bruce Moilanen. Thanks also to former Ontonagon County sheriff Jerry Kitzman for his indispensable input. And further thanks to dozens of others who provided a tidbit here and a tidbit there that helped bring the manuscript to life.

1

A Walk in the Woods

Streak, a happy-go-lucky Springer spaniel, had returned alone to the Blake home after going for a walk in the woods along Cherry Lane. However, he had not gone by himself. He had gone with four other Springer spaniels.

And he had gone with Judy Blake Moilanen.

None of the other dogs returned. Nor did Judy Moilanen.

Mary Ann Blake, Judy's mother, was not alarmed when she saw the dog loping across the clearing. Judy, after all, had to handle all five dogs on their walk in the woods. And this was not one of those citified places where owners had to have their pets on a leash and clean up after them. The dogs cavorted freely when they walked in the woods along Cherry Lane. So what if Streak was back early with his tail wagging in search of approval.

Judy had gone down a wooded trail behind the Blake house on Highway 38, a mile east of Ontonagon, Michigan. The date was Nov. 29, 1992, the Sunday of Thanksgiving weekend, and the ground was only sparsely covered with snow. The trail was familiar because these woods had been a playground to Judy when she was a child.

People also hunted there…and Nov. 30 was the final day in Michigan's firearm deer season.

Mary Ann did not know exactly when her daughter had headed for the woods. She had some bookwork to do after a lunch of turkey casserole, a typical fare for the Sunday of Thanksgiving weekend. Judy, typically for any weekend, volunteered to clean up after lunch.

"You just go to work on your books," Judy told her mother. "I'll wash dishes and then take the dogs for a walk. I'll do some mending for you when I get back."

It was now, finally, relatively quiet in the house.

Judy's younger brother Jerry had been late for lunch. He had hunted until noon before returning to the family home. By the time he got there, the others were finished eating. He put his hunting gear away, grabbed a plate of casserole, visited briefly with Judy and then went down to the basement to take a sauna. He got into the sauna at 1:15 and came back upstairs at 1:30. He did not realize that time would later become important.

Mary Ann came out of the office a little later and Jerry's family was packing for their trip home to Shawano, Wis., 3½ hours almost directly south.

Ontonagon is located in a part of Michigan's Upper Peninsula that, geographically speaking, should almost be part of Wisconsin. It is on Lake Superior, where U.S. 45 dead-ends after a journey from the Gulf of Mexico. U.S. 45 runs through the heart of Wisconsin and Jerry and his family would take that highway most of the way home.

Mary Ann could see that her son was ready to hit the highway.

"Where's Judy?" she asked.

"Walking the dogs, I guess," Jerry said. "She was here when I got into the sauna and gone when I got out."

"She probably wanted to go so she could get back in time to say good-bye," Mary Ann said.

Jerry and his family were getting into the car when Streak came home.

"Here comes one of the dogs," Jerry said.

"Maybe Judy's right behind him," said Anna, Jerry's wife.

She was not…nor were any of the other dogs.

"Well," Mary Ann sighed, "Streak's here and Judy's not. I suppose she's going to be looking all over for him."

Mary Ann later remembered very clearly that it was 2:15 p.m. Mothers remember these things. They remember when children leave because they set their mental clocks forward to when the call should be coming to tell them everyone was home safely. Jerry was anxious to leave for home because he had to teach the next morning.

Mary Ann's mental clock was not set on when Judy should return. Streak's presence did not disturb her because Streak belonged to her and Dale, her husband and Judy's father. Streak was not as disciplined as the four Moilanen dogs. The Moilanens ran Big Creek Kennels near Marquette and Bruce, Judy's husband, was a domineering taskmaster when it came to the dogs. He would snap and they would bark...or sit or heel or roll over.

Streak was lucky. He had the run of the woods around Ontonagon rather than the discipline of Bruce Moilanen's kennels two hours east in Harvey, a community near Marquette.

Bruce Moilanen, unfortunately, was not as disciplined as his dogs. He could not handle financial affairs, he could not handle jobs and he could not handle personal affairs. He could handle guns, and hunting was his agenda for the day.

◆   ◆   ◆

Jerry Blake had been gone two hours, which was too early for his mother to be worrying about the telephone not ringing. However, she was worried about Judy, who had not returned from walking the dogs. The weather was not harsh, not nearly as harsh as it gets in Michigan's Upper Peninsula, but it was a little cold to be out comfortably for so long. There was no way Judy would leave with the dogs before 1:30 and still be gone at 4.

Mary Ann had been busying herself putting up the Nativity set with Elise, Judy's toddler daughter. Grandma Niemi was watching her daughter and great-granddaughter and also glancing nervously at her watch. Her granddaughter seemed a bit overdue, to say the least.

"Mary Ann," she said, "don't you think Judy's been gone an awful long time?"

"When she trains her dogs," Mary Ann said, "sometimes it takes a long time."

"Did she say anything about *training* the dogs?" Grandma Niemi asked.

Mary Ann did not answer the question. She looked out the back window to see if she could see her daughter coming. No, she thought, Judy had not said anything about training the dogs, just going for a walk with them. Her principal fear was that Judy was out somewhere in the woods looking for Streak. She did not think her daughter was lost, because Judy was so familiar with the snowmobile tracks and hiking trails in the woods beyond Cherry Lane toward the old Nieminen farm. However, she knew Judy would be very reticent to return without all of the dogs in tow.

Only one person could search for Judy and tell her Streak was safe. That one person was Mary Ann. She did not know those woods and trails as well as the younger generation, but she made up for that with a hardy and tenacious resolve. She set out, taking her short, choppy steps, to do what she had to do.

Bill Dorvinen, a neighbor who lived across a clearing from the Blakes on Cherry Lane, had just returned from spending the day with his daughter. He noticed Mary Ann Blake and thought she was a little out of her element. He glanced at his watch and it was 4:20. Dusk was gathering and she was headed away from her home toward the woods.

"Isn't it a little late for a walk?" he asked good-naturedly.

"I have to try to find Judy," she said. "She went to walk the dogs a long time ago. Streak came home but Judy didn't and I'm afraid she's looking for him."

"You want me to come with you?" Dorvinen asked.

"No, I'll be fine," Mary Ann said. "I'll come back and get you if I need you."

Mary Ann continued into the woods behind a row of widely spaced houses along Cherry Lane, which intersects with M-38 and runs south through the woods to an eventual dead-end. She knew of a snowmobile trail that began just beyond Dale Brookins' place. She entered the deeper woods past the Brookins' and followed the trail until it hit a depression where an old sandpit had been. It was half puddle and half pond.

When she blew the dog whistle she had brought, all the dogs came running. She went in the direction they had come from and called Judy's name. No answer. She backtracked and called some more. Still no answer.

With the gathering darkness, Mary Ann started to get confused. It was time to ask for Bill Dorvinen's help. She returned to her house, put the dogs in the kennel and then walked across the clearing.

It was 4:50.

"Bill, I'd appreciate it if you *would* come with me," she said. "I'm afraid maybe she's fallen and broken her leg or something. Maybe she can't *get* home."

"Let me get my boots on and grab a flashlight," he said. "Maybe we should take one of the dogs with us. Maybe he can help."

Mary Ann did not even know which dog she took. It was one of the Moilanen dogs and they all looked alike to her. She could tell Streak, but only by his collar.

Once again they walked to the pond, the trail soggy from late rain and early snow. They were calling, but they were getting no response. Visibility, Dorvinen recalled later, was down to maybe 75 feet.

"She has to be around here," Mary Ann said. "This is about where I blew the whistle and the dogs all came quickly."

"Which direction you think?" Dorvinen asked.

"I angled to the right and she's not there," Mary Ann said, her soft voice shattered by nerves stretched like violin strings. "We've got to go the other way."

Together, Mary Ann Blake and Bill Dorvinen found Judy Blake Moilanen.

"Ohhhh," Dorvinen groaned. "There she is."

Judy was lying across the trail on her left side, her head on a little rise and her feet in an icy puddle of water. She was faced in their direction and she was not moving.

Dorvinen raced toward her with Mary Ann right behind him. He gently rolled Judy over onto her back, her arms flopping to the side. Blood covered her upper right chest. Mary Ann screamed. Dorvinen moved the body to get her feet out of the water, a gesture far more considerate and thoughtful than comforting.

Judy Moilanen, wife, mother, daughter and sister, had been shot to death in the woods she loved.

◆   ◆   ◆

Bill Dorvinen, like so many others in the U.P., had his roots in Finland. He was used to hard work and hard weather. He had never encountered what he was now encountering or feeling what he now felt. His thick lips were pursed in anger and anguish. His big, reassuring hands could not reassure the woman at his side as he moved with her away from that horrifying scene.

Mary Ann Blake was hysterical. Her body was wracked with sobs and her soft voice was wailing. The short walk would take forever and it would be over so quickly. She would hardly remember it and she would never forget it. She was a loving, sensitive woman who would have been upset had she come across an injured animal, but that was her only daughter she had found on that trail.

Dorvinen would have to be the one to call authorities. Alvah and Dale Brookins, father and son, lived in the first houses they would encounter on Cherry Lane as they came off the snowmobile trail. Dorvinen ducked into Alvah Brookins' house and called the sheriff's office.

"Yes," he trembled, "I'm sure she's dead."

And then he hastily called his daughter Susan at his house.

"Susan," he said, "Judy's been shot out in the woods."

What he heard at the other end of the line could hardly be described as words.

"She's dead, Susan," he said. "Get out in back and get Mary Ann into our house before she gets home."

Mary Ann was not going home. She had slowed down as she passed the Brookins houses, realizing that her mother and her granddaughter were the only people home. She knew she could not confront them. Susan found her both hysterical and bewildered. Wordlessly, Susan embraced her.

"I can't go home," Mary Ann cried. "I can't tell Mother and Elise. I can't go in. I can't."

Susan could not settle her down, nor could she comfort her. All she could give her were her arms and her heart. She did that.

Susan's father had a chore that was no less heart wrenching. He had to lead authorities to the body of Judy Blake Moilanen.

Dorvinen's call arrived at the Ontonagon County sheriff's office at 5:12 p.m. Deputy Tom Cousineau, who had worked the 9 to 5 shift, was on his way out the door to go home for supper. His evening was about to change very dramatically. A woman had been shot out near Cherry Lane.

Tom Cousineau was the only officer available.

The Ontonagon County sheriff's department was not exactly over-staffed. Twelve officers, including the sheriff himself, had to cover 1,321 square miles of what is essentially forested wilderness. The main highways, to use the description loosely, are lightly traveled two-lane roads on which automobiles are much more likely to run into deer than each other. The woods are also laced with gravel roads, plus 130 miles of groomed snowmobile trails.

Tom Cousineau would not be dealing with a groomed snowmobile trail.

Judy Moilanen's body had been found on what would best be described as a homemade trail. The neighbors had gathered to carve it out of the underbrush to give the children a place to play and a way to access the fields at the old Nieminen farm. It was hardly maintained, much less groomed.

Dorvinen and Dale Brookins met Cousineau and the three of them set out in what was now darkness. The ground was damp and covered with leaves and pine needles. Saplings and scraggly scrubs crowded the trail. Sometimes they could walk two or three abreast, but more often than not they walked single-file with Dorvinen in the lead. They passed the pond and went around a curve in the path and their flashlights caught the body as it sprawled across their path.

Brookins was sent back to await the arrival of the ambulance and Cousineau went to work shooting pictures and assessing the crime scene, which was a difficult chore given the pitch-blackness of the November night. Cousineau could not simply secure the scene and await the imminent arrival of homicide detectives, because the Ontonagon sheriff's department had no such specialists. Circumstances dictated that he do the investigation and, from the standpoint of police work, he would be on his own…at least until the state police were able to get an investigator to Ontonagon.

In these woods at this time of year, a homicide investigation might be nothing more than mere formality anyway. This was hunting season.

What *could* Cousineau do at this scene? He could not ascertain the direction of the bullet, much less determine the exact location of its origin. It could have come from anywhere in those woods and Judy might have been struck on her way out or on her way in and he could not have known when either of those times might have been. The notion that he might apprehend the person who pulled the trigger was absurd. This person was long gone…and might not even be aware of what his or her bullet had done.

"Do people hunt back here?" Cousineau asked.

"Hardly anybody hunts back here that I know of," Dorvinen said. "I never have."

"Why's that?" Cousineau said. "Too populous?"

"Not really too populous," Dorvinen said, "but eight or nine families live along Cherry Lane. It's a little too close to hunt safely."

Cousineau could only take his pictures and check the immediate area for clues. All he found were tracks. Lots of tracks congregated in the area around the body.

Dog tracks.

◆   ◆   ◆

Bill Burgess was not on duty. He was simply on call. He had retired from the paper mill after 35 years in May of 1992, but he was always on call for one thing or another. He was on call for injured souls as a deacon with the Episcopalian Church. He was on call as the medical examiner's investigator. He was on call as an emergency medical technician for Beacon Ambulance. He was on call as a district court officer. He was on call as a special deputy sheriff. A garrulous sort who had been in Ontonagon for 40 years, he was perfect for a village which did not have a need for experts in specific fields but rather enthusiasts with an interest in many fields.

On the evening of November 29, 1992, the gray-haired Burgess and partner Jack Miles would drive the ambulance in the unlikely event that such transportation would be needed.

He had just finished dinner when his beeper told him he was needed…for something. It was 5:20.

"You have to get to Dale Brookins' house," he was told. "There's been a hunting accident."

Burgess, being almost fanatically sincere, did not ask questions. He would simply do as he was told and get to the Brookins' house. He did not need the address. He knew Dale lived on Cherry Lane. Addresses were almost redundant in Ontonagon, at least to long time residents.

When it came to Brookins, he knew where David and Leroy lived. He knew Dale lived next to his father.

The only questions he asked were in his own mind. What had happened at Dale's house? Why did they need an ambulance? The Ontonagon Memorial Hospital was maybe a mile away. They could jump in the car and be at the hospital in less time than it would take him to get to the ambulance.

Why? What? Who?

Dale Brookins and Deputy Cousineau were coming out of the woods when he arrived.

"We have a fatality," Cousineau said.

Cousineau was being very calm, very professional. He had a job to do. Brookins, in contrast, was quite rattled.

"Judy's dead," Brookins said.

"Judy?" Burgess said.

"Judy Blake," said Brookins.

"Judy Blake?" said Burgess, *"Judy Moilanen? My God!"*

Brookins diverted the ambulance into a lane between the house and the woods, a lane that ultimately turned into the snowmobile trail. Cousineau's police car was already in the area, its lights blinking eerily on the edge of darkness. Burgess and Miles pulled the portable stretcher out of the ambulance and Brookins and the deputy led them into the woods.

Dorvinen was waiting there, but it was a painfully lonely scene. A lifeless young woman was on the ground with only flashlights for illumination and five helpless men surrounding her. Burgess noted the blood and checked in vain for vital signs, as both Dorvinen and Cousineau had done. He also noticed that *rigor mortis* was setting in and concluded Judy had been dead maybe 3½ to 4 hours. It was about 5:45.

Dorvinen was explaining, both to Cousineau and Burgess, that he had rolled the body over and pulled the feet out of the icy puddle.

Thus, the crime—or accident—scene was not exactly as he had found it. He described, however, how Judy had been lying.

Collectively, the men decided to remove the body and transport it to the morgue. The area was swampy and covered with wet leaves where it wasn't splotched with snow. They were not comfortable with the thought of leaving Judy Moilanen where she was lying.

"We just have to be sure we've marked the area," Burgess said.

"I know exactly where we are," Dorvinen said. "I'll never forget."

◆   ◆   ◆

Bob Ball, a detective with the Michigan State Police, also got a call that Sunday evening. His headquarters was an hour away from Ontonagon in Calumet and his home a little closer in Hancock, both towns on the Keweenaw Peninsula which juts like a gnarly finger into Lake Superior.

Ball put many miles on his car every year, because he was *the* guy when it came to heavy investigation in the Western U.P. Out of state police posts in Calumet, L'Anse and Wakefield, he had to cover Keweenaw, Baraga, Houghton, Gogebic and Ontonagon counties. That's all.

Here was a man with 21 years of experience with the state police whose bachelor's degree at Michigan Tech was, appropriately for the area, in forestry. He added an associates' degree in law enforcement at Macomb Community College in Warren, Mich., and successfully applied for the State Police Academy class that was graduated in spring of 1972.

All state policemen start as troopers and Ball began his career at the Romeo Post in Lower Michigan. He continued his education at virtually any seminar he could find, as he still does, and scored the highest grade in the state when troopers were tested for promotion to detective. He was promoted to detective sergeant in 1978, beginning that aspect of his career at the Flint Post with five other investigators of that rank.

When an opening occurred at the Calumet Post, not far from Michigan Tech, he volunteered for the assignment and got it in 1984. He was alone, the only detective assigned to what amounted to the western half of the Upper Peninsula.

The call to Ball came at 6:40 p.m. from central dispatch at the Calumet Post.

"We have a shooting in Ontonagon," the voice said. "Sheriff Tom Corda would like assistance."

"A homicide?" Ball asked.

"Don't know, but a woman's been shot."

"I'm on my way," Ball said.

He did not need to ask too many more questions. The State Police were called upon to investigate violent deaths that may or may not be crimes. It would be up to him to figure that out. The bottom line, in terms of Corda's request, was that this death was not cut and dried.

◆   ◆   ◆

Beth Paczesny, Ontonagon County's prosecuting attorney, was at home that Sunday evening when her telephone rang. It was early evening, hardly a foreboding time of day—or night—for the telephone to ring.

Dale Rantala, a sheriff's deputy, was on the line.

This was foreboding.

"We've got a dead body out on Cherry Lane," he said.

Paczesny felt a chill. Any dead body was bad news, but not too many of them around Ontonagon involve the prosecutor. She was unsettled.

"A suicide?" she asked.

It may have sounded like a presumptuous question, but it wasn't. Not in this neck of the woods. No one killed anyone…on purpose.

Suicide, while ugly unto itself, came in a neater package than the alternative.

On his end of the line, Rantala was shaking his head. Suicide did not seem likely.

"Don't think so," Rantala said. "No gun at the scene."

"A shooting?" she blurted.

Obviously. She knew it before she asked the question. The deputies would not otherwise have been looking for a gun. Could a homicidal maniac be on a rampage in this sleepy little village where people leave their keys in unlocked cars in unlocked garages next to unlocked homes? A locksmith, to be sure, would be on food stamps in Ontonagon.

Paczesny was concerned and a little bit frightened, though it quickly occurred to her that she was likely dealing with a hunting accident. Regardless, as she rushed out of the house, Paczesny hesitated and then did something uncharacteristic in Ontonagon. She locked the door.

Ontonagon County's prosecuting attorney since August of 1992, all of three months, Paczesny had been appointed to the position when her predecessor was suspended. Her background was less than extensive, but the $35,500 salary was hardly enough to attract a veteran lawyer from one of the big cities downstate.

Paczesny had gone to Grand Valley State University in Grand Rapids and Thomas M. Cooley Law School in Lansing. She wanted to be a prosecutor and she was not obsessed with big cities. She grew up in Central Lake in the northern part of the Lower Peninsula. To her, a city slicker was someone from Traverse City.

By the time she passed the Michigan bar exam, which she did on her first try, she was already employed as tribal counsel for the Lac Vieux Desert Band of the Chippewa Indians in Watersmeet. Folks in the Western U.P. go to Watersmeet, down by the Wisconsin border, for one reason…gambling.

Beth's office was in the bingo hall.

During her time in Watersmeet, she returned to her rented home to find a flurry of police activity at her next door neighbor's house. The cops were hauling money and guns out of the house.

"What's going on?" she asked.

"The guy was making methcathinone in the basement," she was told.

"Making what?"

"Chemicals…drugs," the trooper told her. "He had enough down there to blow up the whole block."

A "whole block" would pretty much encompass the whole town. That was the first time she had heard of methcathinone, but it would not be the last.

When the Ontonagon position opened, she wanted the job. She had been in Watersmeet only three months, but she wanted to be a prosecutor. Representing the Indians in affairs relating mainly to gambling did not fit into her dream.

Roy Gotham, Ontonagon County's Circuit Court judge, was the man who would make the appointment. Paczesny went to Ontonagon for an interview, but did not find Gotham very encouraging.

"Should I withdraw my name?" she asked.

"Be patient," he advised. "Hang in there and we'll see."

She got the appointment, but soon learned that the position was up for grabs in the November election. The Democratic Party contacted her about getting her name on the ballot.

"I'm really not a politician," she protested.

"You are now," she was told.

She ran unopposed and, naturally, won, retaining her status as the youngest prosecutor in the state and the only woman prosecutor in the U.P. She went out and bought a car.

The question, in Ontonagon, would be what in the world she would be prosecuting. Drugs had spread their tentacles into the area, but it seemed more likely she would be most occupied with drunk drivers and speeders. There were not even any stoplights to run, not one in the whole county.

Murders? She was told there had been one maybe eight to 10 years ago, but the accused had spared the nastiness of a trial by hanging himself in jail. The last trial, as near as anyone could recall, was probably 20 years ago…if then.

Surprisingly, on Nov. 29, 1992, Beth Paczesny was already preparing to try her first murder case. A 28-year-old Bruce Crossing man was accused of a beating death with gay overtones. Ontonagon County was going to have a murder trial, maybe its last for the next 20 years, and Paczesny would be the prosecutor.

Now she was on her way to Cherry Lane, where, in the blandly generic police parlance, a dead body had been found.

Beth Paczesny was 26 years old.

◆   ◆   ◆

Bob Ball was ill. The Thanksgiving weekend can be exacerbating for a person with the flu and this was a bad time of the year for the flu in the U.P. Ball had it and he was tempted on a couple of occasions to turn back and let the local deputies do the preliminary work.

Something drove him onward down M-26.

Sheriff Tom Corda, Prosecutor Beth Paczesny and Deputy Tom Cousineau awaited him at the Ontonagon County Sheriff's Department offices on Conglomerate Street. The building was a sprawling one-story structure in the middle of a residential neighborhood three blocks from River Street, the main drag. Its amenities, at least in terms of investigating crime, were basic. There was no crime lab and even Cousineau's film would have to be sent out for processing.

Cousineau would have to provide whatever briefing he could from his time at the scene as well as time spent at the Ontonagon Memorial Hospital with the family.

When Cousineau had arrived at the morgue, Dr. Steven Gervae, the deputy medical examiner for Ontonagon County, was already there. He had been called at home and advised that there had been a fatal accident and that the mother of the victim needed counseling and sedation.

"A hunting accident?" Gervae asked the caller.

"Probably."

That figured to be a reasonably safe assumption, though hardly a certainty. It had long been a "joke" in the Northwoods that the best time to get away with murder would be during the hunting season. It was up to Ball and Co. to determine if this was an instance when someone actually tried to disguise a murder as a hunting accident.

Gervae treated the hysterical Mary Ann at the Dorvinen house before going to the hospital to make the formal pronouncement that Judy Blake Moilanen was deceased. He would also make a preliminary assessment of the cause of death, though it hardly seemed necessary. It was quite obvious Judy had been shot.

Gervae unzipped Judy's black down jacket and pulled back her fuchsia shirt to examine the chest wound. Burgess helped him as he tilted the body and felt the wound behind the left armpit.

"We have a through and through gunshot," Gervae said. "One entry, in the chest, and one exit, behind the arm pit."

Gervae was finished in five minutes.

"Call the medical examiner," Gervae told Burgess, "and don't disturb the body in the meantime."

Burgess locked the morgue and went to call Dr. Hugo Castilla, the medical examiner for Ontonagon County. Castilla, who lived and worked 45 miles away in L'Anse, was a pathologist who had a private practice as well as his part-time, as-needed work for the county. He seemed in no rush to disrupt his Sunday evening with an autopsy in Ontonagon.

"Notify the state police," he told Burgess, "and secure the morgue. I'll be over tomorrow."

Castilla never said as much, but he too probably viewed the incident as a hunting accident. He might have been a little quicker to react if he thought he had a murder on his hands.

Burgess was at the sheriff's office typing his report when Ball arrived to convene with others to listen to Cousineau's briefing.

"Bob," Paczesny gasped, "you look like death warmed over."

"That bad, huh?" Ball said. "I feel as bad as I look. I almost turned around and went home at Toivola. I'll be okay. What do we have here?"

"Probably a hunting accident," someone said.

Ball learned that the body had already been moved from the scene along Cherry Lane to the morgue. He learned that no evidence had been uncovered in the vicinity of the body. What he learned was that the investigation was essentially about to begin.

"I don't want to upset the family right now," Ball said, "but there's one thing we have to know. It's standard operating procedure in a case like this."

"What's that?" the sheriff asked.

"We have to know where the husband was."

2

The Lost Bowl

Nothing nasty happens in Ontonagon, except for an occasional blizzard…in April. Banks aren't robbed, cars aren't stolen, homes aren't burglarized and people aren't murdered. The police blotter runs more to occasional missing bicycles or sleds, depending on the time of year.

On one occasion, a saloonkeeper called the village police early in the afternoon for help ejecting a disorderly customer on a two or three-day jag.

"Sorry," she was told. "No one's on duty until 3."

Ontonagon surely had a more rough and tumble infancy back in 1843, when James Kirk Paul first established residence on the east bank of the Ontonagon River where it flows into Lake Superior. A band of Chippewa was on the opposite bank. The river had gotten its name, according to local lore, from a Chippewa maiden who lost her bowl to the river's currents. Ontonagon means "lost bowl" in Chippewa and the town came to be named after the river.

Copper was the first attraction in Ontonagon, as it was through much of the Upper Peninsula. A legendary copper boulder, originally estimated to weigh anywhere from one to five tons, was found on a branch of the Ontonagon River. Its presence spawned a boom in mining throughout Ontonagon County.

In those early days, there were more copper mines than there were towns: Victoria, Minesota, Nonesuch, Norwich, Adventure, Mass. Ontonagon itself had no mine, but it had the harbor. Shipping, supplies coming in and ore and furs going out, was central to Ontonagon's economy. There were no highways or railroads.

When the Civil War broke out, the bustling community sent 254 men to serve in the Union Army.

Lumber had come later, when pine forests at the South End of the county began to be harvested. To this day, the largest employer—the dominant company—in Ontonagon is Stone Container's paper mill.

Stone Container's predecessor as Ontonagon's dominant company, in the late 19th century, was the Diamond Match Company, which also had a three-floor company store on River Street. The rough and tumble social structure of a community populated by miners, trappers and lumberjacks was giving way.

Those were grand days along River Street, now a five-block stretch which runs from northwest to southeast. The Bigelow House, a five-story hotel with a grand ballroom, had opened on July 4, 1855 to great fanfare. By late in the 19th century, Ontonagon actually had a philharmonic society.

However, in the summer of 1896, lightning started wildfires in the woods and high winds blew the flames into the Diamond Match lumberyard on the western shore of the Ontonagon River. The resultant inferno tossed chunks of burning embers back into the air and across the river into the town itself.

Nothing was left when the flames died down. The lumberyard was gone from one side of the river and the village, including the Bigelow House and Diamond Match Store, was gone from the other. The expression "high rise," assuming a five-story hotel is a high rise, has never since applied to any structures in Ontonagon.

The biggest building in the village housed a Lake Shore Inc. shipbuilding plant at the end of River Street where Lake Superior and the Ontonagon River intersect, directly across the river from Stone Container. This is an eyesore when empty but an economic boon when occupied. Unfortunately, it is vacant now.

Ontonagon would best be described as a sleepy village, with a population that seems to vary between 2,000 and 2,100 residents. No one happens upon Ontonagon, except maybe en route to the Porcupine

Mountains State Park, 58,000 acres of virgin woods crowned by the Lake of the Clouds. It is otherwise off to the north of the main highways running east to west through the U.P.

This isolation, of course, is part of the village's charm. Visitors were not greeted by a succession of fast food joints lining the highway as they come into town, not in 1992. There were no franchised food outlets. None. The closest thing to a franchised business was probably a mom-and-pop True Value Hardware, except for service stations such as Dale Blake's Union 76.

City Fathers are working to spruce up the community, building a marina for pleasure-boating, a boardwalk along the river and installing street lighting with a look reminiscent of the 19th century. McDonalds really need not apply, thank you.

Of course, pasties are much more in demand in places such as Ontonagon than Big Macs or Breakfast Jacks. A pasty is a meal unto itself, dough rolled and folded back over meat and potatoes and vegetables, such as carrots and rutabagas. They originated with copper miners, but they remain a staple indigenous to the U.P. Ask anyone in Ontonagon where pasties are fresh on, say, a Thursday and they will tell you to go to Henry's in Rockland.

Lake Superior, of course, is right there off Ontonagon's beaches, representing both a beauty and a beast. It can be the source of tremendous enjoyment and beauty, but it has a temperament. Its wrath can bring relentless winter storms and change a brilliant summer day into a glowering blend of thunder and lightning.

The big holiday each year in Ontonagon is Labor Day, when the streets are packed with celebrants. It stands as an acknowledgment that the summer is gone and good times must be had before the first snowfall comes over the horizon. The fabled copper boulder was brought to Ontonagon for Labor Day in 1993, the village's 150th birthday.

Like many of the *people* with roots in Ontonagon, the boulder has moved elsewhere. It now "lives" at the Smithsonian Institute.

◆   ◆   ◆

Murder rarely visited the village of Ontonagon, at least in the latter years of the 20th century. It was as foreign to the populace as beach parties in December. It happened on television or it was splashed across the big city papers which arrive late in the afternoon with seemingly ancient news. It happened also in movies, but Ontonagon had no theaters. However, murder had touched Ontonagon County families three times in the previous three years, but each crime was committed elsewhere.

Steve Tuomi, for example, was a 1981 graduate of Ontonagon Area High School. Many Ontonagon youngsters leave after high school for either higher education or a taste of urban civilization. A few ultimately return to live, but all return to visit. Tuomi was an exception. He would never return.

A gentle, mild-mannered young man, Tuomi never really had a chance in Ontonagon because he was gay. He did not flaunt it and, in fact, had a "steady" girlfriend for awhile. He did auto bodywork for his father. He liked to party and he tried to fit, but he was regularly beaten by intolerant bullies. Ontonagon was not the place for him. He longed for a place big enough to enable him to both lose himself and find himself.

Tuomi's destination was Milwaukee, the closest metropolitan city. He could live his life the way he chose without enduring the glaring microscope of his boyhood home. He dyed his hair purple, crossdressed and got into drugs and drink. Tuomi had an artistic bent, but he never pursued it. He tended bar.

The exact details are hazy, but Tuomi was last seen on Sept. 15, 1987. His older sister, Dawn, checked his apartment and found all of his clothes in place. She checked where he worked and found unretrieved paychecks. As time went by, his father Walter hired private detectives to investigate his whereabouts. Not a clue was left behind.

No one realized it at the time but Steve Tuomi had the misfortune of having met serial killer Jeffrey Dahmer.

The August 7, 1991 *Ontonagon Herald* carried the picture of a handsome young man under the following headline: "Ontonagon Man Identified as Dahmer's 16th Victim."

Gerald Pender, 23, was another young man who left Ontonagon, first to serve four years with the Navy and then to get an education at the Dunwoody Institute in Minneapolis. Pender's family was in the furniture and appliance business and he was studying technical subjects such as air conditioning and refrigeration at Dunwoody. The next generation would take over the business and Gerald was the next generation.

Holidays were special and Memorial Day 1990 was no exception. Gerald would be going home. Minneapolis was six hours by car from Ontonagon, but Gerald could cut that down considerably on his Yamaha 750 motorcycle. He left on Thursday to get home a day early and surprise his family.

Gerald Pender never showed up.

Law enforcement was reluctant to involve itself with a missing 23-year-old, especially a guy as big and tough as Pender who could surely take care of himself. Friends and family did some detective work on their own and learned where he was last seen. They realized he had gotten to within about an hour of home. They organized search parties along M-28 in the southwestern corner of the U.P. They had to deal with woods that were at times almost impenetrable. They slogged through swamps. They persevered.

His aunt, Lynda Uhlig, found the body on June 6, almost two weeks later. It had not been an accident. Pender had been shot to death and buried under branches. His motorcycle was hidden nearby.

Bob Ball was one of the investigating officers, working out of Gogebic County on this case. Gogebic is the next county south of Ontonagon and carries the distinction of being in the Central Time Zone, compared with Ontonagon's Eastern Time Zone. This case would take considerable time by any standard.

The Pender Case was solved by Tip No. 88. It came from a Wisconsin woman who was sitting in a Georgia jail on a murder charge. She was bragging about a killing she had done in Michigan and it fit the circumstances surrounding Pender's murder. Ball made two trips to Georgia to interview the woman. He concluded she was simply trying to get out of Georgia, a state with the death penalty, to Michigan, a state without capital punishment. She was not involved with Pender, but she fingered the guys who were.

On July 22, 1991, the Michigan State Police issued a news release announcing that two Duluth, Minn., men had been charged with Pender's murder. Jonathan Earl Hydall, 23, had been taken into custody in Lower Michigan. Paul Allen Hendrickson, 21, was already in jail on an unrelated charge.

After spending that May 1990 Thursday drinking and target shooting, they crossed paths with Pender at a service station. They did not like bikers and Pender was there on his bike. And Gerald was a mouthy sort who would react poorly to slurs. They chased him for miles before they finally ran him off the road and veritably executed him as he lay moaning in the underbrush with a broken leg.

The arrest hardly ended the trauma for the family. It took four trials to put the murderers away, both getting second degree murder convictions because of the "spontaneity" of their actions. Ball later recalled ruefully that the verdicts wiped out "58 miles of premeditation," the distance they chased the motorcycle.

Murder was getting close to home for Ontonagon and its residents. It would get frighteningly closer in the fall of 1992.

Bruce Crossing, a community 28 miles south of Ontonagon on U.S. 45, is known for its giant—by area standards, at least—general store. On October 28, 1992, the community was the site of a brutal murder. This was a little more than two months after Beth Paczesny had become one of the youngest, if not *the* youngest, county prosecutors in the U.S.

A man named Arthur K. Johnson had been, according to the state police investigation, beaten with the butt of a gun and his head had been mercilessly pounded against the floor. The scene was horrendous, with blood splattered wall-to-wall. There were no witnesses, but everyone in Bruce Crossing knew Johnson was having a "relationship" with a 29-year-old named Mark Mikkola he had picked up as a hitchhiker.

It would be stretching it to say that Mikkola was apprehended after an exhaustive investigation and lengthy manhunt. In truth, about the time investigators were about to start searching for him, they were informed he was already in custody.

Mikkola wrought his havoc in Bruce Crossing and then drove Johnson's car to Ontonagon, where he used money stolen from Johnson to buy rounds for the house at Doc's, the Shamrock and Stubb's. He cut a veritable swath through the saloons on Ontonagon's River Street, getting tossed from one after another. He tried to get his sister to let him borrow her truck while at the Shamrock, but she refused.

Stuck with Johnson's car and exiled from Ontonagon's watering holes, Mikkola headed west out of town on M-64. He got as far as White Pine, where he was arrested for driving under the influence. The arresting troopers had been at the murder scene. When Mikkola sobered up, he was facing much stiffer charges than drunken driving.

Beth Paczesny's first murder trial was swift. Mikkola pleaded that Johnson was pressuring him to have sex and the State Police lab found semen samples on Johnson's sheets that matched Mikkola's DNA. Mikkola complained that hard drinking and heavy pot smoking rendered him unaccountable for his actions. He may have come up with mitigating reasons for murder, but not an excuse. He was convicted of second-degree murder and imprisoned.

Mark Mikkola was sitting in jail, awaiting trial, on Nov. 29, 1992.

◆   ◆   ◆

Three people are missing from an area near Mass City, a small village southeast of Ontonagon. Local lore actually suggests UFOs are responsible because of strange lights sighted in the woods at about the times these people were disappearing from the face of the earth. Other legend has it that a wild mountain man lives in the dense woods. Vehicles have been found, but not their occupants.

A cardboard box rests by itself under a table in the Ontonagon County Sheriff's Department offices. Written on the side, in felt pen, is the label: "Buccanero File."

John Buccanero, a 22-year-old from Ontonagon, was snowmobiling with friends near the long-dormant Adventure Mine on a January day in 1987. His friends got a little ahead of him, but stopped to wait for him to catch up. He never did.

Young Buccanero had been on one of the groomed snowmobile trails that lace the U.P. like mini-highways through the winter months. It is possible to get lost on these trails, but not lost to the point of not being found. They simply handle too much traffic.

After searching for awhile, Buccanero's friends reported him missing to the sheriff's department. Two planes, search dogs and 200 volunteers could find no sign of him. The search area was eventually buried by a 10-inch snowfall and temperatures dropped to minus-20.

All that was found of Buccanero was his snowmobile, which was discovered miles away near the Ontonagon-Houghton county line. A logger found it after the spring thaw. The ensuing search of the area turned up nothing but deflated balloons with the names and addresses of school children inside, undoubtedly from some sort of science project.

In an interview with the *Houghton Daily Mining Gazette's* Amy Starnes, Ontonagon County Undersheriff John Gravier sighed: "We could find these little balloons, but not Buccanero."

Five years passed before Raymond Lewis, a resident of Dollar Bay in Houghton County, disappeared from the area. He was reported missing in December of 1992. Deputies did not take this disappearance quite as seriously as they might have, because they learned Lewis had gone AWOL previously. Reportedly, he once turned up in Ireland.

As with Buccanero's snowmobile, Lewis's truck was found after the spring thaw. Fishermen found it stuck on a two-track road 1½ miles off M-26. The keys were still in the ignition. Search and rescue turned up nothing. If this was an *intentional* disappearance, Lewis has not seen fit to resurface.

Unlike the others, Jan Marie Pattison disappeared in the middle of the summer. She was last seen August 26, 1993. Snowy weather curtailed or inhibited searches for Buccanero and Lewis, but no such adverse conditions existed when the search for Ms. Pattison was launched.

Again, airplanes, deputies, dogs and volunteers were mustered for the search, especially after her car was found abandoned in a ditch six days later. Even with a relatively fresh point of origin, searchers had no luck. All they found was a footprint from an athletic shoe along the east branch of the Ontonagon River.

In spite of intense publicity generated by her family, no sign of Jan Marie Pattison has been found.

The biggest problems are the terrain and the sparse population. A person getting disoriented in the woods can go miles and miles without seeing either a cabin or a road, even though, at times, he or she could well be within shouting distance.

Jerry Kitzman, who replaced Tom Corda as Ontonagon County sheriff Jan. 1, 1993 after winning the November election, is dismayed but not surprised that people should so thoroughly disappear.

"I'm sure there are places in this county," he said, "where no person has ever set foot or seen…not even deer hunters. There are places where it's more like a jungle than just woods. Looking for people is like looking for a needle in a haystack."

Airplanes, Kitzman said, have disappeared into the woods and never been found.

Gravier, the former undersheriff, was Ontonagon County's sheriff when a forester found Buccanero's remains in 2002, more than 15 years after he had disappeared. He was two miles from where his snowmobile had been found. How had he gotten there?

"We don't know for sure," Gravier said. "I guess we'll never know."

Kitzman, meanwhile, had picked through his memory and come up with maybe a dozen stories of other persons who had been lost in Ontonagon County. Some had been found alive. Some had been found dead. Some...

Two—Pattison and Lewis—have not been found at all.

UFOs?

A wild mountain man?

Disorientation?

Or some other fate?

3

The Hunters

Thanksgiving in Ontonagon is a holiday within a happening. Venison is much more on the minds of the populace than turkey. The Happening is the firearms deer season, which runs the last two weeks of the month of November. The hunt for bucks is an all-consuming passion.

The nearby Porcupine Mountains are an all-season tourist attraction, but nothing draws as many strange faces to the area as the hunting season. Storefronts are plastered with banners welcoming hunters from all over the Upper Midwest. Locals disappear into hunting camps hidden deep in the woods, where they hunt through daylight hours and play cards, drink brandy and tell tall tales at night.

Conversations take new twists. "Hello" takes a vacation. People meeting on the streets invariably ask: "Did you get your buck, eh?"

The dress code is orange. The old green, brown and gray camouflage is out. Hunters wear orange hats, orange overalls, orange jackets and orange gloves. They do this to protect themselves from each other.

Schools celebrate the hunting season. The first day of the season is a school holiday. It may as well be, because teachers and students alike would play hooky anyway. One young man at Ontonagon Area High School missed the first four days of school in the 1993 hunting season. Dana Brookins, one of his teachers, did not even have to ask where he had been.

"Did you get your buck?" she smiled.

"Sure did," he said. "That's why I'm back."

A unique part of the phenomenon is that area women, those who aren't hunters themselves, get dressed up and go out to meet visiting hunters while their husbands or boyfriends are at camp. They drink with the visitors. They dance with them. They cook for them. Friendships forged are renewed each November, come hunting season.

"You can't come out," a non-hunting *male* newcomer was advised. "No husbands are allowed in town during the hunting season."

◆   ◆   ◆

Jan Marie Pattison's family and friends saw the 1993 deer season as an opportunity to learn what the fate of the missing woman might have been. A massive search had been conducted in the aftermath of her disappearance, but perhaps the random meandering of hundreds of hunters might turn up a clue.

Stores, gas stations, restaurants and saloons throughout the area had stacks of yellow leaflets:

Dear Hunter,
A 38 yr. old woman has been missing since August 26th, 1993. Her car was found six days later on a four wheeler trail 1/2 mi. off Vista road on the north side of the East Branch River. Please if you find any articles or pieces of clothing, a shoe, jewelry, watch or anything, call the Ontonagon County Sheriff's Dept. @ 884-4901.

She was believed to be wearing a teal shirt with short sleeves, blue jeans or dark blue shorts, white shoes, several gold bracelets, necklace, watch and a gold ring.

Please keep your eyes open, we need your help.

Thank you,
The Family and Friends of Jan Marie Pattison

"That's about the last hope we've got until spring," Jan's father Jack told Starnes, the reporter for the *Houghton Daily Mining Gazette*. "This is the first year I really don't want to see the snow come. It's the last hope before the snow blankets the earth."

The snow did not come until late in the 1993 hunting season. It hit over the Thanksgiving weekend. No traces of Jan Marie Pattison were found.

◆   ◆   ◆

A year earlier, it was a normal Thanksgiving at the Blake household at the intersection of M-38 and Cherry Lane. Son Jerry, his wife Anna and their children had arrived on Tuesday, but Jerry left early Wednesday morning to join the men at the family hunting camp located southeast of Ontonagon between Greenland and Rockland.

The Moilanens were having a little problem with transportation. Bruce had totaled their Subaru station wagon the opening day of firearm season when he struck a deer on the way home from shooting his buck. This left them with no vehicle capable of hauling the four dogs as well as luggage for a weekend.

As fate would have it, they found an '87 Chevrolet conversion van the day before Thanksgiving. They made a $500 deposit and Moilanen explained that he would like to use it for the weekend to get the dogs and gear to Ontonagon.

"No problem," Moilanen was told. "Go ahead."

With that approval, Bruce Moilanen had all the room he needed to take all he needed for the weekend to Ontonagon.

"So it was helter skelter," he said later, inadvertently using a term associated with Charles Manson a few years earlier. "Pack everything in the van."

The Moilanens arrived in Ontonagon at mid-day on Thanksgiving. They were there for the weekend.

Bruce never did go to hunting camp. He spent his evenings at the Blake home. The Blake women, Judy included, were conservative and religious and their nature was to stay by the home fires. If they went to town, it was for cherry pie. This was their weekend to cook and chat and, to use one of Mary Ann's favorite words, "monkey" with the children.

Judy, however, was an outdoor lover who was not automatically left behind when it came to hunting. She had guns of her own and she joined her husband when he hunted Friday and Saturday. Indeed, they put in two *full* days of hunting.

The Moilanens took off early Friday morning for the Dishinaw Creek area and promptly got the new and unfamiliar van stuck. They decided to abandon it, temporarily at least, and go to hunting blinds. Neither had any luck, so they returned to the van and got help dislodging it from an anonymous Good Samaritan. They needed matches for the heaters in the blinds, so they drove to the Rousseau Bar, a hard-drinking shack in the backwoods foreign to both of them.

When they got back to hunting, they decided to "drive" deer. They moved through the woods, trying to spook deer in the direction they wanted them to go. They came out into a field full of pine trees…perfectly shaped Christmas trees.

Judy walked up to one and smiled.

"Boy," she said, "I'd love to have this in the dining room this year."

They settled back into their respective blinds—shacks where hunters sit and wait rather than stalk—as darkness started to fall. The coyotes began to howl and Judy became unnerved. She headed out of the blind, thinking to herself, "God, I don't know why I'm nervous. I'm the one with the gun here."

Then a gunshot went off.

It was so close, Bruce came bolting out of his blind. A couple of deer ran by. He was convinced his wife had shot her first buck. He splashed across a creek and ran up a hill and stood looking around. Judy was coming toward him with a flashlight…and no buck.

On Saturday, Judy and Bruce joined the Niemis—Uncle Ed Niemi and cousins Gary and Mike—in search of a buck Gary thought he had wounded on Thanksgiving Day. They tracked him under a power line down the Rockland Road from Mass, Ed and Gary trying to get a position behind the deer while and Judy, Bruce and Mike were trying to drive him in their direction. The buck eluded all of them.

The remainder of Saturday was spent either driving deer or waiting for them in blinds, all to no avail. At all of 5-foot-4, Judy was a trooper. She kept up with the men in the family.

Everyone was a little weary by Saturday evening, when the family gathered at Mike Niemi's house in Mass City for hamburgers. Bruce was there, talking about the following day's hunting.

"We're going to have to be really careful moving through the woods tomorrow," he warned. "With only two days left in the season, people are going to be shooting like crazy trying to fill their permits."

Gary Niemi, Mike's brother, thought the caution sensible at the time. He did not think much about it until months later, when it struck him that his cousin's husband could have been planting the notion of an accidental shooting in the back of their minds.

Judy was particularly pleased that evening to have company when she returned to her mother's house. Sheri Groitzsch-Bishop, an old classmate and a friend since they were 12, was in town for the holiday. They could not visit as often as they liked, because Groitzsch-Bishop was married and living in Minneapolis.

This was an evening when they were able to get off by themselves and spend quality time together. The conversation took a serious turn. Judy was talking about her relationship with Bruce, whom her friend did not particularly like. Judy had previously confided that she and Bruce were having some financial difficulties.

"Bruce is involved in some kind of a lawsuit over his work," Judy said. "He didn't follow his attorney's advice and I think it's going to end up costing us money. He has a way of holding things like this inside."

Judy told Groitzsch-Bishop that they were going to counseling for more than financial difficulties, but insisted Bruce was a good husband

and father. She talked of needing to communicate more, an age-old marital problem.

"Bruce," Judy said, "just won't talk about his childhood."

◆   ◆   ◆

Bruce Robert Moilanen's childhood was not much to talk about, it would seem. His contemporaries at Ontonagon Area High School, Class of '73, remember him because he was there, not because of anything he did. Classes were small enough that everyone knew of everyone else, even if they didn't get to know everyone else. The only place his name—or picture—appeared in the 1973 Boulder, the yearbook, was with his senior class.

The Moilanen family came from Mass City, an outpost off M-38 that made Ontonagon seem like Detroit in comparison. There were a couple of bars, a general store, a motel-cafe and Frank's Barber Shop, which was hardly big enough for both a barber and a chair. The Moilanen home was next to the grade school garage.

Bruce, 37, was the youngest child born to Wiljo and Huldah Moilanen, the others being Ron, 52; Wayne, 49; and Joanne, 45. Moilanen's parents were married when Huldah was 17 and divorced 37 years later. Bruce was the only child living at home when the parents were divorced.

To hear Huldah tell it, it is amazing the marriage lasted 37 years. In an interview with police investigators, she said Wiljo was an alcoholic when they were married. She described her ex-husband as a man of few words whose drinking did not affect his work, but did affect his family. She said his paychecks went to his bar bills first and groceries second, on one occasion leaving only $2 for a week's groceries.

Bruce's mother described him as a kind, gentle, loving kid who kept everything inside. She said he never fought with his siblings, but then the next youngest was seven or eight years older than he was. However, when the divorce occurred, Huldah said Bruce seemed to change his attitude toward her. He became, in her words, real cold and angry.

After those nondescript high school years, Bruce went away to Northern Michigan University in Marquette. He did not get a four-year degree, but he did get a vocational certificate in auto body repair. He worked as a body repairman at several dealerships and repair shops before going back to NMU for certification as an emergency medical technician (EMT). He also held a job as radio operator at the Negaunee State Police Post.

Moilanen's knowledge of auto repair eventually caused him to form his own business, North Country Claim Service, which he worked at part-time for assorted insurance companies. It was this business which supposedly got him into the problems Judy alluded to in her conversation with Groitzsch-Bishop.

Though not involved in organized athletics, Moilanen did have one sport he loved. And he was very good at it.

Skiing.

Ontonagon was not particularly socially stratified, but the ski slopes at the Porky Mountains eliminated what barriers might have existed. The Moilanens from Mass City were "out" geographically, economically and socially. Bruce developed an "in" because of his skiing. He met Judy Blake on the ski hill. Judy was no social butterfly, because it was not the nature of her upbringing, but she came from a solid and respectable family.

Judy was two years behind Moilanen in school, but they ended up at NMU at the same time. Bruce was later to confide in a friend that they "semi-cohabited" without Mary Ann Blake's knowledge…or at least acknowledgment.

"She didn't catch on," Bruce said, "or maybe she just played dumb.

It was not exactly a match made in heaven.

When Judy Blake married Bruce on June 24, 1978, the consensus of those close to the families was that Mary Ann Blake was against it.

It seemed, however, that Bruce came to favor the Blake family. When he and Judy were in Ontonagon County, they stayed with the Blakes and stopped for visits with Huldah Moilanen in Mass City. They never stayed in Mass City.

In late April of 1993, when interviewed by police investigators, Huldah said she had not seen her son since the previous Christmas Eve. He had shown up at her front door, crying, to deliver a Christmas card and gift for her ex-husband, who was staying in nearby Rockland with Bruce's brother Ron.

"Judy wrapped this," Bruce blurted, and then ran off sobbing.

At that time, Bruce and Ron were the only sons who *could* show up at Huldah's front door. Wayne was in the Waupun Correctional Institute in Wisconsin, serving three 15-year terms for first degree sexual assault on a child. He had had no contact with his brother since he was incarcerated Jan. 13, 1992.

Interestingly, Wayne Moilanen's pre-sentencing report included a comment from his brother Bruce.

"They should give him life in prison," Bruce said, "and throw away the key.

◆   ◆   ◆

Judy Moilanen had been reassuring to her friend Sheri Groitzsch-Bishop Saturday night. She told her there were bumps in the marital road, but things would surely smooth out. All would be fine.

When Sunday morning dawned, Judy was feeling lazy. Bruce made coffee and returned to the bedroom to find her half awake.

"I feel like sleeping in," she said. "I think I'll stay home today."

"Want me to come back and pick you up at lunch?" he said. "I can just go sit in a blind this morning."

"No, I think I'll just stay here."

"You want me to leave your gun?" Bruce asked.

"Yeh, why don't you do that," she said.

"I'll leave your gun by the bathroom and your shells on the counter," he said, "in case you want to go for a walk this afternoon behind the house or something."

Bruce left the Blake house somewhere around 7:30 that morning and headed for Mass City, where Mike Niemi lived. Maybe halfway down M-38 toward Greenland and adjacent Mass City, Moilanen pulled into the yard at the Wilbur Farm. This was the old Penegor spread, which sprawled on both sides of the highway.

Clarence Wilbur, who was doing chores in the barnyard with his wife Margo, had not seen Moilanen since Bruce had baled hay for him as a youngster back in high school.

"Could I cross your property on the other side of the road?" Moilanen asked. "I'm trying to get to Dale Blake's land."

"Sure," Wilbur said. "There's a gate maybe three-quarters of a mile down the road."

The Wilburs would later be on an "alibi list," but a contact so early in the morning would hardly be helpful. What's more, Moilanen had not bothered to ask if the gate was locked. It was, with a padlock. Wilbur drove past later and noticed the Moilanen van was not parked on the outside of the gate.

Obviously, Bruce did not turn at the gate and head for the Blakes' land, either on foot or in his van. He continued on to Mass City to meet Niemi, who had become an increasingly good friend over the last few years. They golfed together and went to hockey games together and, of course, hunted together. Mike had stayed with the Moilanens in Harvey during one brief period when he moved away from Mass City.

Moilanen came over a hill between Greenland and Mass and a buck darted in front of him. He swerved and hit his brakes and the deer ran off into the woods. He accelerated, anxious to get to Judy's cousin's house.

Niemi, a cherubic man with an easy-going nature, was actually asleep when Moilanen knocked on his door sometime after 8 o'clock.

Understand that fanatical hunters have this thing about being "in the field" at the crack of dawn.

"Mike," Bruce said, "get up and get dressed. I just saw a buck cross the road by the old dump."

This was enough to alert the sleepiest hunter. The old Mass City dump was maybe a half a mile from Niemi's house. Bruce was talking about a very fresh sighting of a buck. They went looking. If the ground had been covered by snow, they could have tracked him and likely shot him. As it was, they never found him.

Breakfast was starting to sound good and the Adventure Motel and Cafe was only a few blocks away. Mike Niemi, being a regular, was well known by owner Donald Withrow. Moilanen was not a familiar customer. It was around 10 a.m. when they walked in, wearing their hunting orange.

"Getting a late start, eh Mike?" Withrow teased.

"Slept in a little," Mike said, "but we've been looking for a buck Bruce saw by the old dump."

Any luck?" Withrow asked.

"Naw."

Bruce and Mike got back to the Niemi house about 10:45 and Mike expected his father Ed and brother Gary might be back from the morning hunt. No one was there.

"What are you going to do, Bruce?" Mike asked."

"I don't know," Moilanen said. "I may go park up by Wilbur's farm and walk in there. I may go to the Gardner Tower area or I may just walk into camp."

Of course, walking into camp would likely put him in the company of Judy's father, brothers and uncle as well as others such as Bill Dorvinen and Carl Yanke. If someone wanted to be alone for whatever reason, camp was nowhere to be.

"I'm going to feed my deer blinds," Mike said.

A "camp" is, in truth, a cabin, normally a bit on the primitive side. It has a stove, table and bunks and the rest room is usually a one-holer out in back. Hunters use camps as headquarters, of sorts. They don't hunt in the camp.

Hunters do hunt from "blinds," which are basically camouflaged sheds not unlike the forts youngsters build when playing in the woods. Hunters start feeding, or baiting, deer in the vicinity of their blinds long before the hunting season. Deer are territorial and habitual animals and the idea is to get them accustomed to coming near the blind for food. Mike Niemi would be taking apples or carrots or corn to restock the piles next to his blinds.

Bruce Moilanen did not go to any hunting camp. He parted company with Mike Niemi about 11 and headed off on his own. The next contact he said he had with another human being was around 2:15. It later became a question of what human being he "contacted" at 2:15…and in what manner.

◆   ◆   ◆

Marie Lyons is an elderly woman who packs enough spunk in a four-foot something body to energize a room full of kindergartners. She wraps herself in oversized coats, scarves and knit hats and wanders wherever her feisty whims might take her.

On this Sunday afternoon, Ms. Lyons was walking along M-38 on her way to a supper club called The Candlelight. Russell Reid, 90-plus years old himself, was appearing with his band at the restaurant a couple of miles outside Ontonagon on M-38. Medication prohibited Ms. Lyons from having a cocktail, but she did not want to miss a party.

She was near the intersection of Cherry Lane and M-38, just east of Jack and Elly Hawley's house, en route to that party. This was a rather lonesome area for anyone to be walking, but Marie was not actually walking. She was *hitchhiking*. She heard a shot. She stopped.

"My God," she said to herself, "I'm wearing my tan coat. This is a bad place to be wearing a tan coat during the hunting season."

She looked at her watch. It was between 2:10 and 2:15.

She made it to the party.

At that moment, at a home one-quarter mile past the Brookins houses on the west or opposite side of Cherry Lane, Jerry (Wally) Schoch was doing fall cleanup. He was in the front door threshold, washing the outside of the window.

A shot rang out from the woods on the east side of the road.

"Geez," he said, "someone's hunting across from the house. Somebody got a deer."

While it may seem presumptuous to equate a gunshot with a fallen deer, that is generally the way it works with modern firearms. Unless a hunter is shooting from some pie-in-the-sky distance or firing at a deer in full flight, it is hard to miss with a scoped rifle.

Schoch did not look at his watch, but he knew his friend, Kim Wilber, was in the shower. She and a friend were getting ready to leave the house at 2:30.

Others along M-38 remembered hearing a gunshot around the two-minute warning near the end of the first half of the Green Bay Packer football game. A check with WJMS-WIMI, the Ironwood outlet telecasting the game, revealed that the first half actually came to an end at 2:16.

◆   ◆   ◆

Bruce Moilanen was back at Mike Niemi's home in Mass City by mid-afternoon. He missed Mike, who been there a little after 2:30 to pick up deer feed. Moilanen was also there to pick up deer feed.

Gary Niemi, Mike's brother, was there, but he was finished hunting. He had a brief telephone conversation with his wife Theresa, who was at home in White Pine. They were going to a movie at a Houghton mall early in the evening.

"I'm going to feed the dog," Theresa said, "and then I'll be over."

Theresa had a 40-minute drive to get from White Pine to Mass City. She was there at 3:30.

Shortly after he left Mike Niemi's house, Moilanen almost literally ran into Wade Johnson. A Mass City resident who drove a truck for the Ontonagon road commission, Johnson was heading into the Tank Creek area to hunt.

Tank Creek is a desolate area that would become inaccessible to "street" vehicles after the snows came. Johnson was driving down a narrow road when he noticed Moilanen coming around the back of a van parked nose-in from the road. He was pulling in behind the van to see if Moilanen needed help when the van lurched backwards. It almost backed into his pickup truck.

No greetings were exchanged and Moilanen drove away, heading out of the area.

Moilanen next encountered Lori Johnson, Wade's wife, in what would later become a significant coincidence. She started a shift at the Elms General Store in Mass City at 3 p.m. Lori did not really know Moilanen, but she recalled that a relatively unfamiliar face stopped in to buy a Pepsi and visited on the way out with a local named Harvey Ahola.

At some point, Moilanen drove by the Mass City home of Butch Macy and left a two-page note on the door: "Butch, Diane and Crystal...Love, Bruce, Judy and Elise."

Who knows why it took two pages to convey such a simple message...or why Moilanen felt compelled to leave such a message in the first place.

At some other point, undefined as to time, Moilanen saw a blue 1989 Chevrolet pickup with "Mars Sales" written in brown and white on the side. The driver, Terry Neal, was, in fact, hunting in the area that Sunday. He never saw Bruce Moilanen.

Another vehicle Moilanen saw was the squad car of State Trooper John Raymond. Moilanen was coming out of the woods on M-38 near Simar-Wasas Road when he saw Raymond drive past. He set the time at 5:10. Raymond did not take note of seeing either Moilanen or his parked van on the shoulder of M-38. Vehicles, both strange and familiar, were always parked along roads during the hunting season.

Not too long after dark, Moilanen stopped at the residence of Irene Leimantine. Ask anyone about Bruce's boyhood friends and the name George Leimantine is almost invariably the only one mentioned. George had moved to California, but he was home in Mass City for the hunting season. It made sense that Bruce would want to visit him.

What did not make sense to Leimantine was that his buddy walked right past him and went up to Butch Macy.

"Did you get my note?" Moilanen asked.

Leimantine was taken aback. He was surprised he had been ignored. He was startled by the insistent, almost adamant tone in Bruce's voice. He thought his friend was uptight for some reason.

◆   ◆   ◆

Mike Niemi had finished hunting. He was in the camp and it was dark. His cousin David Blake's wife Yvonne came running into the camp with a flashlight. It was unusual that one of the women would be coming to the camp, especially after dark.

"Something serious has happened to Judy," she said. "We have to find Bruce and get to Ontonagon."

She did not say what had happened. She had heard Mary Ann screaming and she thought she had heard Mary Ann say, "She's gone." However, she wasn't sure and she just wanted to get the men moving back toward town.

"I'll see if I can find Bruce," Niemi said.

Niemi raced home and was just pulling off his wet boots when Moilanen drove up.

"Something serious has happened to Judy," Mike said. "We have to get to Ontonagon right away."

"What?" Bruce asked.

"I don't know," Mike said.

"Is she dead?" Bruce asked.

"I don't know," Mike said. "We just have to get to Ontonagon fast."

◆   ◆   ◆

Judy's father Dale and brother David were already at the hospital. Her cousins Gary and Mike and uncle Ed were there as well. Gary had been paged at the Houghton mall before he and Theresa had gotten to the theater.

Deputy Tom Cousineau was there. So was Bill Burgess.

Cousineau was doing a thankless job in the face of tremendous grief. He was asking the family where they had been that day.

"We were at the camp," David said in hushed tones.

"All of you?" Cousineau asked.

"All of us," David said.

Everyone was in a state of shock. They were not in the mood to be detailing everyone's whereabouts for every minute. Cousineau knew that. Hunters tend to get spread all over the landscape. They could be at one camp or one blind one hour and at another the next. This group was in no frame of mind for more insightful recollection.

When the door burst open and Bruce barged in, he had a panicked look on his face.

"What happened? What happened? What happened?"

Dale Blake, his father-in-law, told him.

Bruce's first question was strange.

"Was she wearing orange?"

No one answered.

Moilanen sat down on the floor and lowered his face into his hands.

"How can your life go from being so full one moment to so empty the next?" he asked.

Moilanen asked to view the body. Burgess told him that would be okay, if he really wanted to. Moilanen asked David if he would accompany him. They followed a nurse down the hall.

"Can you handle this?" Moilanen asked his brother-in-law. "It's probably going to be a little gruesome, but I'm used to it."

Used to it? Used to viewing the body of his dead wife?

"What do you do?" the nurse asked.

David noticed Moilanen brighten.

"I work in the O.R. at Marquette General," Moilanen said.

This made him immune to feeling?

He certainly showed feelings when he walked out of the morgue. He stood in the hallway and leaned his forehead against the wall and banged his fists. Surely, he was very upset.

◆   ◆   ◆

George Leimantine and his girlfriend had left his mother's house and gone to visit another Mass City friend named Mark Maki. They were there about an hour when the telephone rang. George's mother was on the line and she was crying.

"Bruce just called," she said. "Judy was killed in a hunting accident."

Leimantine was angry.

"I hate to say it," he said to his girlfriend, "but I think that slippery son of a bitch shot his wife."

How long was it that George Leimantine had been Bruce Moilanen's best buddy?

Leimantine and the others started talking.

"He told me about a year ago that he was having an affair," Leimantine said. "He just ranted and raved about how beautiful this woman was. He left me with the impression the affair was over, but you just never know what to believe with him. He can look you right in the eye and lie to you and do a good job of making you believe him."

George Leimantine did not know whether the affair was a lie or whether the termination of the affair was a lie…or both. More importantly, he had voiced aloud his suspicion that the "hunting accident" may be the biggest lie of all.

◆   ◆   ◆

Det. Sgt. Bob Ball met the Blakes, and Moilanen, for the first time at about 10:30 Sunday night. Deputy Cousineau accompanied him.

Ball was not there to interrogate. He was there to introduce himself to the family and he was there to extend condolences. He was also there to try to get an impression of Judy Moilanen's husband.

When he came through the door, Bruce approached him with his right hand extended.

"I'm Bruce Moilanen, Sgt. Ball," he said. "We've met before. I was a dispatcher down at district headquarters in Negaunee a few years ago."

Ball did not remember, but he nodded his head in polite acknowledgment. He did not want to bother the women, so the men adjourned to the kitchen. Dale and David Blake stood with Ball and Cousineau in the kitchen and Moilanen sat with his chin on his folded hands at the nearby dining room table.

Dale and David did the talking while Moilanen sat quietly at the table. They would make a statement and Bruce would nod his head in agreement. Ball did not press. It was not an occasion to press or even suggest that he might have suspicions, which he really didn't. He came away thinking the men had all been together at the hunting camp.

David Blake was curious. Not suspicious, maybe, but curious. Bruce Moilanen, after all, had just sat there and let he and his father leave the impression he had been with them. He had not as much as hinted to the contrary.

"Bruce," he said, "where were *you* hunting all day?"

Bruce Moilanen recited such a comprehensive list of places he had been and people he had seen that David Blake was dumbfounded. And David Blake was unsettled.

4

Suspicious Minds

Bob Ball had expressed interest in "The Husband" almost immediately. He did not have suspicions about Bruce Moilanen, at least not yet. It was just a standard procedure to wonder about spouses.

Tom Cousineau had encountered Moilanen at the hospital shortly before he left to join the other officers at the sheriff's offices. A barrel-chested officer with sandy hair and a wispy mustache, Cousineau scratched his chin. He too was unsettled.

"I've been an officer for 15 years," he told Ball, "and I've delivered a lot of 'death messages.' The way Bruce acted was strange. He wasn't the grieving husband. I can't help but think something is wrong here."

"Was he showing emotion?" Ball asked.

"I'll tell you what it was like," Cousineau said. "It was like he was sobbing without tears. He came out of the morgue and I asked him if he was okay and he said yes. I told him I'd like to get some information and he came out of the sobbing part so quickly that he caught me off guard. Then he answered my questions with total clarity."

◆   ◆   ◆

Det. Sgt. Ball would normally start his investigation at the scene of the incident, but the dampness and darkness had prompted Cousineau and Burgess to remove the body to the morgue. Consequently, Ball chose to stop at Ontonagon Memorial Hospital's morgue before going to the woods along Cherry Lane.

Burgess, the medical examiner's investigator, unsealed the morgue, ignoring Gervae's instructions under Ball's orders. Cousineau, Paczesny, Trooper Amee Ives, Burgess and Ball entered the little room and found Judy lying on a gurney. She was wearing a black waist-length jacket, a fuchsia pullover shirt, green pants and Sorel hiking boots. The jacket was unzipped.

"It was zipped when we found her," Burgess said. "Dr. Gervae unzipped it to examine the wound."

Ball examined the damage to the jacket and found a 5/16th of an inch hole in the right chest and a jagged, irregular hole in the back left. He noted their consistency with damage created by entry, in other words the front, and exit. He peeled back the jacket and found that the bullet had shoved a bit of the shirt into the entrance wound in front.

Unfortunately, as Ball peeled back the shirt, the piece forced into the wound by the bullet came out. With it came a piece of tissue maybe one inch long. This would cause confusion later.

Ball found that the hole in Judy's chest was oval-shaped, maybe one-half inch by three-quarters of an inch. The hole behind her left arm was seven-eighths of an inch by one inch. These measurements reinforced his conviction that entry had been through the front and exit from the rear.

The morgue was cleared and sealed. Dr. Castilla, accompanied by Burgess and Cousineau, would perform the autopsy Monday afternoon. Ball, who had police business in Gogebic County, could not be there.

◆   ◆   ◆

It had been easy, for Gervae and Ball at least, to determine where the bullet had entered the body, but the scene of Judy's death presented a more complex problem. It was complex because almost nothing of consequence could be found.

Nine people were involved in the search of the area, nine people looking for anything they might find in the darkness. They were looking for footprints, shell-casings, candy wrappers and even a foolishly dropped wallet. They carefully fanned out maybe 200 feet in all directions from where the body had been found.

"We're not going to have much luck with this leaf cover," Ball said, "unless we can find footprints in snow or mud."

A shell casing was an even more far-fetched possibility.

"Wait a minute," said Ontonagon Sheriff Tom Corda. "Take a look at this tree."

Corda, who had little more than a month left of his term in office, was standing under a maple tree. A graze mark, possibly made by a bullet, was on the northeast side of the tree. It was obviously fresh. Deputies measured the tree at 37 feet to the west of where the body had been found.

If the bullet that killed Judy had made the mark, it had to have come from east of the path. Ball felt that the bullet had first passed through Judy. He came to this conclusion because the entrance wound would have been as jagged as the exit wound if the bullet had been damaged by first hitting the maple tree.

◆   ◆   ◆

Ball and Cousineau made their stop at the Blake house and then joined the others at the Sheriff's Department offices. It was after 11 p.m., but they huddled to make sure there was nothing left to do which could not wait until morning.

Ball and Corda decided they could use the services of a tracking dog. They called State Trooper Phil Stanton.

"I don't think the dog will be much use tracking a shooter out of the area," Stanton warned. "It's probably too late."

"What about picking up on something we might have overlooked?" Ball asked.

"It's possible," Stanton said.

He and his companion would be there at 9 a.m.

"What about a news release?" someone wondered.

They decided to put together a release that would depict the shooting as a hunting accident, which may have been exactly what it was. They wanted to know if anyone had been in the area or knew of anyone who had been in the area. They worded it so as to encourage anyone who had been inadvertently involved to come forward with information.

The story in the Dec. 2, 1992 *Ontonagon Herald* was reported in the desired tone.

Headlined *"Shooting under investigation,"* it read in part:

"A possible hunting accident is under investigation by the Ontonagon County Sheriff's Department...Responding officers found the body of Judy D. (Blake) Moilanen, 35, of Marquette, about one-quarter mile south of M-38 and about 300 yards east of Cherry Lane in an area frequented by hunters...Moilanen had been walking her dogs and was wearing dark clothing at the time of the shooting."

◆   ◆   ◆

While hunting-related accidents are commonplace on the Upper Peninsula landscape, murders disguised as hunting accidents are not. The most recent had occurred in 1988 in Republic Township and it had actually happened in front of a camp four days *before* the hunting season started.

Republic, located in Marquette County, two counties east of Ontonagon, was just down the road from Michigamme, the setting for the famed "Anatomy of a Murder" book and film.

A schoolteacher had been found shot and police suspected it had been a hunting accident, but a 16-month investigation resulted in the conviction of the teacher's wife, her brother and two others.

Game wardens had been fair game earlier in the century, according to research by the *Marquette Mining Journal's* Greg Peterson. Four, he found, had been killed in the U.P. by either poachers or unlicensed hunters. Two were shot and dumped into Lake Superior with cement blocks tied to their feet, one was shot and blown to smithereens by dynamite and the last run over by a truck.

Judy Moilanen's death seemed to fit into the accidental category, but investigators had some work to do before they settled on that conclusion.

◆   ◆   ◆

Ontonagon County Sheriff's Deputies had their track shoes on Monday, Nov. 30. They interviewed residents along Cherry Lane and M-38 in search of anything they might deem helpful, be it suspicious vehicles or persons or simply the sound of gunfire. And they interviewed hunters in the field for the last day of the firearms season.

Judy Moilanen's death was not being treated as a homicide…nor was it being treated as a hunting accident. Questions had to be answered.

Undersheriff Robert Tulppo knocked on Jerry Schoch's door on the west side of Cherry Lane and learned that Schoch had indeed heard a gunshot. He also learned that Schoch had a houseguest who had hunted Sunday, but the houseguest had left before noon to return to his home in Iron River.

Tulppo also noted that the "witness" seemed nervous. This became understandable a few months later, when Schoch was arrested and pled guilty to the use and manufacture of the drug methcathinone. He was perhaps fearful that the officer at his door was investigating *him* rather than the gunshot across the street.

Down Cherry Lane from Schoch's house toward M-38, Tulppo found that Marsha LaFernier and her children had seen a couple of men and a pickup truck in the area. He marked the LaFernier family for further contact.

Other deputies working along M-38 encountered people who had heard a gunshot, some specific as to time and some not. They also learned of hunters on the north or opposite side of M-38 and another possible hunter further east along M-38 at Turpeinen's clear-cut, an area stripped by logging activity.

Deputy Cousineau and Trooper Stanton, meanwhile, were having no luck with the tracking dog. The human eye had picked up as much as the canine nose, basically nothing. Fifteen months later, the State Police assigned a tracking dog and handler to Ontonagon County… but that was too late to be of help finding who shot Judy Moilanen.

These early investigative thrusts made it seem that no one but Judy Blake Moilanen—and five Springer spaniels—had been in the woods behind Cherry Lane that fateful afternoon. Everyone was elsewhere, including Bruce Moilanen.

◆   ◆   ◆

Dr. Hugo Castilla arrived in the afternoon to conduct the autopsy, which seemed to be a mere formality in such a circumstance. It was not likely he was going to find that anything other than a gunshot killed Judy Moilanen, and he didn't.

Utilizing police reports as much as anything else, he determined the time of death to be 3 p.m. He stressed that it could actually have been an hour or two in either direction. It was too late, in his mind, to use such gauges as *rigor mortis* or lividity or body temperature as more precise barometers. What's more, lividity would have been affected by the moving of the body.

Castilla noted that the bullet did massive damage to the interior upper body, virtually tearing the top off Judy's heart. His findings were a reflection of his feelings that a rather high-powered gun had been involved in the incident.

In examining Judy Moilanen, Castilla curiously noted the one-inch piece of tissue extending from the wound in the upper right chest. In his report, he wrote that the bullet had entered from the left rear and exited from the right front. He concluded that the tissue had been forced out of the wound by the bullet as it left the body.

◆   ◆   ◆

Bob Ball was back on the case Tuesday and he was about to have his interest piqued. He was on the telephone with Lt. Henry Steede of the Marquette Police Department. Steede had been contacted by a source who asked to remain anonymous, but the lieutenant thought Ball should be made aware of what he had been told.

"The Moilanens have been receiving some kind of marriage counseling," Steede said. "And Judy made a comment to my informant that the marriage is in trouble, but not quite to the point of divorce."

"Go on," Ball said.

"Two to three weeks ago," Steede continued, "Judy came to my informant all upset and crying and said, 'You won't believe what Bruce has done this time.' But she clammed up without saying what."

Ball was already listening intently, but Steede had not yet dropped the real bomb.

"Twelve to 14 months ago," he said, "when Judy and Bruce were doing some work on their home, Bruce was on the roof and Judy was on the ground. A large chimney block fell from the roof, hit Judy on the head and damn near killed her. My informant thinks the block was dropped intentionally."

Ball was aghast.

"Was it investigated?" he asked.

"It was ruled accidental."

◆   ◆   ◆

Det. Sgt. Bob Ball had a mild manner about him. He was as comfortable as a baggy sweatshirt. It was hard to imagine that even suspects he was investigating could dislike him. Ball could ask a suspect if he had murdered his wife and make it sound like he was offering a choice of steak or lobster for dinner. His manner was more that of an insurance salesman than a hard-nosed cop.

If anything gave him away, it was his eyes. They seemed constantly on the alert for something no one else could see. When it came to intense eye contact, Ball could stare down the devil.

In his job, that was something he often had to do.

Ball, a 45-year-old native of Buffalo, N.Y., was fresh from an 11-month chase of the devils who murdered Gerald Pender. He had not expected to be kept quite as busy in the Upper Peninsula as he had been down in Flint, with its 50 or so murders a year.

Two investigations that stick in his craw to this day were downstate, one an execution-style murder in Flint and the other the death of a 20-year-old woman who disappeared from a bar. Neither has been solved and he takes those "failures" in a most personal way.

"I know the one in Flint was connected with organized crime," he said. "It's the other one I feel so badly about. In my mind, I know who killed her. We gave the guy a polygraph in Texas and he passed. You just can't rely completely on those tests."

This man who fails so grudgingly was going to know for sure that Judy Blake Moilanen's death was a hunting accident before he would let the case go. The chimney block incident, to him, was a red flag the size of Lake Superior.

How many "accidents" did it take before they were no longer accidental?

◆   ◆   ◆

When Bob Ball drove to Ontonagon to renew his investigation on Tuesday, Dec. 1, he had company. Det. Sgt. Don Poupore, headquartered at the Negaunee Post, would be his partner until the case was resolved.

Poupore, like Ball, had started his State Police career in Lower Michigan. He had been a trooper in Mount Pleasant, in the central part of the state, and Erie, down near the Ohio border, as well as Detroit. However, he was a U.P. native, born in L'Anse and educated at Suomi College in Hancock.

Given an opportunity to go home to the Upper Peninsula, he moved to Negaunee as a trooper in 1985. He became a desk sergeant and then a detective sergeant, working out of Negaunee but living in L'Anse.

Poupore was younger than Ball and more slightly built, but their temperament was much the same. He seemed more open-faced and maybe less suspicious, but a naive countenance disguised an intensity to rival Ball's in the heat of an investigation.

If there was anything that might be considered unusual about this alliance, it was that these detectives could not really stage one of those dog-and-pony, good cop-bad cop routines. Their nature was the same when it came to approaching suspects, schmoozing and maybe soothing rather than challenging.

Bob Ball and Don Poupore could make a suspect feel like they were checking him into a luxury suite when they were booking him into a jail cell.

5

Remembering Judy

Mike Niemi accompanied Bruce when he returned to the Marquette area from Ontonagon the day after Judy was shot. It was a long, gloomy drive from late afternoon into dusk. Twenty-four hours had passed since the world tumbled down upon life as it had been for the family.

Before returning to the Moilanen house in Marquette, they stopped at the Photo Outlet in the Marquette Mall. Bruce wanted to have some photographs of Judy enlarged for display at the funeral service Wednesday in Ontonagon and the memorial Thursday in Marquette.

After visiting briefly with a couple of friends, such as Bill Nemacheck, Judy's supervisor at Marquette General Hospital, they drove on to Harvey.

Niemi, a compassionate man, had taken time off from his sales work at Courtesy Chevrolet in Ontonagon to help his cousin's widower, even if help only meant being there.

When they got to the house, luggage, dogs and guns had to be unloaded. Bruce was taking care of the dogs while Mike lugged hunting clothes into the basement and then came back for the guns. He carried three cases, one he knew contained Bruce's 33 Winchester and another Judy's 6mm. The third, stuck down between the kennels, had not been opened, but Bruce had mentioned that he brought his muzzle-loader as well.

◆   ◆   ◆

The night before, Bruce Moilanen had had the sad task of explaining to Elise what had happened in terms a three-year-old could understand. David had been with him when he called Elise into one of the bedrooms at the Blake house.

Bruce started by refreshing his daughter's memory of a dog named Quincy, the first dog he and Judy ever trained. They had started accumulating too many dogs, so they gave Quincy to David and Yvonne.

A year earlier, Quincy had died.

"Lisa," Bruce said quietly, "it's just going to be you and Daddy from now on. There's not going to be any more Mommy."

"Why?"

"Well," Bruce said, choosing his words carefully, "do you remember when we told you, when Quincy died, that Jesus needed a real good doggy to go live with him? And then Jesus took Quincy?"

Elise nodded, but her look was more of confusion than understanding.

Bruce plunged onward.

"Well, Jesus needed a real good Mommy to take care of somebody, so he picked your Mommy."

He stopped for a second and looked at his daughter and then continued reassuringly.

"Of course, we're going to see her again some day. It will be a long, long time, but you and Daddy will see her again some day."

It would be a long, long time before Elise understood…if ever.

◆   ◆   ◆

Judy's funeral service was Wednesday in Ontonagon, though her remains could not be buried until spring because of the frozen ground. She would rest in a vault. The Redeemer Free Lutheran Church in

Ontonagon was packed. David Blake's wife Yvonne played the organ. Bruce held Elise and seemed in a daze.

It is hard to imagine a sadder occasion than a funeral service for a 35-year-old mother, struck down by a seemingly random bullet during an innocent walk in the woods. Such senseless tragedy was so foreign to the Ontonagon community.

Judy Blake Moilanen had been part of that community virtually all of her life, growing up in the cozy white house at the corner of M-38 and Cherry Lane. Ontonagon is a wonderful place for children, a playground that begins at the back door and stretches to the horizon.

The woods behind Cherry Lane were a perfect place to play without getting into trouble. The world back there belonged to the kids.

Judy's best friend as she was growing up, a neighbor from two houses away on M-38, was Lee Anne Daniels. Judy was a year older, but that was hardly an insurmountable barrier. They played together and went skiing together and went to school together and joined the same clubs together. When Judy died, they were working at Marquette General together because Judy had gotten her friend a job.

When it came to activities, Judy would try anything. She was not particularly athletic, but she would try playing football or softball. She was usually one of the last persons chosen when a game was being organized.

What she really liked to do was read and do artsy-crafty projects. She was perfectly happy at home with her nose in a book. And friends still have things Judy made them while still in high school.

Basically, Judy Blake was a homebody. She was popular because she was so nice, but she was not remotely obsessed with being socially active. If high school classmates were gathering at the Township Park to sneak a surreptitious beer, Judy was more likely to be at Syl's Cafe eating a piece of cherry pie with a glass of milk.

While Judy was serious, she was not stodgy. She would not be the person telling jokes, but she would laugh heartily when she heard a good one…as long as it was not off-color.

Much of her attitude toward life was imbedded by her upbringing. The Blakes were comfortable unto themselves, religious and conservative. It would be safe to bet that neither Dale nor Mary Ann has ever set foot into any of the saloons that line River Street and the same can likely be said of their offspring.

Mary Ann was particularly protective of her only daughter and oldest child. She set the rules and Judy abided by them. If she was involved in an evening activity, she had her curfew and she adhered to it.

Judy's pictures in the Ontonagon Area High School yearbook, the Boulder, were almost repetitive. All four years she was pictured as a pretty blond with soft waves and curls in her hair and a wide smile. She was always wearing a sweater and over-sized glasses and she had a simple necklace with a cross in all but her senior picture.

Elsewhere in the yearbooks, she could be found each year with the Future Health Careers Club, Candy Stripers and Girls Athletic Association Mod Squad. At times, she was also involved with the newspaper, yearbook and pep club. Notably, she did not involve herself in student government, her shyness likely inhibiting her interest in such socially based activities.

She did give track a fling at one stage in her high school years, but fell on the cinders and came up with all of the scrapes a cinder surface inflicts. That was it for her track "career."

Although both pretty and pleasant, Judy did not get into the dating game. She went out infrequently, never with one boy to the exclusion of others.

The one summer job she held for a few years was waitressing at the Ontonagon Golf Course. Most of the members at the time were older and conservative and it was a safe place for a young woman to work, in spite of the presence of a bar.

Another interest Judy developed was skiing. The Porcupine Mountain Resort was maybe 20 minutes west of Ontonagon along M-64 and presented a wholesome and convenient form of winter recreation. She became a very good skier, coming down those tree-lined slopes with their magnificent views of Lake Superior.

It was on the ski slopes where Judy Blake met Bruce Moilanen.

The Moilanen family was considered somewhat a motley crew in Ontonagon, but this was not a community with a snobbish attitude. Judy would have had none of that anyway. What's more, Bruce brought an infectious enthusiasm to the ski slopes, because that was his turf.

Judy and Bruce started going together, regardless of whether approval was forthcoming.

Mary Ann Blake may not have approved, but she could not really argue with a daughter who was so much like her. Judy was strong-willed, stubborn and feisty and she was at a time in her life when all of that might have combined to create just a bit of rebellion.

Judy Blake married Bruce Moilanen.

◆   ◆   ◆

When the Ontonagon service was over, Bruce Moilanen found himself visiting with two of Judy's closest friends. One was Lee Anne Daniels Wysocki, a divorced mother who lived in Marquette, and the other was Sheri Groitzsch-Bishop. They were friends of Judy's from the days of Cherry Lane and cherry pie.

All were deeply into hurt, but Bruce was the one in search of sympathy.

"I hope she loved me," he said, "because I loved her so much."

Sheri was touched. She had talked with Judy the night before the "accident" and listened to her friend's heartfelt concern about where the marriage might be going. Judy *had* made the point that she knew they were going to get through all the bumpy roads and that the marriage would be fine. Given the circumstances, Sheri could sugarcoat her recollections just a bit.

"Bruce," she said, "you know Judy and I talked for a long time Saturday night. She did love you. She talked about it. She told me how much she loved you."

Bruce shed tears as Sheri was reassuring him.

The conversation went on and, as happens on occasions such as this, recollections started flowing and the name "Wysocki" came up on a couple of occasions.

"Who *is* this Wysocki woman?" Sheri asked.

"Me," Lee Anne said. "That was my married name."

They all enjoyed a brief moment of bemusement.

Meanwhile, Bob Ball and Deputy Cousineau were having their first conversation with Dale and David Blake since that painful Sunday evening in the kitchen. In the most casual of manners, they were talking about Sunday afternoon's hunting...and exactly where the men had all been.

◆   ◆   ◆

Yvonne Blake, David's wife, played the organ at the memorial service the following day in Marquette, as she had done at the funeral in Ontonagon. An accomplished musician, Yvonne played the organ, piano and guitar and sang and wrote music as well. She was in demand, particularly at churches, around the area.

As if she could not feel enough compassion already for her husband and his sister's widower, she could also relate through personal tragedy of her own. Nine years earlier, her 25-year-old brother had drowned while swimming in Lake Superior off the Ontonagon shores.

This particular service was unusual in that Bruce Moilanen sang with Yvonne, which was totally uncharacteristic of him, and also delivered a eulogy. He talked more of the last few days than of their life together and it began to sound more and more, towards the end, like a thinly veiled alibi for where *he* had been and what he had been doing.

Mourners looked at each other in bewilderment as Moilanen spoke, wondering what he was trying to say and why he was trying to say it. In this eulogy, they were trying to find the tribute to his deceased wife.

After the services were over and they were back at the Moilanen house in Harvey, Bruce called David off to the side. He offered Judy's double-barreled shotgun to his brother-in-law.

"Bruce," David said, "I appreciate it. It may be a good idea to keep it in case you need to sell it."

"Huh?"

"Don't start giving things away," David continued. "You may need to sell things to help support you and Elise."

Bruce turned somber.

"It may not be any of my business," David said seriously, "but what kind of shape were you in in terms of life insurance?"

Bruce shook his head and frowned.

"I think we had between $40,000 and $45,000," Bruce said. "There's really not even enough to pay off the mortgage."

"See what I mean? I think you should be careful giving things away."

◆   ◆   ◆

Wiljo (Bill) Moilanen, Bruce's father, was at the service. Bruce had stayed closer to his father, who had a farm in Kiva a short distance down U.S. 41 from Harvey, than he had to his mother. His father was quietly mingling with guests.

The older Moilanen felt tremendous hurt for his son. He knew the turmoil at home and the resultant divorce had given Bruce a less than idyllic boyhood and he felt a share of that responsibility. And now this senseless hunting accident had come along and destroyed what Bruce had built on his own as a man.

Before that calamitous Sunday, his son had a beautiful home and beautiful child and a beautiful wife and the most important part of all was now gone.

Wiljo Moilanen came upon David Blake and embraced him.

"David," Bruce Moilanen's father said, "you people are the only real family he's ever had."

6

On the Ball

Det. Sgt. Bob Ball was thinking of Bruce Moilanen as someone to be eliminated as a suspect. He was pursuing leads, confiscating weapons, or at least borrowing weapons, and, in one case, administering a lie detector test…to one of Jerry Schoch's house guests.

Leads had to be checked.

What about these people Marsha LaFernier had seen?

"I was leaving the house with my boys at about 2:45 on Sunday," she recalled. "I looked to the right, down toward Schoch's house, and I saw two men and a pickup truck. The men were walking toward the pickup truck."

"Can you describe them?" Ball asked.

"One was tall with a medium build," she said. "He didn't look like he'd been hunting, but he looked like he was in a hurry. The other was a little shorter, but huskier. He was wearing hunting clothes and carrying a rifle."

"What about the truck?" he asked.

"Full-sized," she said. "Older. Late 70s or early 80s. Dark blue or brown. No cab."

"Were they at Schoch's?" Ball wondered.

"I don't think so," she said. "They were parked kinda halfway between our houses, facing my direction."

"You noticed quite a bit pausing to come out of your driveway," Ball offered.

"It bothered me to think anyone was hunting so close," she said. "I had a deer shot in my yard last year. That was *much* too close."

Ball talked to one of LaFernier's young sons, who told him the men had come out of the woods on the west side of the street. This was opposite the side where Judy had been found, though a stray bullet could have carried that far. Ball, however, was convinced that the bullet had come from the other direction.

Schoch's house was the next stop. Ball, who was accompanied on this expedition by Det. Sgt. Poupore, knew that Schoch had a houseful of guests on Sunday, but one in particular interested him. He wanted to know about the hunter.

"He got here Saturday night with a couple of friends," Schoch said. "They live in Iron River and they were gone by noon Sunday. John was the only one who hunted. He was back from hunting by 10 or 11."

"Where did he hunt?" Ball asked.

"Both sides," said Schoch's friend Kim Wilber. "I looked out the window and saw him cross the road."

Butch Ark was another of Schoch's friends who had been at the house that day, but he did not get there until noon. The Iron River guests were gone. Ark did not hunt, but he was a burly man of medium height. Ball thought he could have been one of the men the LaFerniers saw down the road toward Schoch's.

Maybe it was a matter of being stubborn or maybe it was a matter of grasping at straws, but Ball decided to further investigate the houseguest from Iron River who had supposedly departed. He was the only person investigators had uncovered who hunted the area at any time that Sunday.

◆   ◆   ◆

On the Wednesday afternoon of Judy's funeral service in Ontonagon, a telephone tip was called into the State Police. Ball returned the call from a woman who requested anonymity.

Her recitation went somewhat like this: "I know a woman who knows a woman who seems to be close to Bruce. He is making quite an effort to have a relationship with this woman. Sends her flowers and calls her all the time."

This may have seemed like a real-life enactment of that game where a story starts at one point in a circle and comes back completely different at the other end, but Ball did not shove it on a back burner. He had no circle, but rather a seeming million points of darkness.

Ball contacted the next link in the "telephone chain" and got a woman who worked afternoon shifts in the admitting office at Portage View Hospital in Hancock.

"Everyone in the admitting office is familiar with Bruce Moilanen," she said. "Up until a year and a half ago, he was over here all the time from Marquette General with a mobile C.T. scan unit. We got a unit of our own about that time. Everyone assumed he was single by the way he acted. I didn't know he was married. I went out with him for a drink."

"Does he have a girlfriend at Portage View?" Ball asked.

"Not really," the woman said. "He has a friend, but it's more like he is stalking her. She doesn't do anything to egg him on. She might be able to help you. Her name is Gayle Lampinen."

◆   ◆   ◆

After the funeral service, Det. Sgt. Ball and Deputy Cousineau paid a visit to the residences of Dale Blake, Judy's father, and David Blake, Judy's brother.

The Moilanens, Dale explained, had been married since June 24, 1978, both working at Marquette General at the time Judy died. Judy had been there since shortly before they were married in 1978 and Bruce since 1980. He talked about his daughter and son-in-law and then volunteered how hard Bruce was taking Judy's death.

"He told me he had lost not only a wife but his best friend as well," Judy's father said.

Dale Blake had run Dale's Service Station in Ontonagon for years. He fueled cars and serviced cars. He also sold fuel oil for homes. Many locals know him on sight, but don't really know him. He is a private man, even among the cronies who gathered at his station each morning to drink coffee and exchange manly gossip. He also is a religious man who could not lie if he was boiling in his own fuel oil.

When Bruce Moilanen told Dale Blake how much he hurt, Dale could feel Bruce's hurt. He could also believe it, because a man he trusted had said it. A man can bestow no greater trust than to give away his daughter in marriage.

Ball was not so trusting. His job did not leave a lot of room for trust.

"So the men were all together down at the hunting camp," he said matter-of-factly.

"Most of us," Blake said. "Bruce was either hunting on his own or with Mike Niemi."

"When did he leave the camp?" Ball wondered.

Blake scratched his chin as if making sure his memory was on target.

"Actually," he said, "Bruce never came down to the camp. He stayed at the house and went off either with Judy or by himself."

Ball was not exactly stunned by the revelation. It could, in fact, prove to be totally meaningless. However, based on Sunday's brief meeting, he had concluded that all of the men had been together. What it did was make him more interested in learning about the chimney block incident and the woman at Portage View Hospital.

"I was the person who had to tell Bruce about Judy," Blake was saying, "and he took it very, very hard."

Ball droned on, asking questions and taking notes.

"No problems between the two of them?" he said, almost apologetically.

"Not a bit of a problem," Dale Blake assured.

◆   ◆   ◆

David Blake was much like his father, medium of height and slim of build…and quiet. He had gone away first to a Lutheran college in Minneapolis and then vocational training at Moorhead State in Minnesota before coming home to join his father in the family business. David was only 29, but he had the maturity to basically take over preparations for Judy's funeral service.

Ball had been surprised to learn that Bruce had not been with the men that Sunday, but then again not surprised. The mood Sunday night at Dale and Mary Ann Blake's house had not been right for a detective to ask penetrating questions.

On this Wednesday night, he approached David as he had approached Dale Blake. He just wanted some background. In truth, he had no specific direction to look. That was his problem. Ball asked a few question about guns, a few about Judy's girlfriends, a few about dogs, a few about the trails behind Cherry Lane and a few about Bruce.

"Bruce was either hunting alone," David said, "or maybe with our cousin Gary Niemi. He didn't make it to the camp."

◆   ◆   ◆

Bob Ball had unfinished business in Iron River. He wanted to question Jerry Schoch's houseguest. As it turned out, he questioned two houseguests. And he "borrowed" a rifle for test firing.

John, a 32-year-old construction worker, had heard from Schoch and he was expecting that detectives would be visiting him. He was at ease, as though the experience was routine. He had, in fact, been arrested earlier in the day on an unrelated bench warrant and released.

"I never hunted east of Cherry Lane," he told Ball. "I know the area. I know where the houses are. I was about a half-mile west of Cherry

Lane hunting near a power line. I saw a couple of deer blinds and I got nervous. I don't like to hunt near someone else's spot."

John went on to tell Ball how Butch Ark had been sent down Cherry Lane to try to find him and hurry him up because the others wanted to get back to Iron River. He told of seeing children playing in the street in front of the old Gordon residence. LaFernier lived in the old Gordon residence.

Ball now had a possible explanation for the two men, one a hunter and one in a hurry, whom Marsha LaFernier and her kids had seen, but the time was wrong. And he had been told the Iron River guests had been gone when Ark arrived.

Unanswered questions will drive a detective nuts and Ball was getting answers that raised more questions.

"John," he said, "I think it's very important for you to come up with documentation for either the time you left Ontonagon or the time you got back to Iron River."

◆   ◆   ◆

Judy had worked for 14 years at Marquette General Hospital as administrative assistant to the assistant administrator and Bruce joined her at MGH in 1980, first as an emergency medical technician (EMT) and later as an instrument technician in the operating room. To find out more about the victim and her widower, Det. Sgt. Ball went to the hospital on Dec. 8.

Accompanied by Lt. Henry Steede of the Marquette police and Poupore, Ball first dropped in on Judy's boss. Bill Nemacheck had hired Mrs. Moilanen and she had become a friend as well as employee.

"I think there were financial problems in their household," Nemacheck said, "but I don't really have details because Judy was very private about things like that."

He had heard of problems involving a business or partnership, possibly relating to Bruce's North Country Claim Service. He also knew that the Moilanens had been trying to refinance their house, but could not seem to get the deal closed.

"I picked up from Judy that Bruce wasn't taking care of business," Nemacheck said. "I told Judy our employee assistance program might be of help, and I think she talked to them. I know she made some schedule changes to take advantage of the counseling."

"What happened?" Ball asked.

"Well," Nemacheck said, "Judy told me that she and Bruce had talked to an attorney about bankruptcy as an option. I ran into one of the bank executives I knew and asked him about maybe being more flexible and working with the Moilanens. It must have worked itself out because Judy thanked me for helping."

"What do you know about the chimney block incident?"

"My wife and I were called to the emergency room after it happened," Nemacheck said. "I don't know all the circumstances, but I know Judy was lucky to be alive."

Ball and his colleagues went down the hall to interview Roger Brooks, an employee in risk management. He really knew nothing of the Moilanens in a personal sense, but he had taken a Gordon Setter to them for training.

"Judy was good," he said, "but I had problems with Bruce. I was working my dog at their place one day when I saw Bruce kick another dog very hard. It bothered me. I never took another dog over there because I was afraid it might be mistreated."

Brooks had already lined up Robin Bartanen, who could help with information on the hospital's group insurance programs, and now he also suggested that the detectives talk to Mary Andes, a good friend of Judy.

Bartanen was helpful, but nothing they learned was particularly startling. The hospital's plan, underwritten by Safeco, would pay $20,000, plus another $20,000 for accidental death. Bruce had been telling friends and relatives that he had $40,000 to $45,000 worth of insurance and this must be it. That he had been to see Bartanen about how to make a claim the previous day did not seem outrageous either.

Mary Andes was more enlightening.

Judy had come into her office crying and distraught in late October or early November. She wanted to talk. She wanted to confide. She told Mary that she and Bruce were facing bankruptcy, suggesting Bruce might be involved in something fraudulent.

"I might be held responsible too," Judy told her.

Mary sat and listened while Judy told her about a lawsuit involving one of his businesses and an error or omission he made in his claim service business.

"I keep finding out more and more about Bruce," Judy told Mary. "I've thought about leaving him, but I don't want to take his daughter away from him."

Judy had had only one reservation about confiding in Mary. She was adamant that her parents not become aware that any problems existed. Mary's understanding was that Judy's mother never cared for Bruce and she did not want to cause any problems in the future.

For all of her uncharacteristic openness, Judy had still managed to keep most of what was bothering her inside. Mary Andes knew her friend had problems and her friend was upset, but she had no clue exactly what the problems might be.

Ms. Andes had a three-page, single-spaced memo with her dated Dec. 4, 1992. It detailed her conversations with Judy, what had and had not been said. It was a thoughtful, concerned memo, in which she recalled specific suggestions she had made to Judy. She gave the detectives a copy of the memo.

Poupore looked at Ball as they awaited an elevator. They were reading each other's minds.

"Judy kept finding out more and more about Bruce, huh?" Poupore said.

"That's what we're going to do too," Ball responded.

◆   ◆   ◆

Patricia Blake, the nurse supervising the operating room, did not talk about Judy Moilanen. Blake, no relation to the Ontonagon Blakes, told the detectives about Bruce Moilanen. He was no friend of hers. She had a lot to say about Bruce.

Moilanen had started vacation on Nov. 25, but he had since applied for unpaid personal leave until Jan. 18, 1993. The application was granted. Pat Blake would not miss him. She described him as an employee who was chronically late for work and often inexplicably away from his job when he was supposed to be on duty.

"People are irritated with him," she said, "because he causes problems regarding job description and he's not dependable. I tried to find him another position, but his reputation precedes him. No one wants him. Either nothing fazes this guy or he doesn't care."

The detectives were astonished at the calmly delivered evaluation of Bruce Moilanen, the employee.

"Other supervisors," she continued, "ask me what it is he does because they see him all over the hospital. In short, he's the worst employee I've ever had."

On the way down the hall, Ball was shaking his head.

"We can't put the guy in jail for being the worst employee in history," he said.

◆   ◆   ◆

Katie Kuopus had only been at Marquette General for a year, but she worked side-by-side with Judy in Bill Nemacheck's office. She too noticed in late October that Judy was upset. Judy would take a telephone call and then excuse herself to talk in a private office. When she came back, it was obvious she had been crying. When Katie offered to help, Judy just shrugged her shoulders and said she was having some problems.

Katie apparently knew Bruce Moilanen just well enough to know she did not want to know him.

"He came into the office one day," she recalled, "and he and Judy were having some sort of difference. On his way out of the office, he turned to me and said something like, 'Don't worry, I'll make *you* cry someday soon.'"

Bruce Moilanen could make a lot of people cry.

Judy Moilanen was doing most of the crying in late October and early November. Sharon Olsen, employed in purchasing at Marquette General, noticed it as well. It was totally out of character for Judy to be letting emotion come to the surface, other than joy at something nice happening to a friend.

Olsen was also very unsettled by the fact that Judy had been the victim of two freak accidents little more than a year apart, especially after she overheard a maintenance man talking in the cafeteria.

"He didn't get her with the brick," he said, "but he got her this time."

Bob Ball and Don Poupore had gotten an earful at Marquette General Hospital. Obviously, problems existed with this marriage. Obviously, Bruce Robert Moilanen was not the most beloved individual in the building. Their job would be to unravel what it all meant.

◆   ◆   ◆

Marquette, a college town with Northern Michigan University, was very strongly dependent on the K.I. Sawyer Air Force Base for its economy. The university and the air base combined to make Marquette the most robust community in the Upper Peninsula, but it was a community in a quandary because Sawyer was on the list of bases scheduled for closure.

People in Ontonagon, and other areas of the Western U.P., liked to take shopping trips to Marquette because stores were bigger and there were more of them. However, the drive takes more than two hours, dependent on the weather, so people with chores in Marquette try to schedule them in clusters to save trips.

Det. Sgts. Ball and Poupore were men with chores. Lt. Steede had helped them schedule a full day on Wednesday, Dec. 9, 1992.

Getting started early in the afternoon, they drove to Frei Chevrolet GEO on U.S. 41. Jim Grundstrom, the owner, had known Bruce Moilanen as both an employee and a customer. Lt. Richard Goad, the chief State Police detective in the U.P., thought Grundstrom had some interesting information about Moilanen, the customer.

"After all we've heard at the hospital," Ball remarked to Poupore, "let's ask this guy about Bruce as an employee."

Grundstrom explained that it had been some years since Moilanen had worked in his body shop, but he had been a memorable employee.

"He wasn't a good employee," Grundstrom said, "because he did everything his own way. It was Bruce's way or no way."

"So he came back to you later as a customer?" Poupore said.

"Right," Grundstrom said. "He came in last summer for some service work, which we did. We came in the next morning and the vehicle was gone. Bruce picked it up at night and left without paying a $240 bill."

"So what's come of it?" Ball asked.

"We tried to take him to small claims court," Grundstrom said, "but we were never able to serve him. All the paper work kept coming back."

"So nothing's happened?"

"The small claims hearing was scheduled for last Monday," Grundstrom said. "The day after Judy's death. We backed off."

The detectives were on their way out the door when Grundstrom called.

"I've never liked dealing with Bruce Moilanen," he said. "He's more trouble than he's worth."

Ball and Poupore looked at each other with arched eyebrows.

◆   ◆   ◆

When the detectives pulled up in front of the Janofski home on Riverside Road, they did not know what to expect. Irene Janofski ran a baby sitting service in her home and the Moilanens had been customers almost since Elise was born. Bruce and Judy could be virtual strangers who dropped a child off daily and wrote checks once a week or they could be more than that.

Irene and John were both there when the detectives knocked on the door. The Janofskis sat down and leaned forward, as if anxious to help.

"Judy," Irene offered, "had become one of my closest friends. Bruce, though, is a difficult person to get to know. He's a very secretive person."

"I don't know quite how to put this," John said, "but he has actually called us stupid people."

"Stupid people?" one of the detectives frowned.

John shrugged. That was just Bruce.

"We really love Elise," Irene said, "so we don't want to cause any problems between us and Bruce."

The Janofskis echoed what the detectives had heard at Marquette General. A change in Judy had taken place maybe six weeks earlier. Judy crying. Judy emotional. Judy confused. Judy worrying. Judy not elaborating. They sensed it was something financial.

"I noticed something strange after this started happening," Irene said. "They'd always paid us off a joint account, with both names on the check. Judy started paying us with checks written on an account in her name only."

"What makes you think there are financial problems?" Ball asked.

"About a month ago," John said, "they were selling things such as a Jeep, an ATV, a van and, I think, a camper. Then they turn around and pick up a new van the Monday before Thanksgiving."

The Moilanens would seem to have been going in contradictory directions, if it was assumed they were selling assets to pay bills. It might have been that they were raising money to pay for the new van.

The conversation eventually steered away from the financial aspects of the Moilanens' life. And these people were not done talking.

"We've been suspicious of Bruce since the chimney block incident," they said. "We think Elise might have seen more than she has been able to tell. She was there."

And the chimney block incident was not the only one that stirred the Janofskis' suspicions.

"Judy was here once later that fall," Irene said, "and she told us she woke up one morning and the house was full of smoke. She checked the basement and found that hot ashes from the wood stove had started the woodpile on fire. Bruce had dumped the ashes before he went hunting."

Irene Janofski could see by the expressions on their faces that Ball and Poupore had not heard about this...a third freak "accident."

"Judy and Elise," she said, "were *both* asleep in the house when he left."

Ball and Poupore were consistently encountering people with just one more thing to say, one more comment or one more suggestion, as they were preparing to leave.

"You should talk to Jennifer," they said. "She's our 21-year-old daughter."

And so they did.

Jennifer was an ambitious young woman who worked for Marquette General, at a job Judy had gotten her, as well as at a First National Bank branch. She was also a student at Northern Michigan. She had occasionally helped her parents when they were watching Elise.

Bruce did not impress her.

"He is hard and out-spoken," she said, "and downright rude at times."

The previous Saturday, the first Saturday after Judy's death, Jennifer had run into Bruce at ShopKo. He told her of how he felt so alone in the big house. He told of how he longed for adult companionship. He said something about how much Elise would like to see her.

"I got the impression he wanted me to spend the night," she told Ball and Poupore. "I told him I might stop by some evening for a couple of hours."

She hesitated only briefly.

"But I would have taken a girlfriend with me."

She never went.

◆   ◆   ◆

Bob Ball and Don Poupore had plenty of time to talk as they drove back to headquarters from Marquette. Their notebooks were full of suspicions and opinions, none very positive when it came to Judy Blake Moilanen's husband. Undeniably and inexplicably, something had caused Judy to be uncharacteristically upset to the point of shedding her veneer of privacy when it came to personal matters.

"She confided in an awful lot of people," Poupore said.

"But she never got specific about what was troubling her," Ball said. "Getting hold of their financial records may be helpful."

"And now we have that fire in the basement to go with the chimney block incident," Poupore said. "We've got a lot of 'accidents' involving Judy Moilanen."

"I think tomorrow we better sit down and have a talk with Bruce," Ball said.

They certainly were not closing the door on other aspects of the investigation. The man from Iron River was not off the hook. What's more, Tom Cousineau had learned of tire tracks and foot prints leading toward Cherry Lane from a clearing nine-10ths of a mile to the east. They were far from focused, not only regarding potential suspects but also in terms of whether they were dealing with a hunting accident or homicide.

◆   ◆   ◆

Tom Cousineau's information came from Jason Warren, a 17-year-old whose family owns Turpeinen's clear-cut. He had been in the area late the afternoon of Judy's death and he had noticed fresh tracks in the area.

After young Warren showed him the tracks, Cousineau arranged to have State Trooper Greg Wardman, a crime scene technician from the Wakefield Post, take plaster casts, photographs and measurements. They might be meaningless and innocent, but the investigators could take no chances.

The imprints were sent to the Marquette crime lab.

◆   ◆   ◆

Ball, Poupore and Det. Lt. Goad, their boss, drove to Bruce Moilanen's home in Harvey for the first time the evening of Dec. 10, a Thursday. They were unannounced "guests" so Moilanen was not there when they arrived at 8 o'clock. They backed out of the driveway and parked along U.S. 41 to wait and watch. Moilanen and his daughter arrived an hour later.

Ball introduced his colleagues and gave Moilanen a brief summation of the investigation. It had to be brief, because they really had nothing they wanted to tell him. They did not tell him how popular he wasn't at Marquette General.

"Bruce," Ball said, "one of the things we have to do is go through the formality of eliminating you as a possible suspect. We don't have you accounted for that afternoon, at least not all of that afternoon."

"I understand you have a job to do," Moilanen said.

"We have to eliminate your firearms as well," Ball added.

"Do you want to take my guns with you tonight?" Moilanen asked.

"If we could," Ball said.

"Fine."

Moilanen signed a "permission to search" form and took the detectives to the gunroom in the basement. He turned over a Remington 6mm, a Winchester 33, a Remington 7mm and a Sturm-Ruger 357 magnum.

"I have a muzzle-loader and a couple of shotguns," he said, "but this is all my high-powered stuff. You want ammunition for test firing?"

"If we could," Ball said. "We'll replace what we use."

When they sat down to talk, Moilanen delivered what the detectives came to call The Destiny Speech. He talked of an automobile accident and a four-wheeler accident, as if to suggest his wife was accident-prone. He talked of how Judy had gotten the Christmas shopping done early and packed some of her clothes for delivery to St. Vincent De-Paul. He was suggesting to his visitors that his wife must have had a subconscious and ominous premonition.

The "visit" had been brief. Its purpose, basically, was to retrieve high-powered weapons in such a way as to inhibit Bruce Moilanen from being able to remove or hide any particular weapon. The detectives, to be sure, did not even know what weapon they were seeking, other than a high-powered rifle.

"You notice what he did not mention?" Ball said to his colleagues when they got to their car. "He didn't mention the chimney block incident. *That* was probably the most life-threatening experience she had. *That* wasn't important enough to mention. To me, *that's* a red flag."

◆   ◆   ◆

A "formal" interview had been scheduled for Friday morning at the Negaunee State Police Post, where Poupore was headquartered and where Moilanen had worked a few years earlier as a dispatcher. Bruce knew his way, but he was still almost an hour late.

"We understand what you're going through," Ball said, "but you've said you understand that we have our job to do."

Moilanen expressed appreciation for the seeming sympathy.

"Not only have I lost my wife," he said, "but I've lost my best friend."

This was a sentiment that seemed almost rehearsed. Ball wanted to get to the point of the interview.

"Tell us about your activities that day," he encouraged.

Moilanen described the morning, the breakfast with Mike Niemi and then a trip to the Tank Creek area for a couple of hours of hunting starting at maybe 11:15 to 11:20 a.m. He marked on a map where he parked his 1987 Chevrolet van, which he said he and Judy had just purchased. He talked of almost backing into Wade Johnson at around 2:15. His recitation took him back to Niemi's house to pick up deer bait and onward to hunting until after dark.

Bruce Moilanen produced a long list of people he had seen and places he had been…and people he was sure had seen him.

"Are you familiar with the Turpeinen clear-cut?" Ball asked.

"Sure," Moilanen said. "I know that area."

"You didn't hunt there that day?"

"Never," Moilanen said with emphasis.

"Did you and Judy have marital problems?"

"I honestly don't think there's a perfect marriage," Moilanen said, "but I'd say we got along better than maybe 90 per cent of your marriages."

"Financial problems?"

"Nothing big or major. The hospital cut out our overtime this year, so, of course, that made our incomes a lot less, but you know, no major problems."

"What do you have in terms of life insurance coverage?"

"Well," Moilanen said, "we have a policy with Lutheran Brotherhood that I think's about $60,000, but we have $5,000 of that out in a loan for remodeling our house."

"Does that have double indemnity?"

"Right," Moilanen said. "It's for accidental. That's what I was about to tell you. And they're in the process of setting up a trust for my daughter. And my wife and I, about two years ago, purchased a single-pay policy for $75,000, should something happen to one of us, for her education."

"Which company is that through?"

"Northwestern Mutual Life. But it's designed to go into a trust for Elise."

"Okay," Ball said. "Any other policies."

"I think the hospital has one that's $5,000. And then there's a $1,000 policy through the credit union."

Ball and Poupore did not even look at one another. They had previously heard of only $40,000 in life insurance, that being Judy's double indemnity through work. These people were not exactly under-insured. Without doing the math, they could see Judy was covered by more than $200,000 worth of insurance.

"How about assets?" Ball said.

Moilanen listed property, checking accounts, savings accounts, businesses and a tax-sheltered annuity Judy had through Marquette General. He told detectives he and Judy had been refinancing their home to consolidate payments and reduce the interest rate.

"Any other women in your life?" Ball asked.

The look on Moilanen's face suggested such a question was totally inappropriate and distasteful.

"None," he said. "Never."

"Any traumatic events?"

"None. Ah, a year ago in September, we were fixing the chimney on the house and Judy fell off the house roof and spent four days in the hospital."

"She fell off the house roof?"

Ball wanted to make sure he had heard right.

"Yeh," Moilanen said. "She was up cutting flashing for around the chimney, landed on the patio, wound up with a concussion."

"Holy smokes," Ball said with sympathy. "That's a real high house."

"I wouldn't want to fall off the house," Moilanen said.

Ball did not pursue this subject further. He had to know more about this chimney block incident. To this point, his understanding had been that Judy was on the patio and the block fell from the roof and hit her on the head. Bruce Moilanen had come up with a completely different version.

"You had nothing to do with Judy's death?" he asked off-handedly.

"Nothing whatsoever," Moilanen said.

"Well Bruce," Ball said, "we would like to take a look at your financial records and have a look around your house. We have a couple of consent forms we'd like you to sign."

Moilanen had no problems. He signed the forms and returned them.

"And," Ball said, "we'd like you to take a polygraph examination this afternoon. We'll get this wrapped up so we can get on with our investigation."

"That would be fine," Moilanen said, "but I have to check with the baby sitter."

"Feel free to use the phone in the next room," Poupore offered.

Moilanen made the call and returned to the room. Unfortunately, the baby sitter was unavailable. Maybe he could take the test on Monday instead. They scheduled him for 5 p.m.

After Moilanen left, Ball called Irene Janofski.

"I told him I had a party tonight," Mrs. Janofski said, "but I was available all afternoon."

Bruce Moilanen had lied to get out of taking a lie detector test.

◆   ◆   ◆

At about the time Moilanen was denying that he had been in the Turpeinen clear-cut area the day of Judy's death, state troopers were taking impressions from the tires of his van out in the parking lot.

If he had, in fact, been at that location, these tracks were useless as evidence.

They did not match.

◆   ◆   ◆

Having retrieved Moilanen's rifles on Thursday night, Ball, Poupore and Goad drove to Harvey for a more thorough search Friday afternoon. They had the consent forms, of course, and they showed these to Ed Niemi, Judy's uncle, who was the only person there when they arrived. They waited for Moilanen to arrive with Elise.

Looking around, they could see the house better in the daylight than they could the previous evening. It was a brick ranch-style house, set back from U.S. 41 behind a wooden rail fence. The yard was open to the highway, but wooded in the back.

What the detectives did not know as they waited was that Bruce Moilanen had stopped at the house *before* they got there. He had gone down to the basement and come up with a brown paper bag. He went out the door and told Niemi he had to go to the Janofskis' to pick up Elise.

Once Moilanen arrived, Ball took him to check the basement to be sure they had not missed any rifles. Moilanen had insisted that the guns he had given the detectives were all that he owned and all that he had ever owned. Ball found no more weapons, at least no more high-powered rifles.

Some instinct caused Ball to grab a stool and reach blindly into what amounted to a crawl space between the gun room ceiling and the rafters. He felt a packet of papers and pulled them out.

"Bruce," he said, "what's this?"

"I don't know how that got there," Moilanen said.

Ball hustled upstairs to get a taller stool. He didn't know exactly what he had, but, most importantly, he did not want to alarm Moilanen to the point where he decided to throw them all out of the house. They had a "consent to search" form, not a search warrant.

At about this time, Ball's beeper went off. It was Hank Steede's number at the Marquette P.D.

"Irene Janofski called," Steede said. "Bruce ran in to get Elise, but he put something in the garage first."

Ball did not know what "something" might be, but he was anxious to find out. He kept the call's purpose to himself, since Moilanen was standing only a few feet away waiting to go back down to the basement.

The taller stool gave him a better view above the gunroom and he found another packet of papers. It seemed an unusual place to be storing what appeared to be financial records and insurance policies. At a quick glance, Ball noticed telephone bills...unopened. He took both packets.

Poupore and Goad, meanwhile, were searching the office area in the breezeway between the house and the garage. They found the usual clutter on the desk, but clutter could be meaningful. They seized bankbooks, deposit slips, statements and credit cards. Goad found two life insurance policies in a file cabinet.

Searching in the basement, Ball went through another file cabinet and found more life insurance information.

While the others continued searching the main floor, where they found Judy's bureau drawers empty, Ball discovered a panel to the attic. He poked his head into the attic, but the dust was thick. It was obvious there had been no activity for quite some time.

Ball looked out the window and realized the consent form also covered the van parked in the driveway. He went outside and threw open the doors. He found five boxes and sorted through each of them.

All he found were articles of a woman's clothing.

One box contained nothing but sweaters.

"What's this stuff?" Ball asked.

"It's some of Judy's clothes," Moilanen said. "Mary Ann packed them for me a few days ago. I'm gonna take them to St. Vincent De-Paul."

When the detectives finally got into their car, Ball had some news. He was so anxious that he momentarily forgot that Bruce had told him less than 24 hours earlier that Judy had packed clothing for St. Vincent DePaul.

"I couldn't wait to get out of there," he said. "We have to get to the Janofskis'. Bruce got here before we did and took something over to their place."

"A gun?" Goad asked.

"She didn't look," Ball said, "but she said Bruce seemed to be awful anxious and in an awful big hurry."

The detectives went to the baby sitter's house and found the brown paper bag. It was full of pornographic tapes.

◆   ◆   ◆

Bruce Moilanen was unnerved by the interview and the search. The family was taking turns keeping him company and it was Uncle Ed Niemi's turn. He went to sleep on the living room couch after the detectives left. From the couch, Niemi could see Moilanen pacing back and forth between the entryway and the bedroom.

"He never said anything," Niemi recalled. "He just paced back and forth."

7

The Sweater Letter

Gayle Lampinen's interest was piqued when she came home from work the Monday night after Thanksgiving and read in the *Houghton Daily Mining Gazette* that a woman named Moilanen had been killed in Ontonagon. The woman's name was Judy, but that did not ring a bell with her. She had known a Bruce Moilanen for a couple of years and had heard from him more often than she cared to hear from him. She and her husband Paul considered him to be a pest.

"Do you remember Bruce's wife's first name?" she asked Paul.

He didn't.

Moilanen was a relatively common name in the Upper Peninsula and, besides, this shooting had occurred in Ontonagon. She knew that Bruce lived near Marquette. She scanned deeper into the article and soon realized that Judy Moilanen was, indeed, Bruce Moilanen's wife.

"Paul," she said, "Bruce's wife was shot down in Ontonagon. I *think* it's the same Bruce."

"What?" Paul said, startled at the news.

"They think it was a hunting accident," she said.

"Oh God," Lampinen said. "They have a little girl, don't they?"

"I think I should try to call him," she said. "See if you can get the number from information."

Gayle Lampinen had known Bruce Moilanen for maybe two years since he first showed up at Portage View Hospital in Hancock with a mobile scanner unit. Gayle was a supervisor at Portage View and he had come in all cocky and chatting up the women in the office. She was happily married and, consequently, did nothing to encourage his attention.

Gayle could not stop Bruce Moilanen from taking a liking to her. He started dropping into her office whenever his mobile scanner was in Hancock. If he wasn't scheduled to be in Hancock, he would call her at the office. The crutch he used, the excuse, was that he was a dog trainer and Gayle was an American quarterhorse trainer and this caused them, in his mind, to have much in common.

In the summer of 1991, Moilanen walked into Gayle's office and announced that he and Judy were getting a divorce. He did not say when and he did not say why. It was as though he was announcing his imminent availability, as if anyone eminently cared.

During that same summer, Paul met Moilanen for the first time. Sort of. Bruce showed up at the Lampinen's home on his bicycle. Paul, vice president of the Superior National Bank in Baraga, realized he had met Moilanen a few years earlier when he had hired him to appraise a used car for possible loan.

"He was always around," Paul said later. "If he wasn't calling, he was visiting."

Paul Lampinen, an affable sort with prematurely graying hair, was not one to feel threatened by Moilanen's contacts with his wife. He was very secure with himself and he felt very secure with his relationship with Gayle. He could tolerate Bruce if Gayle could. If Bruce's intentions went beyond friendship and he was using an insincere friendship with Paul to disguise those intentions, Paul knew the dog trainer was barking up the wrong tree.

In the summer of 1992, Moilanen arrived unannounced, as was common with him, at the Lampinen house in Chassell. Elise was with him. So was Judy. Bruce had long been claiming a divorce was in the works, but the Moilanens' demeanor did not suggest the trauma of a divorce was on anyone's mind.

Paul came out of the house and said hello. Gayle, who was exercising one of her horses, got down and said hello. Moilanen introduced his wife and daughter. The encounter might have lasted five minutes. The Lampinens never saw Judy Moilanen again.

Later in the summer, Moilanen showed up at Paul's bank in Baraga. He had three sheets of North Country Claims letterhead paper. One sheet had a formula for a concoction Moilanen purported would eliminate a person's scent. The other two sheets listed a detailed itinerary for a hunting trip to Texas. Moilanen was excited about the formula.

"This product," Moilanen said, "should sell like crazy during the hunting season. I'm looking into how I can manufacture and market the stuff."

If he was interested in the bank's backing, he didn't say anything. He might have been hoping Paul would offer. Paul didn't.

However, Bruce had come up with an idea that would surely get him into Paul's good graces. The proposed hunting trip was for two. Bruce and Paul. Bruce would pay all of the expenses for his good buddy. Paul declined. In retrospect, he could be excused for wondering exactly what—or who—the prey might have been.

In October of 1992, while Gayle was "vacationing" at a horse show, Moilanen again popped in on Paul at the bank. This time he wanted to borrow money.

"I'm trying to buy a pickup," he said, "but GMAC turned me down. My wife has run the credit cards to the max and she's late on loan payments. You know I'm good for it, Paul."

"Bruce, I can't lend you the money," Paul said. "You're out of our loan area."

Gayle was no sooner home from her vacation when the telephone rang at her home in Chassell.

"Judy's left me," said a distraught voice on the other end of the line. "Bruce..."

"She left me," he said, crying.

"What about Elise?" Gayle asked.

"I have her," he said. "I can't talk any more. I'll call you later."

Gayle hung up the telephone. God, he was a pest, but he did not seem to have any other friends. He was certainly not numbered among the many she and Paul considered close friends, but they—Paul too—seemed so important to him. It may not be easy for them to explain or others to understand, but they were just not the kind of people who easily turn their backs on someone reaching out.

Not too long after that conversation, Bruce called and wanted to meet Gayle for lunch. They met at Gino's, a popular restaurant in Hancock. It was now November, 1992. Moilanen wanted to talk about the divorce and what Judy was doing to him. He was a bitter man. He was beyond crying and now he was angry.

"She took off with $33,000 from North Country Claims," he said, "and she's run all three credit cards to the max. I have to do my work for Marquette General, run my businesses, train my dogs and take care of Elise."

Just before Thanksgiving, Gayle got a call at work. Bruce told her he was going downstate to show a dog over the Thanksgiving weekend. Elise would be fine, he assured her. She would be staying with her Grandma and Grandpa Blake in Ontonagon.

"By the way," Bruce said nonchalantly, "why don't we go to the Ojibwa Casino? Paul won't mind you getting out while he's gone."

He knew Paul was at a hunting camp. He seemingly knew everything. What Gayle did not know, since she assumed the Moilanens were separated, was that Bruce was taking advantage of a "window of opportunity" to get out without having to explain to Judy. All of the Blake women take a shopping trip to Green Bay the weekend before Thanksgiving.

Judy was gone alright. Shopping.

Regardless, Gayle was not interested. She said no, making up a story about a weekend trip to Iron Mountain.

Her telephone rang a couple of days later and it was Bruce: "Gayle, I want to apologize. I wasn't really inviting you on a date. I don't want you to get the wrong idea. It's just that you're so easy to talk to."

This call had come early in Thanksgiving week. Bruce was supposedly "alone" with Elise. Judy was gone. Somewhere. Now she had the *Daily Mining Gazette* in her hands and Bruce had been in Ontonagon, where his wife had been killed in a hunting accident. Had he lied to her about showing a dog? Had he lied to her about the separation and all those horrible things Judy had done? If he expected friendship from her, was he betraying it with lies? Or maybe the spirit of the upcoming holiday season had just salved the wounds between the Moilanens.

Never before had Gayle called Moilanen, either at home or work, but now she was dialing the home in Harvey. She got the answering machine.

"I can't answer the phone due to a death in the family," Moilanen's voice said. "Please leave a message."

"I'm sorry to hear about your wife," Gayle said. "If you need anything, call us."

About 20 minutes later, the Lampinens' telephone rang. Bruce was calling, but he was so despondent he could hardly speak. He thanked her for thinking of him. The conversation lasted all of 15 seconds.

The Lampinens found a flower shop in Ontonagon and called the next day to order an arrangement for the funeral. Friends do that sort of thing. Even for a pest.

◆   ◆   ◆

Exactly 12 days after his wife's death, Moilanen was on the telephone to the Lampinens. It was Friday, Dec. 11. He had to see someone…them. He had to talk. Would they please meet him for lunch? Like the next day. They agreed to meet him at The Chippewa Restaurant in Chassell.

With Elise in tow, Bruce showed up with Christmas presents. He gave a key chain to Paul and a collector's plate to Gayle. They had no presents for Bruce and felt uncomfortable accepting what he brought for them.

"I have good news," Moilanen announced. "I'm in the process of selling my insurance business and I'm going to retire from Marquette General."

At a time when Moilanen had excused himself to use the rest room, Paul whispered to Gayle: "Are you as surprised as I am about how upbeat he is?"

"Very surprised," she said. "I can't believe this stuff about retiring. He's been talking all along about financial problems."

Conversation went on and on about horses and dogs, but nothing about the hunting "accident" that had left him a single father. Maybe he just couldn't talk about it. Maybe he was uncomfortable talking about it in front of Elise.

When lunch was finished, Moilanen asked if he could follow the Lampinens home.

"I have some things for you in the van," he said. "It'll just take a second."

◆   ◆   ◆

Gayle was not in any particular hurry to open the five boxes Bruce had dropped off at the Lampinen home in Chassell. They sat there Saturday night and they were still sitting there Sunday morning. They were actually getting in the way underfoot, so she decided to see what was in them.

She opened the first box and it was full of sweaters, nice sweaters of varying colors and styles. Tucked in among the sweaters she found an envelope. It contained a letter written on yellow-lined notebook paper. She unfolded it and began to read…

6/6/92

Gayle:
These are for you, Bruce wouldn't let me send them to St. Vinnie's. He thought you or your girls could wear them. Enjoy them if you can use them.

He sure thinks a lot of you, I guess it's the animals you have in common.
Sometimes it makes me jealous but at this point it shouldn't matter I guess.
He really is a great guy, actually none better. After 14 years we just don't
see things the same anymore. He loves those dogs, I love my work & free-
dom. However, I do need a favor from you. At this point, you are the only
woman he trusts. And I'm sure of that. Help him find a woman to take
care of him, one that loves animals as much as he does. I'm sorry we never
got to know each other better…you sound like a great lady.!

Love
s/Judes
P.S. don't tell the prospects, but, believe it or not he's incredible in the
sack…

Gayle Lampinen was shocked. The letter tucked in with all those
sweaters baffled her and stunned her from the top of the page to the
bottom. She called Paul into the room. While he read the letter, she
hastily poked through the other four boxes. All of them were filled with
clothes, obviously clothes that belonged to Judy Blake Moilanen.

"I can't believe this," she said. "His wife has been dead two weeks
today. It looks like he's emptied her closets."

"This letter," Paul said, "is bizarre."

It was bizarre right from the date. It had been purportedly written
more than six months earlier, presumably during one of those times
when Moilanen was telling the world that his marriage was on the
rocks.

"Why me?" Gayle said.

It was probably a better question than Gayle realized. After all, both
of Judy's brothers had wives she surely would have thought of before
sending five boxes of clothes—and a letter—to a veritable stranger.

"I hardly knew Judy," Gayle continued. "Paul, you were there the
only time I met Bruce's wife. And what girls?"

"The girls at the office?" Paul said.

"I suppose," Gayle said. "And my name is spelled right. I would expect anyone who knows me so casually to spell it G-A-I-L."

Paul was scanning through the letter again, shaking his head.

"It sounds to me like she's giving him to you," he said. "I can't believe a woman would write a P.S. like that to a stranger."

"I can't believe Bruce's wife wrote that letter," Gayle said.

Gayle Lampinen went to the telephone.

"Paul," she said, "I'm calling Detective Ball."

8

The Chimney Block Incident

"Hon," said Candy Floyd, *"what* happened to you?"

Judy Moilanen had walked into Wagar's Apparel in Ontonagon early in the fall of 1991. She had a wide brace on her neck and, it appeared, stitches in her head. She looked like she had been in a wreck.

Candy, the clerk, was one of those people who could take "Hon" and turn it into a three-syllable word. Everyone was "Hon" to Candy, but she could make it a bright and upbeat greeting or a concerned and sympathetic greeting. Obviously, she was concerned and sympathetic about whatever ill fortune had befallen Judy Moilanen.

"Just an accident," Judy said, brushing it off.

Into each life a little rain must fall…even if it comes in the form of a chimney block.

In December of 1992, detectives were not treating this injury as "just an accident." The chimney block incident had become a mystery within a mystery. It kept coming up in interviews. It kept coming up as a very suspicious event in the minds of those who knew Judy and Bruce Moilanen.

And what about the fire in the basement wood pile?

Had these events been investigated?

Don Poupore would do the legwork. He would see what, if any, paper work existed on the chimney block or the fire. The detectives were already wondering about the chimney block incident *before* Moilanen himself had told a different version from what they had been hearing.

Ball and Poupore had already heard…

- That the block slipped off the edge of the roof and landed on Judy.

- That a scaffolding collapsed and the block tumbled off the roof and fell on Judy.

- That Judy fell off the roof and struck her head on the patio below.

Each version had originated with Bruce Moilanen. Poupore, at this point, was scratching *his* head in befuddlement as to exactly how Judy Blake Moilanen had injured hers.

◆   ◆   ◆

What Poupore discovered was that State Trooper Don Brown had been called to the Moilanen residence on Sept. 23, 1991 to assist an ambulance run at the address on U.S. Highway 41. Paramedics were already there.

"What happened here?" Brown asked Moilanen.

"I was working up near the chimney," Moilanen told him, "when a block I'd set near the edge of the roof fell. I didn't realize anything had happened until I heard my wife moan. She'd been working down below."

Judy was lying on the patio, conscious but groggy. She told the trooper she had been cutting flashing for the chimney when she was hit.

Brown was not there in an investigatory role, but he looked around. He climbed the ladder leaning against the eaves until he was high enough to look up onto the roof. He did not consciously note at the time whether there was scaffolding on the roof, because Moilanen had not mentioned anything about a scaffold collapsing. Instead, he took note that there was nothing on the roof but one more chimney block.

The paramedics, Thomas Flynn and Brad Wyman, were both from Marquette General, Judy's place of employment. Their role was pretty clearly defined, which was to treat her at the scene and get her to the hospital if needed.

"What happened, Judy?" Flynn asked.

"That brick fell on me," she said.

Flynn looked at the block lying next to her, which was so large it had gouged a two-inch hole in the patio after it had hit Judy. It had to be a glancing blow. Paramedics would not be necessary if it had been a direct hit.

Dr. Scott Emerson was the attending physician in the Marquette General emergency room when Flynn and Wyman arrived with Judy. Poupore asked him to review his report.

"It states here," Emerson said, "that the cement block fell on Judy when a scaffolding on the roof collapsed."

"Where did you hear that?" Poupore asked.

"It doesn't indicate," the doctor said. "It had to come from one of the EMTs, Judy herself or Bruce. I don't recall."

Poupore knew neither of the paramedics had asked about what caused the block to fall and Judy was so woozy she hardly knew what hit her, much less how it happened to get there. That version had to come from Moilanen and it was different from what he had told Trooper Brown on the scene.

"Could an 80-pound block falling from a roof have been fatal?" Poupore asked.

"Definitely," Emerson said.

When Poupore left the hospital, he had the physicians' reports on Judy's stay. She was not checked out until Sept. 26.

"Mrs. Moilanen is not clear about the exact details of her injury," Emerson wrote that first evening. "She has total amnesia for the event and does not recall whether she was struck in the head, the neck or the back. Her husband was outside near her at the time of the accident, but did not actually witness the event."

Judy had a five-inch laceration in her scalp, which was flushed and sutured. She had a concussion, but no fracture. She was admitted to the neurological unit. Dr. J.L. Lehtinen released her Sept. 26 with instructions that she not return to work until Sept. 30.

During none of this time did Judy Moilanen recall exactly what had happened to her. All she had was her husband's explanation that it was an accident and she never suggested it was anything but. However, her friends and colleagues were quietly suspicious…on her behalf.

◆   ◆   ◆

Bruce Moilanen, meanwhile, was busily making an insurance claim covering the damaged patio and Judy's broken glasses. He filed a claim for $508 with Farmers and Merchants Mutual on Sept. 26, $275 for the patio and $233 for the glasses.

The preliminary claim report filled out by the insurance company said: "Judy & Bruce on the roof of there (sic) house making some repairs on the chimney when somehow a brick came lose (sic) and hit Judy on the back of the head!"

Perhaps the exclamation point indicated a measure of disbelief on the part of the person filling out the claim form…or maybe just astonishment.

Regardless, a Farmers and Merchants representative wrote Moilanen and suggested $275 seemed high for repairing a four-foot by four-foot area of a patio.

Moilanen fired back a memo, complete with pictures of the damaged area: "It is actually more than just repairing the 4x4 area. When the timber is removed, all patio bricks must come off & new sand replaced & leveled. Then it must be regrouted."

Moilanen finally got a check for $408, his original claim minus $100 deductible.

When it came to making insurance claims, Moilanen was not shy. When his neighbor's house burned down in 1989, he cashed a check for $730.81 to compensate for damage the fire did to his fence and fruit trees. A broken water line to the dishwasher produced a $1,902.80 insurance check for damages earlier in 1991.

At one point, Farmers and Merchants cancelled the Moilanens' homeowners insurance because of a dispute over whether a premium had been paid. When Bruce made the payment with a $279 check, it came back because of insufficient funds. The policy was cancelled again.

◆　　◆　　◆

Ironically, no claim was filed with any insurance agency after the fire in the basement later in the fall of 1991. And no report was filed with a public agency, such as a fire department.

Judy had apparently gotten to the basement and extinguished the fire in the woodpile before either the fire itself or smoke did any reportable damage. Moilanen, obviously, would not have been reticent about filing such a claim.

The only way anyone even knew that the fire had occurred was through Judy discussing it with friends such as the Janofskis.

Only Judy and Bruce know how she reacted to him when he returned home from hunting that day. Only they know if she confronted him with what was obviously negligence of a most dangerous nature, given that she and Elise were both asleep upstairs when he left that morning.

In none of her conversations regarding either the chimney block incident or the fire in the woodpile did Judy ever indicate that she suspected Bruce had done anything purposeful and wrong. Perhaps she thought it possible and kept it to herself, hence her sudden openness when she was confiding to friends that there were problems with the marriage in the months before her death. She never *was* specific in discussing those problems.

One thing detectives were never told in any of their interviews was that Judy was ever subjected to spousal abuse, either verbal or physical.

There were apparently no instances of beatings, for example, which would suggest the potential for the relationship to come to a violent conclusion. Police had never been called to the Harvey home to settle a domestic disturbance of any nature and Judy never reported such incidents in her most open moments with friends, albeit she was guarded even then. Instead, investigators were hearing only of financial problems, which seemed more troublesome than drastic.

Yet this was a woman who had been struck from above by a falling chimney block and awakened to a fire in her basement, both under circumstances which would seem to be suspicious, at best.

Maybe Judy Moilanen just did not see those red flags waving. It was remarkable that it did not strike her as strange that such bizarre events should come so closely on the heels of a drastic increase in life insurance coverage. She had not initiated those policies, but she had to sign the papers. Maybe all else, with the exception of the financial woes, was so tranquil that it never occurred to her that her life was in danger.

If Bruce Moilanen was, in fact, an assassin, he was a most quiet assassin.

◆   ◆   ◆

One person *did* witness the chimney block incident and, much later, innocently blurt to family, friends and strangers alike what she had seen.

"I saw Daddy drop a brick on Mommy's head."

That person was Elise.

9

The Marble Man

Bruce Robert Moilanen could not have known it, but Gayle Lampinen had met Det. Sgt. Bob Ball the Friday after Judy Moilanen had been shot. He went to Portage View Hospital and interviewed her in her office. He had to know if the relationship between Bruce and Gayle was such that The Other Woman could be a motive for murder.

"This could very well be a hunting accident," he explained, "but we always have to look at the spouse in a situation like this."

Gayle understood. She explained the duration and nature of the friendship.

"Bruce can really be a pest," she said. "He calls sometimes two and three times a day. I think he considers Paul and I to be his close friends, but it's not quite that way with my husband and I. We just don't have the heart to tell him how we feel, because he does seem like a nice guy. We don't want to hurt his feelings."

Gayle Lampinen told Ball about the Moilanens' financial problems and the separation and the impending divorce. She told him about the three times Bruce had sent her a single rose as a congratulatory gesture, usually for some success she had enjoyed showing her horses. She told him about rejecting Bruce when he asked her to accompany him to the casino in Baraga and she told him of Bruce's call to apologize for any misconception he might have caused. She told him of calling to offer her condolences after Judy's death.

Bob Ball came away from the interview convinced there was nothing romantic about this relationship, except perhaps in the recesses of Moilanen's mind.

"I don't know how Bruce perceives this relationship," he told Don Poupore, "but there's nothing there from her end. She's a down-to-earth, honest, religious person. She's just too good-natured to hurt anyone."

Gayle Lampinen promised to stay in touch with the detectives and keep them advised of any further contact she might have with Bruce Moilanen. And she agreed she would not terminate the friendship…at least not yet.

◆   ◆   ◆

Bob Ball was developing suspicions, but there were a couple of major holes in his investigation. He had no gun. And he had no bullet. If he could somehow find the bullet, he would at least have a clue what kind of gun he was seeking.

Finding the bullet, in those woods, would seem to be a longshot, at best. Ball had returned to the scene shortly after Judy's death and performed a sodium rhodizonate test on the blaze mark Sheriff Tom Corda had found on the maple tree. The blaze mark tested positive for the presence of lead residue, reinforcing Ball's conclusion that the bullet passed through Judy from the east and ricocheted off the tree to the north.

But where?

On the Tuesday after Judy's death, Ball called Dan Castle and asked him to help. Castle, who worked for the Copper Range mining company in nearby White Pine, had a potentially helpful hobby. He had a metal detector and Ball knew he had previously helped law enforcement agencies recover hard-to-find evidence. Nothing could be more challenging than finding the bullet that killed Judy Moilanen.

Castle got off work and made the 16-mile drive to the Ontonagon County Sheriff's Department. He met Ball and Deputy Cousineau and they drove to the woods along Cherry Lane.

"I really need the bullet," Ball told him. "Or at least the shell casing."

Conditions were far from the best. It was getting dark and it was cold. Castle started in the area where the body was found and slowly expanded the perimeter.

"I've got something," he said.

Ball was excited. This could be a major break for the case. They carefully cleared the leaves away. They had a bullet. Unfortunately, it was not *the* bullet. It was under a one-inch matting of leaves and it was badly corroded. They sighed.

"Can we give it another try?" Ball asked.

"I'll call work and see if I can get tomorrow off," Castle agreed.

Castle got the day off and headed back for the woods, this time with Department of Natural Resources officer Jackie Strauch. They worked the area between the tree and where the body had been found, again without success. They expanded the area, moving to the east side more in hopes of finding a shell casing than a bullet. They went over and over where they had already been, but they had no success. They spent six hours and covered a circle with a radius of 100 feet.

"The bullet just has to be here somewhere," Castle told Strauch.

Castle was determined. He returned to the scene over the weekend with Deputy Terry Dove, but snow now covered the ground. Dove was not dressed for the weather, which had changed for the worse, so the search was cut off once again without success.

Doggedly, Dan Castle would return one more time on Sunday, Dec. 13, 1992.

"How about if I go back out there by myself?" he asked Ball. "Maybe I'll have some luck if I'm just doing it my way at my pace. There's no need to tie one of you guys up. I'll take a radio with me in case I find anything."

"Give it a try," Ball encouraged him. "If we can't get it this time, we'll probably have to wait until spring."

In doing it "his" way, Castle would provide one of the most interesting twists to the entire investigation. He took a slingshot with him. And he took marbles.

"I was getting frustrated," he explained later. "I knew where the body had been and I had the mark on the tree. The bullet couldn't have jumped around to the *other* side of the tree. It had to be close to where I'd been looking."

Castle started where the body had been found and walked in a straight line toward the maple tree, which was 37 feet away. He got part way along the path the bullet traveled and took out his slingshot and marbles. He fired marbles off the blaze mark and watched as they bounced off to the right.

This was almost literally a shot in the dark. Castle didn't even expect to find the marbles, much less a bullet, but he found a couple of marbles glistening atop the snow at about the point he suspected the bullet might have landed. Castle marked the area and turned on his metal detector.

He found two bottle caps.

He found a coin.

He got another reading on his detector and used his foot to brush away two inches of snow. A fresh slug was lying on top of the leaf cover, 77 feet from the tree. Excitedly, he reached for his radio.

"I've got a fresh bullet," he said. "Can you get an officer out here?"

Dan Castle stood like a sentinel over the bullet. He knew better than to touch it or move it. It would rest exactly as he had found it until Bob Ball arrived.

◆   ◆   ◆

Bob Ball was home that Sunday, eating an early supper. Exactly two weeks had passed since Judy's death. He was wondering how Dan Castle was doing as he was eating his pork chops.

His telephone rang.

"Dan's got a bullet," Cousineau told him.

"Bingo," Ball said.

Ball had just finished his first pork chop. He grabbed another and headed for his car. He could not have gotten out of his house any faster if it had been on fire. He was in such a hurry he probably would have eaten mashed potatoes in his car.

Det. Sgt. Ball, as excited as he already was, would have been much more elated if he knew about the letter Gayle Lampinen was digging out of a box of sweaters at about that very same time on that very same Sunday.

◆   ◆   ◆

First thing Monday morning, Ball was on his way to the Marquette State Police crime lab. He had handled the bullet with rubber gloves and sealed it in an evidence envelope for delivery to Lt. Ray Kenny, who would have the task of examining it for fibers and tissue and trying to ascertain what type or brand of weapon had fired it.

Kenny, a 23-year veteran of work in the crime lab, had worked with Ball and Dr. Castilla, the medical examiner, in removing bullet fragments from Judy Moilanen's body. He also had samples of material from her jacket and the fuchsia shirt. He would use a stereoscopic compound microscope, which would give him a three-dimensional look at the bullet itself and whatever it was carrying.

In examining and measuring the jacket, Kenny had already made an interesting discovery. The entrance wound was 17 5/8 inches from the bottom of the jacket and the exit wound was 18 1/4 inches from the bottom of the jacket.

"The bullet," he noted to Ball, "went through the victim with an upward trajectory."

This told the detective that the bullet was not a "spent" bullet coming into those woods from out of the area. A spent bullet would have been sinking rather than rising. He knew now with certainty that the gun that fired this bullet was not very far from the victim when the trigger was pulled. It was looking less and less like an accident.

However, Ball could not be sure that the bullet he delivered to Lt. Kenny was the bullet that passed through Judy Moilanen's body.

"I've got some tiny red fibers," Kenny said, pulling away from the microscope. "There's also some white material and some material that looks like it might be wood."

"Bingo," said Ball.

Nothing was cast in stone, but, in all likelihood, this was the bullet that passed through Judy Moilanen's dark jacket with the white down feathers, continued through the fuchsia shirt, exploded through her body and caromed off the maple tree before coming to rest where Dan Castle found it.

"I want to send samples down to Connie Swander in Grayling," Kenny said. "I want her to do a serological and trace evidence exam. We could do it here, but we'd have to wait for Dennis Napes to get back from vacation."

"How long would that be?" Ball asked.

"Three weeks," Kenny said.

"That's too long," Ball said. "Let's get the stuff to Connie."

Lt. Kenny removed the trace samples, which had been snagged when the copper jacket peeled back from the bullet's point as it entered the body.

"Now, Ray, can you tell me what type of weapon fired this bullet?" Ball asked.

"It's 30 caliber," Kenny said, "but it's going to take some time to pin it down. Let me call you."

"I really need to know if it matches any of the guns we've got," Ball said. "Especially Bruce's."

Bob Ball had things to do. Specifically, he had to prepare for a polygraph examination of Bruce Moilanen, which had been scheduled for late afternoon that Monday. He was getting organized when Kenny called him.

"The bullet could not have been fired from any of the weapons we have," Kenny said, "but I have a list of possibilities for you, at least in terms of brands."

Kenny had checked the bullet's lands and grooves, the tell-tale marks along its side that carry the "fingerprints" of its manufacturer. This bullet had six lands and six grooves and a distinctive right-handed twist. He compared his findings with a technical bulletin produced by the Federal Bureau of Investigation.

"Bob," he said, "I come up with seven 30-caliber class rifles: A Remington 30-06, a Stevens 30-30, a Remington 300 Savage, a Weatherbee 300 magnum, a Remington 300 Winchester magnum, a Remington 308 Winchester and a Savage 30-30. I'm going to research to see if there are any other possibles."

Bob Ball had guns, but they were the wrong ones. He had the right bullet, he was sure, but he could not connect it to any specific brand of weapon, much less any specific gun. As frustrating as all that was, now he had Bruce Moilanen on the telephone from Ontonagon.

"Sorry, I can't make it," Moilanen said. "I'm over here with the Blakes. We have an appointment in the morning with Tom Corda."

Bob Ball called the Ontonagon County Sheriff's Dept. No one knew of any Tuesday morning appointment. Moilanen had lied again to avoid a lie detector test.

◆　　　◆　　　◆

Bob Ball was having one of those days when he did not know whether to laugh or cry. He had been so buoyed on Sunday by Castle's news, but nothing was falling into place on Monday, Dec. 14, 1992.

He checked with his office and got a message that Gary Niemi had called and wanted him to call back. He did not get the message that Gayle Lampinen had called.

"What's up, Gary?" Ball asked.

According to Ball's recollection, Gary was calling to read him the riot act for suspecting his cousin's husband. Bruce, as Ball figured it, had gone to Ontonagon to rally the troops on his behalf and maybe elicit some sympathy.

"I don't think it's fair how you are picking on Bruce," Niemi said.

"We're just doing our job," Ball sighed.

"If you'd called me," Niemi said, "I could have told you Bruce was hunting in my dad's blind that afternoon. And I saw him at Mike's house when he was there to pick up deer bait around 3 o'clock. That's when Judy was killed. Bruce couldn't have been there."

"Where did you come up with 3 o'clock as the time of death?" Ball asked curiously.

"That's what it said on the death certificate," Niemi said.

Ball knew by now that 3 o'clock was erroneous, regardless of what the death certificate said. He knew a lot of things, such as the presence of financial and marital problems, that he chose not to share with Gary Niemi, at least at that time. He saw Gary as an unwitting ally of Bruce and he was not ready to burst any bubbles.

"Gary," Ball said, "were *you* with Bruce that afternoon?"

"No," Niemi said.

"Gary, you don't know where he was, do you?" Ball said.

"I know where he was at 3 o'clock," Niemi insisted.

"But you don't know for sure where he was the rest of that afternoon, do you?"

"Not for sure," Niemi admitted.

"Then just let us do our jobs," Ball said. "It's for Bruce's benefit. If he wasn't involved, we'll clear him."

◆   ◆   ◆

Bob Ball's telephone was jumping that Monday. Moilanen had obviously been a busy man. A man who lives out in the Simar-Wasas area, not far from Mass City, had seen Bruce the afternoon Judy was killed, but he could not remember exactly when. A Mass City resident called to say he had seen Bruce between 8 and 9 a.m. that Sunday. No one was accounting for the time Jerry Schoch and Marie Lyons heard gunshots.

Ball also heard from State Trooper John Raymond, a one-man State Police detachment in Bruce Crossing. Moilanen and David Blake had come to his house.

David handled the introductions and then Bruce got to the point.

"I was coming out of the woods along M-38 near the Simar-Wasas Road a little after 5," Moilanen told Raymond, "and I saw you go by in your squad car."

"I don't really recall," Raymond said.

"You didn't notice a gray van?" Moilanen asked.

"I don't recall," Raymond said, "but I could check my daily activity sheet. I don't think I observed that vehicle."

"It may have been as late as 5:30," Moilanen offered.

"I don't know," Raymond reiterated. "Why are you asking?"

"Sgt. Ball is hassling me about my whereabouts at that time," Moilanen explained, "and I remember seeing you as I was coming out of the woods. I get the impression his investigation is focused on me. I gave him a list of witnesses, but they're not being contacted."

"Well," Raymond said, "I'm not involved in that investigation so I don't know anything about it. Has Sgt. Ball offered you a polygraph test? That could eliminate you."

"I went through a three-hour interrogation," Moilanen said, "and he offered me a polygraph test, but I don't think I could handle it. I'm still pretty stressed over Judy's death."

"That would be best for you," Raymond said. "When you can handle it."

Bruce Moilanen had a bright idea.

"How about 3 p.m.?" he asked. "Did you notice my van parked on M-38 at 3 o'clock?"

10

"Bingo"

When all else seemed to be failing, or at least frustratingly elusive, Det. Sgt. Ball knew evidence could be found in the simplest of places. He could find it on paper. Some of it might, in fact, be circumstantial, but enough numbers might add up to a solid case.

After reviewing the two packets of papers he found over the gunroom in Moilanen's basement, he concluded that financial problems did, indeed, exist in the household. He also came up with insurance policies totaling $229,000 on Judy's life. Bruce had been insisting all along, mainly to Judy's family, that he had maybe $40,000 to $45,000 coming from life insurance.

"Why," Ball wondered, "does he feel a need to lie about this?"

Of considerable importance at this point was that Ball had "consent forms" from Bruce Moilanen, which would allow him to obtain records from banks and insurance companies. His next trip would be down a trail of paper.

Michael Skytta, the executive vice-president of the First National Bank of Marquette, told Ball and Richard Goad that he had had limited contact with the Moilanens.

"I talked with Judy shortly before Thanksgiving," he explained. "She told me she was taking over the finances because Bruce had gotten them into a mess without her knowledge. I'm going to get you with Mike Fedrizzi and Kim Hall, a couple of our assistant vice-presidents who worked much more closely with the Moilanens."

The Moilanens' financial picture was about to unfold, and it was not a pretty picture.

. Fedrizzi's realm was consumer credit and he had personally worked with Bruce Moilanen since 1987. The Moilanens had been customers of First National since 1977.

"They didn't start having significant problems until 1991," Fedrizzi told the detectives. "Up until a month ago, I had dealt strictly with Bruce. I met Judy for the first time when she came in concerned about the financial situation they had gotten into."

"How was it dealing with Bruce?" Ball asked.

"He wanted to refinance," Fedrizzi said. "He wanted about $60,000. He wanted to take care of the land contract on his home, pay off delinquent loans of almost $19,000 and take care of delinquent credit card loans."

"How was this refinancing going?"

"I personally had a little problem because of a situation we had in July of 1991," Fedrizzi said. "Bruce borrowed $9,000 to buy a 1989 Buick. I had dealt with Bruce in the past without any problems coming up, so I issued the check without securing title. When Bruce became delinquent on the loan, I set up a meeting to talk about it. This was the one Nov. 13, when I met Judy for the first time."

"Go ahead."

"Bruce never bought the Buick. He never did explain where the money went, but I got the impression Judy wasn't even aware that he had secured the loan. I told him what he had done was illegal and put me in a bad spot."

"How did he react?" Goad asked.

"He got all emotional and cried," Fedrizzi said.

Even before this meeting, Fedrizzi explained, the bank had repossessed two of Moilanen's vehicles. After numerous unsuccessful attempts at repossession, First National took title to a 1983 Skamper Travel Trailer and a 1982 GMC Conversion Van.

"We let Bruce take them back on the condition he sell them and apply the money toward his outstanding loans," Fedrizzi said.

Fedrizzi had been dealing with Moilanen for a few years, but Kim Hall's bailiwick was mortgages. She would assess the request for refinancing. Ball and Goad sat down with her and started sifting through papers Moilanen had given her in April of 1992. The packet Moilanen provided including a cover letter on his North Country Claims stationery, an appraisal on the house, a home mortgage request form and a list of personal assets totaling $20,700. Hall added a four-page credit report and a First National worksheet to the package.

"It didn't take me long to determine that the Moilanens were not going to qualify for refinancing," she said. "The rule of thumb is that housing expense plus other debts cannot add up to more than 36 per cent of monthly income. They were at 56 per cent."

Hall called Bruce and told him the appraisal was too low, debts were too high and, further, there were problems with the credit report. Judy's credit was good, but joint credit was bad and Bruce's was worse.

"What you might do," she suggested to Bruce, "is obtain a copy of your credit report and try to clear up any discrepancies."

By November, however, the bank was working with the Moilanens toward trying to put together a workable solution to their problems.

"Do we really have a chance to get this done," Judy asked in a telephone conversation with Hall, "or are we wasting our time?"

"We hope to have a written proposal in a couple of weeks," Hall told her. "We're working toward a closing date of Jan. 4, 1993."

Those negotiations were still underway on Nov. 29, 1992, when Judy died in the woods down Cherry Lane.

Ball and Goad were sorting through the paperwork when something jumped out at Ball. An entry on the list of assets uncovered yet another lie by Bruce Moilanen. He had insisted all along that he had disclosed all of the guns he possessed or had possessed.

There on the list of assets was the following entry: *"Savage Model 110, 30-06..........$300"*

"Bingo," Ball said, sliding the sheet to Goad with his finger on the entry. "By God, Bruce never told us about this gun."

"And," Goad smiled, "it's on the list of 'possibles' Ray Kenny gave us, right?"

"It sure is," Ball said. "Remember what Don Poupore said? 'You put Bruce Moilanen in a room with 999 other people and he assumes he is the smartest person in the room.'"

"This," Goad said, tapping his finger, "was not very smart."

"It's typical of Bruce," Ball said. "He thinks we're a bunch of dumb country cops. His problem is telling lies we can check out so easily."

◆   ◆   ◆

The next stop on the paper trail was at the Northern Michigan Bank in Marquette. In various forms, the Moilanens had a number of savings accounts. Some of them were rather dusty.

Peter Treml could only find one loan on record, a $6,446 transaction paid off in June of 1990. However, Judy had two accounts, a 24-hour instant cash account and a Christmas Club account. Bruce had both checking and savings under the names of Big Creek Kennels and North Country Claims, his two businesses. The average monthly balances of Bruce's "business" accounts ranged from $23 to $259. The bank officer said the North Country Claims checking account No. 808-6 was plagued by, in his words, a multitude of overdrafts.

"Judy had one other account of her own," Treml said, "a savings account opened Nov. 21, 1990."

The detectives were told that Bruce Moilanen pulled up to Northern Michigan's drive-up window on Dec. 4, the Friday after his wife's death, and tendered a withdrawal slip for $1,000. Judy's purported signature was on it. The head teller checked the signature card and saw that the account was payable upon death. Moilanen drove away with $1,000 in cash.

The next week, he came in at the bank's request and closed the account. He left with another $1,200.

◆   ◆   ◆

Det. Sgt. Ball was still sorting through the packets he found in Moilanens' basement. Life insurance, he noted, was certainly in ample supply. He took a legal pad and a calculator and did the mathematics.

Judy was covered by…

- Lutheran Brotherhood..............$ 60,000
- Northwestern Mutual*...............150,000
- Northwestern Mutual…............. 70,000
- Safeco*................................. 40,000
- First of America Bank................ 10,000

*Includes double indemnity for accidental death

He shook his head. Judy Moilanen's life was insured for $330,000 in the case of accidental death. Bruce had been bemoaning how modestly his wife had been covered, all the while "collecting" insurance policies almost like a kid might collect baseball cards.

Would he insist that he did not know of these policies? Would he insist that Judy must have purchased them without his knowledge? Exactly how naive did he think these country cops were?

◆   ◆   ◆

On Thursday, Dec. 17, Ball and Poupore drove to Ontonagon to meet with Dale and Mary Ann Blake and their son David. They did not really have a pre-planned approach. They would provide an update, but they didn't know how much or how little they would actually reveal.

The drive took them through an occasional village, but most of the highway to Ontonagon was a two-lane road with occasional farmhouses and gas stations, most of the stations closed for the winter. Even the main highways can be treacherous in the winter, so the best of driving is conservative driving.

"I don't know how we're going to be greeted," Ball said. "Remember that Bruce was here over the weekend rallying support."

"You haven't talked with Mrs. Blake yet, have you?" Poupore asked.

"No," Ball said, "and I haven't talked to anyone else in the family since right after it happened."

They met at Dale and Mary Ann's house, the pretty white house that sits back from the intersection of M-38 and Cherry Lane. It was a warm, receptive residence. It seemed such an unlikely place for tragedy to come home.

"Mrs. Blake," Ball said, "how closely can you pinpoint when Judy left the house to walk the dogs?"

"It couldn't have been any later than 2," she said. "It was probably earlier rather than later. Maybe as early as 1:30."

"Do you know if Judy and Bruce had discussed walking the dogs that day?" Ball said.

"I don't know of any talks they might have had," Mary Ann said.

Mrs. Blake seemed agitated. Ball sensed it. They had been asking questions about Bruce, but they had couched their questions gently and carefully. They were trying not to let their suspicions surface.

"I have some things I want to get off my mind," Mrs. Blake said. "You people have made a horrible mess out of this situation, the way you've treated Bruce. A horrible mess."

"How much do you know about the marriage and their financial condition?" Ball asked, again trying to soft-pedal and maybe even back-pedal.

Mrs. Blake related how she and Judy talked almost every day and how great the marriage was. She described Bruce as a good husband and father. The Blakes had little financial insight, other than that they were unaware of any problems.

"Do you people know how much insurance Bruce had on Judy's life?" Ball said.

"He told us $40,000 to $45,000," they responded. "He said it wasn't even enough to take care of the mortgage."

"Do you know where he was when Judy was shot?"

"He has a good alibi for the time period when Judy was shot," they said. "We're not too happy that you haven't bothered to talk to some of the people who saw him that day."

"Let me share a few things with you," Ball said. "This was not a 'perfect' family. There were financial problems. There was talk of bankruptcy. There had been talk of a divorce. The information we have is that there was $330,000 worth of insurance on Judy's life. These are the kinds of things we're looking into...and we'd like your help."

He was firm, yet understated. He wanted to get the family's attention without hammering it over the head. He did not, for example, disclose Bruce's fixation with Gayle Lampinen. He needed allies, not antagonists.

The room was quiet. Ball recalled later that the atmosphere at the table took a 180-degree turn. They shared a prayer.

"What can we do?"

"What we're going to ask you to do is going to be very difficult for you," Ball said. "I don't want you to share what we've told you with anybody. I mean *anybody*. I want you to welcome Bruce and listen to what he has to say. You might even be able to convince him to take a polygraph exam to clear his name."

"What about Elise?" Mary Ann asked. "Can't we get her away from Bruce?"

Rightly so, she was wrought with concern for the welfare of her granddaughter. Ball patiently explained that he had no basis for taking the child from her father. They would have to encourage Bruce to spend as much time with them as possible to give them time with Elise.

Ball had asked the Blake family to welcome with open arms a man who very well could be the murderer of Judy Blake Moilanen. It would be an agonizing charade, a traumatic period beyond comprehension. They would have to act like they loved a man who, in turn, was obviously acting like he loved their daughter.

Det. Sgt. Ball would come to realize that he was dealing with a family so imbedded with faith in God that they could survive and, ultimately, conquer as their ordeal stretched on through the winter and into the spring.

11

Another "Other" Woman

Bruce Moilanen, with the Blakes, had kept the appointment he didn't actually have with Sheriff Tom Corda in Ontonagon. He had put together a three-page "memo" detailing his purported whereabouts on Nov. 29. Corda contacted Don Poupore and forwarded the information to the State Police.

It was easy to look at what Moilanen had put together and understand why the Blakes had been perturbed at the investigation's focus on their son-in-law. He had rather elaborately accounted for his whereabouts, almost to the point of overkill. What the police would have to do is check his version against reality.

Two of the three pages had dealt with witnesses who should have or could have known that Moilanen was at a certain place at a certain time. The third page dealt with times and distances, according to Bruce's measurements, from the Blake residence to the assorted other places he had been, an obvious attempt to prove that he could not have been in the vicinity of Cherry Lane at the time when Judy was shot.

"I don't know what this list is supposed to do for him," Ball told Poupore. "These people do nothing to account for the time he was supposedly hunting alone. I think this is a tactic to divert the focus of what we're trying to do."

◆　　　◆　　　◆

Det. Sgts. Ball and Poupore were continuing on their fascinating and informative trip down the paper trail Bruce Moilanen had left in his wake. Their next stop was at the First of America Bank in Marquette.

Moilanen had been busy at First of America.

"The week after Judy was shot," explained First of America's Colleen Schmeltzer, "Bruce came into the bank and wrote a $500 check on Judy's account. He deposited it into *his* account."

The Moilanens, Schmeltzer told the detectives, had had a number of accounts with First of America, checking and savings for Bruce, checking for Judy and a joint checking and trust account for Elise.

A day or so after Moilanen switched the $500 from Judy's account to his, he showed up at the drive-up window with a $7,200 check made out to Judy from Lincoln National Life Insurance. It was dated Nov. 23, 1992. It had both Judy's signature and, even though he was not on the check, Bruce's signature.

"How do we handle this?" teller Donna Lancour asked Schmeltzer.

Schmeltzer checked the file and concluded that Judy's signature was not authentic.

"What does he want to do with it?" Schmeltzer asked. "Cash it or deposit it?"

"Deposit it," Lancour said. "He said he's using the money to buy a van."

Schmeltzer shrugged. She did not see any red flags flying. The poor man's wife had just been killed. Why cause unnecessary anguish hassling him over a check.

"Let him deposit it," she said.

Bruce had found a way to pay for the van…with Judy's money. Bob Ball was scratching his chin. He wanted to find the source of that $7,200.

Colleen Schmeltzer had another tidbit of news for Ball and Poupore. Judy's checking account had been one of First of America's "first class" accounts. It came with an automatic $10,000 accidental death benefit.

"Would Bruce have known about this?" Ball asked.

"They both had it," Schmeltzer said. "They both had to sign an insurance card when they opened the accounts. We gave them each a packet of information on the policies."

◆　　◆　　◆

On Friday, Dec. 18, Bob Ball finally got the message that Gayle Lampinen had called. It had been a busy week, much of it spent on the road between Calumet and Marquette and between Marquette and Ontonagon. These are lengthy drives, in excess of two hours, meaning the detectives were on the road for between four and five hours of their working days. Of course, neither was working eight-hour days or 40-hour weeks at this point.

"Heard from Bruce?" Ball asked.

"He called last Friday," Gayle said. "He wanted to have lunch with us at The Chippewa on Saturday. He showed up with Elise, driving a new van."

"Anything else interesting?"

"He told us he had retired from the hospital," Lampinen said, "and he told us he was selling his claims-adjusting business."

"Retiring?"

"Sounds funny, huh?" she said. "We thought it was odd. He'd been telling us about all his financial problems. I think I told you he had come to Paul and asked about a loan."

"That's interesting…"

"And he had these boxes he wanted to drop off at the house," Gayle said. "They were full of clothes."

"I saw them," Ball said. "I thought they were going to St. Vincent's."

"Did you notice the envelope in the box with the sweaters?"

"It wasn't there when I looked," Ball said. "I went through them Friday night."

"I've gotta read you this letter," she said.

Bob Ball listened for the first time to what would become known as The Sweater Letter. He was flabbergasted. He suspected immediately, to be sure, that Judy Moilanen had not written the letter, but he did not share his thoughts with Gayle.

"How well did you know Judy?" he asked.

"I just met her once," Gayle said, "and I didn't even remember her first name. When I read about the accident in the newspaper, I didn't even know she was Bruce's wife until I got near the bottom of the article."

"That's what I thought. And the date was June 6, 1992?"

"Right."

Moilanen had to be lying about something. When Ball searched his van on Dec. 11, Bruce had explained that Mary Ann had packed the boxes a few days earlier. Had that been the case, Judy could not have written a letter June 6 giving her clothes—and, for all intents and purposes, Bruce—to Gayle Lampinen.

"Do you want the letter?" she asked.

"I'll be right over," he said.

Bob Ball did not even hang up the telephone. He hit the button to cut off his call to Gayle Lampinen and punched in Don Poupore's number.

"Don," he said, "you've gotta read this letter Moilanen sent to Gayle Lampinen. If I had any doubts about this son of a bitch, they're gone now."

◆　　　◆　　　◆

Bob Ball wanted to interview Paul Lampinen. For whatever reason, Bruce had befriended him as well as his wife. It mattered not that it was likely a smokescreen to disguise Moilanen's real agenda.

Ball made the drive down U.S. 41 to Lampinen's bank in Baraga Monday morning, Dec. 21. It is one of the prettier drives in an area with nothing but pretty drives, leaving Calumet and driving along Portage Lake and the Keweenaw Bay.

"Tell me about Bruce," Ball said.

"I've known him a couple of years," Lampinen said. "He's always been a friendly guy. He'd even invited me on a hunting trip to Texas, said all I'd have to pay for was my license."

"When was this?" Ball asked.

"It was supposed to happen next month," Lampinen said.

"Next month?"

"He actually invited me last summer. He sent me a two-page itinerary. I have it right here."

"You're not going, though?"

"He hasn't said anything since last summer," Lampinen said. "I told him I appreciated it, but I didn't think I could get away anyway."

Lampinen offered the itinerary to Ball, as well as the formula for disguising a deer hunter's scent. Ball accepted them. He wanted as many samples of Moilanen's handwriting as he could get.

"You were with Gayle at the lunch at The Chippewa?" Ball asked.

"I was there," Lampinen said, "but he seemed to direct all of his conversation toward Gayle. It does seem to me that he's interested in Gayle."

"Does this bother you?"

Lampinen laughed.

"Gayle can handle herself…and him."

"Have you seen him since then?" Ball asked.

"Yesterday," Paul said.

"Yesterday?"

"He just dropped in. No call. I was on my way out to the sauna when he pulled up in his van."

Paul waved and continued to the sauna. Moilanen went up onto the front porch and entered the house without knocking. He walked through the house and found a very surprised Gayle in the kitchen.

"I dropped my clothes in the sauna," Paul said, "and went back into the house. I was afraid Gayle might be a little nervous."

He found his wife and Moilanen in the kitchen, Moilanen talking once again about retiring from Marquette General.

"I found out I have to give them 30 days notice from when I return to work," Moilanen said.

"When's that?" Gayle asked.

"Jan. 18," Moilanen said.

"What are you doing with your time?" Paul asked.

"I've gotta go down to Traverse City for a couple of days to take care of some stuff."

"What kind of stuff?" Paul asked.

Det. Ball had asked them to help "monitor" Moilanen's activities. Maybe he could learn something helpful.

"Just stuff," Moilanen said.

"Where you headed now?" Gayle asked.

"We're going to Ontonagon," Moilanen said.

"We're?" Gayle asked. "Where's Elise?"

"In the van."

◆   ◆   ◆

Bob Ball picked up the Dec. 21 *Houghton Daily Mining Gazette* and thumbed through it casually. He was not interested in anything in particular, just browsing through the news of the day.

An advertisement jumped out at him.

INFORMATION SOUGHT
MASS CITY AREA

Anyone seeing a gray chevrolet van parked on M-38 next to the Simar/Wasa Road in the Firesteel River area on the afternoon of Sunday, November 29th, 1992 between the hours of 3:15 and 5:30 P.M....Please call...

Bob Ball looked at the telephone numbers. They seemed familiar. He took out his book and checked. One was the Blake residence in Ontonagon. The other was Bruce Moilanen's residence outside Marquette.

He scratched his head. Moilanen was always up to something. He chuckled to himself. Why in the world was Moilanen trying to find someone who had seen his van between 3:15 and 5:30? Obviously, he was still trying to cover for the erroneous time of death in the medical examiner's report.

Bruce Moilanen spent $500 running the ad in three Upper Peninsula newspapers and no one was being asked to cover him on his whereabouts between 2 and 2:15.

◆   ◆   ◆

The investigation was focused on Moilanen, to be sure, but not to the exclusion of other possibilities. Deputy Tom Cousineau had heard of some scuttlebutt in an Ontonagon coffee shop that a 15-year-old boy from nearby White Pine had been hunting at his grandfather's Christmas tree farm across M-38 from Cherry Lane on the day Judy was shot. Cousineau tried to check it out, but got little cooperation. Nettled, he informed Ball.

"All I've been able to determine," Cousineau said, "was that the kid had hunted on the Christmas tree plantation during the deer season. I heard he was probably hunting with a 20-gauge shotgun, unless he borrowed his grandfather's 30-06."

Ball and Poupore drove to White Pine High School to interview the boy, who was gangly and bespectacled and hardly seemed the outdoor type. He looked like he would have been much more at home in a library, but he presented a surprisingly tough front.

"I didn't hunt at the farm the day the woman was shot," he said, "and that's about all I can tell you. My dad told me not to talk about this to the police unless our attorney is with me."

So there.

"Why in hell does this kid—or his father—think they need an attorney?" Ball wondered.

"And why were they expecting to be contacted by police?" Poupore responded.

Attitudes such as this are exactly what pique the interest of detectives such as Ball and Poupore. A simple explanation might have put a wrap on the matter, but now the State Police wanted to talk to the youngster's parents and grandfather.

"All three of our boys were grounded that day," the mother explained. "One of them had taken some money out of his dad's semi and none of them would admit it."

"They were home with me here in White Pine watching the football game that afternoon," the father said.

"It would have been impossible for our son to have been involved," the mother said.

After interviewing the grandfather as well, Ball and Poupore were convinced that there was nothing to the Ontonagon scuttlebutt. The kid had not been hunting because he and his brothers were in trouble with their parents.

"Maybe," Poupore laughed, "he thought we were investigating the money missing from his old man's truck."

◆   ◆   ◆

Of all Moilanen's alibi witnesses, the most troublesome to the investigators was Wade Johnson. Moilanen placed his near-collision with the blond, tousle-haired young man at 2:15, which gave him an alibi for about the time the detectives knew the shooting had occurred.

Johnson had been at the Adventure Cafe in Mass City the Sunday after the shooting, when he ran into Judy's cousin Mike Niemi.

"Wade," Niemi said, "Bruce said he saw you last Sunday. Do you remember?"

"Sure," Johnson said. "He almost ran into me down in Tank Creek."

"We think the police might suspect Bruce," Niemi said. "Could you do us a favor and give them a call?"

Johnson said he would, but he hadn't gotten around to it when his telephone rang Tuesday night. It was Moilanen.

"Hi Wade," Moilanen said. "Mike told me he talked to you. Did you get a chance to call the police?"

"Not yet," Johnson said, "but I will."

"Do you remember what time we saw each other?"

"Not really."

"It was around 2:15."

"Seems about right to me," Johnson said.

"By the way," Moilanen said, "your wife saw me too."

"I don't think she knows you."

"Tell her I came in around 3 and bought a pop. I talked to Harvey Ahola outside for awhile. She'll remember."

When Ball and State Trooper John Raymond interviewed Johnson at the Ontonagon County Road Commission garage in Mass City on Dec. 23, he confirmed that he had seen Bruce Moilanen on the afternoon Judy was shot.

"What time?" Ball asked.

"I'm pretty sure it was around 2:15 to 2:30," Johnson said.

Ball pulled out a map of Ontonagon County and asked Johnson to mark the location. He slid the map across the table to the detectives and Ball noticed that the location was almost exactly the same as Moilanen had pinpointed.

For the few minutes it took Ball and Raymond to drive from the garage to the Elms General Store, Bruce Moilanen was looking like he had the alibi he needed for the time when Judy had been shot.

Lori Johnson was standing behind the counter when the two policemen walked in.

"I didn't realize the guy was Bruce Moilanen until later," she said, "but I remember he was one of my first customers. My shift started at 3."

Lori replaced Julia Kemppainen, whose shift ended at 3. Kemppainen would recall later that she and Lori visited for 10 or 15 minutes before she left. Lori's first customer had yet to arrive.

Obviously, Moilanen arrived after Julia left.

"He bought a two-liter bottle of Pepsi," Lori said.

"You have a pretty good memory," Ball said.

Lori smiled.

"It cost $1.69," she said, "plus a 10-cent deposit."

"You're sure on the time?"

"I remember that day," she said. "Wade and I met at the store in Greenland around 2. He went home ahead of me because he wanted to shower before he went hunting. I got home at 2:30 and he was just getting out of the shower."

"Wait a minute," Ball said. "Wade was in Greenland at 2 and coming out of the shower in Mass at 2:30? Wade wasn't down near Tank Creek at 2 or 2:15?"

"No way," she said. "He left for hunting camp just before I left for work. He couldn't have been in Tank Creek much before 3, probably later."

Bingo!

Bruce Moilanen's best witness, a witness who had unwittingly been "coached" into believing the near-collision happened at 2:15, would be of no help at all. Wade Johnson had been standing in the shower in Mass City at the moment Judy Moilanen was shot.

Only one troublesome question remained: Why would anyone take a shower before trudging into hunting camp?

♦   ♦   ♦

Christmas was a dismal occasion at the Blake house. Jerry and Anna and their children were in town from Shawano. David and Yvonne were over, of course. And Bruce Moilanen was there with Elise.

Judy Blake Moilanen's absence was the strongest presence in the house.

The family knew by then that police investigators strongly suspected that Moilanen was a murderer. He did not know that they knew, so they put on a warm facade in the midst of their gloom.

What was most important to them was that Elise was there. They could embrace Bruce Moilanen until the end of time if it meant having Elise with them. Mary Ann only felt comfortable with her granddaughter's safety when she could see her and feel her and hug her. The price she had to pay was a feigned affection for Bruce.

Thus, the family sat around the living room that Christmas morning and exchanged gifts and cards, all the while burdened by who was there and who wasn't there. Bruce, perhaps looking forward to the wealth he would come upon in the form of Judy's life insurance, was particularly generous. Judy's cousin Mike Niemi, for example, was given a muzzle-loader rifle.

When the presents had been opened and the family had settled into quiet conversations, Moilanen went to the telephone and dialed the Portage View Hospital. Jerry Blake overheard him ask for Gayle Lampinen.

"Ha ha!" Moilanen said. "Merry Christmas! You're at work and I'm not."

Jerry could not believe his ears. Everyone was depressed and subdued and here was Judy's widower making a taunting, jocular telephone call to some woman. It seemed so out of place and out of taste to have made such a call from any place, much less in the midst of grieving relatives.

"Who was that?" Jerry asked.

"Just a friend," Moilanen shrugged, passing it off as nothing.

Christmas was like a lot of other days when it came to what Moilanen did to keep himself occupied. He always seemed to have a yellow legal pad in front of him. He was filling the pages with names and times and places, looking for the right combination to get the detectives off his trail.

"Mary Ann," Bruce said, "what time was it Judy left the house?"

Mary Ann Blake had heard this question repeatedly, beginning the day after Judy had been shot. It was wearing on her, particularly now that she knew what she knew. She was exasperated, but she tried not to show it.

"I told you I was in the office when she left," she said. "She was gone when I came out to say good-bye to Jerry."

"Two o'clock?"

"That's when I came out."

"Okay," Moilanen said. "Let's stick with the 2 o'clock story."

"Fine," she lied.

◆   ◆   ◆

Bob Ball was feeling his way. He was accumulating suspicion piled on suspicion and bits and pieces of evidence, most of it circumstantial. He was very religiously attempting to contact people who had been part of the Moilanens' life.

One such person on his list was Lee Anne Daniels Wysocki, a friend of Judy's since they were pre-schoolers. The Daniels family had lived two houses down from the Blakes along M-38. Judy had gotten her friend a job 6½ years earlier in the medical records department at Marquette General Hospital.

On Jan. 7, 1993, Det. Sgts. Ball and Poupore drove to Wysocki's apartment near the hospital. They found an attractive woman with dark shoulder-length hair, fragile-looking and soft-spoken. They were to learn that life, in part a divorce and raising her daughter Stephanie as a single parent, had reinforced her with an inner strength.

"We were friends all the way through school," Lee Anne said, "but we really didn't talk much over the last few months."

"Problems?" Ball asked.

"Not really," Lee Anne said. "Not between us, anyway. I was involved in union activities at the hospital and Judy, being in administration, was on the other side. We just decided it would be better in terms of appearances if we kept our distance until it was resolved."

"That had to be hard?"

"It was," she said, "because we've always been so close."

"So you really don't have any insight into the last few months of the marriage?"

"Judy didn't usually talk about that kind of thing. I'd heard rumors around the hospital that they were having financial problems and might be getting a divorce, but Judy never confided anything like that. It was like she and Bruce were off in their own little world."

It was beginning to look like this might be one of those dead ends.

"Do you know Bruce very well?" Ball asked.

Wysocki frowned.

"Bruce Moilanen," she said, "can be a very aggravating person. He bothered me because he was always cutting me down. I tried to visit Judy when he wasn't around."

She hesitated.

"The funny thing," she continued, "is that he started calling me after Judy died."

"He *what?*" Ball said.

"He started calling me. I just put it off to him being lonely and in need of a friend."

"That was strange, huh?"

"It was strange, considering how he always treated me. Then he came over New Year's Eve day and shoveled my walk for me. After he finished my walk, he came to the door and we talked."

"About what?"

"He asked if we could ever be more than just friends."

Ball and Poupore exchanged glances. The Sweater Lady had company, at least in Bruce Moilanen's mind.

"I asked him if that meant sex," she said, "and he seemed flustered. I guess he thought of me being naive and quiet, which I guess I had been when I was younger. He said, 'Hmmm, maybe somewhere down the road.'"

She shook her head, recalling his brashness...and maybe hers, as well.

"I told him I didn't think so. I tried to be nice about it. I told him our lifestyles were just too different."

"And that was the first time he'd been over?"

"No, he'd come over a couple of days earlier and asked if I could watch Elise for a couple of hours. I told him that would be fine. When he came back, he took us all out for pizza. Stephanie and me and Elise."

◆   ◆   ◆

The pizza did not taste very good that evening.

Bruce was talking about Judy's death. He had a napkin in front of him and he was drawing a diagram of a human body. He was talking about the trajectory of the bullet.

"It was a matter of inches where it hit to do the damage it did," he said.

He stood up, swinging his arms in a walking motion. He demonstrated the backward swing of his right arm and how it had to be in just such a position for the bullet to enter the right side of the upper chest without hitting the arm first. Lee Anne's stomach was queasy.

"You couldn't *try* to make a shot like this and do it intentionally," he said, supporting his insistence that it had indeed been an accident.

What Lee Anne could not have known was that the medical examiner's report, upon which everything Moilanen knew theoretically had to be based, had erroneously described the wound behind the *left* armpit as the entrance wound. Moilanen was describing to her what had actually happened.

Regardless, Lee Anne Wysocki had come to her own conclusion about her friend Judy's death.

"When we left the Pizza Hut," she said later, "I knew Bruce had done it."

◆   ◆   ◆

Now Bob Ball and Don Poupore were sitting in her apartment. She had not previously come to them, because she had reached her conclusion based solely on intuition. These detectives, for whatever reasons, seemed to have reached the same conclusion she had.

"Bruce called again yesterday," she told them. "He wanted to know if I'd be interested in any of Judy's craft items. He invited me to come over and look at them and I went. I noticed then that he wasn't wearing his wedding band. That bothered me."

Moilanen directed her to the basement, where he said Judy's handicraft items were stored in boxes. She didn't find much, causing her to wonder to herself if he just used the crafts as a come-on to get her to the house. When Lee Anne returned to the kitchen, Moilanen was sorting through the cabinets. They talked.

"I told him I was having some problems with my apartment," she said. "He asked me when my lease was up and I told him it was in the spring. He asked me if I wanted to move in with him. I told him I didn't think so."

"Insistent guy, huh?" Ball said.

"Annoying," she said.

"Anything else interesting?"

"His life insurance policies," she said. "He was bummed out about them. He said payment was being held up until the police were done with their investigation."

Ball had one more question.

"Do the Moilanens have any other friends we should contact?"

"If you find any," Lee Anne said, "they'll actually be Judy's friends. Not Bruce's."

◆   ◆   ◆

The detectives had been gone for less than an hour when Ball's pager buzzed. He called the post and got a message that Lee Anne Wysocki had called for them. They hurried back to her apartment.

"Ten minutes after you left," she said, "Bruce showed up. He had been sitting over in the bank parking lot, waiting for you to leave."

As with the Blakes, Lampinens and Janofskis, Bob Ball had asked Lee Anne to work with them and keep them advised of Moilanen's activities. Naturally, she agreed, though not without some trepidation.

"What did they want?" Bruce asked. "Did they ask if Judy and I had had any marital problems?"

"I'm not aware of any marital problems," Lee Anne said. "Bruce, they're only trying to do their jobs. They have to investigate you to clear you. You're the husband."

"Did they call you ahead of time?"

"No, they just showed up. I'd never talked to them before."

"They've been all over the place," Moilanen grumbled. "They've been to the hospital, they've talked to my neighbors, they've talked to Gary Niemi. They talked to Dale and David Blake after the funeral."

"They didn't say anything to me about who they are talking to."

"I don't know why they are after me like this," Moilanen complained. "I'm alibied for the whole day, except for between 1 and 2 o'clock. I called the coroner and he told me Judy was killed at 3. It's on the death certificate."

"You shouldn't be worried then," she assured him.

If Bruce Moilanen had an alibi for the time of the shooting, she thought to herself, these two detectives would not be sitting in her living room.

"I'll keep you posted," Lee Anne told them for the second time that day.

She did.

Don Poupore's telephone rang later that afternoon. It was Lee Anne Wysocki.

"Bruce invited us out for pizza again," she said. "We accepted."

12

Jean Claude Moilanen

Bruce Moilanen was spending virtually every weekend with his in-laws in Ontonagon. Make that, *at* his in-laws rather than *with* his in-laws. He spent almost every Saturday and Sunday on the ski slopes at the Porcupine Mountains, using the Blakes as baby sitters for Elise. This was fine with the Blakes, who could not have cared less if he dropped Elise off and disappeared from the face of the earth.

Once the Porkies open, usually around Christmas, Moilanen was out the door and on his skis. In the winter of 1992, the Porcupine Mountain Ski Resort was groomed and ready the weekend after Christmas.

Being a member of the National Ski Patrol, Moilanen logged in and out each day. Ball asked Deputy Cousineau to discreetly monitor Moilanen's activities at the ski hill. Cousineau quietly checked the logs, carefully keeping his interest general in nature.

Moilanen, according to Cousineau's investigation, went skiing Dec. 27, Dec. 28, Jan. 2, Jan. 3, Jan. 9, Jan. 10, Jan. 17, Jan. 24, Feb. 6, Feb. 13, Feb. 15, Feb. 27 and Feb. 28.

"The first weekend it was open, he was there," Cousineau said. "We just wanted to know what he was up to. There were so many times he wasn't where he said he was going to be when we were trying to find him. There were times he was on the ski hill when he had used an excuse to get out of an interview, and the excuse had nothing to do with skiing."

The dates were almost invariably weekends. He might have been at the ski hill seven days a week if the Blakes did not both work Monday

137

through Friday. Someone had to watch Elise and he could hardly drop her off at the Janofskis when the snow started falling and pick her up in the spring.

◆   ◆   ◆

Det. Sgts. Ball and Poupore were finding that Moilanen's paper trail was almost as long as U.S. 45, which begins in Mobile, Ala., and ends in Ontonagon.

They stopped to see Jim Lori at the Marquette First Federal Credit Union on Jan. 7. They presented the release form that Moilanen would have been wishing he had not signed back on Dec. 11 had he known how much information could be gleaned from bank files.

Lori knew Moilanen from a personal standpoint because of mutual interest in raising and training dogs. The business side was troubling.

"Bruce isn't considered a good risk," he said. "He's usually late and bounces a lot of checks. We have to hound him for payments. We've always gotten our money from Bruce, but it's never been easy."

"Is there any insurance linked to your accounts here?" Ball asked.

"Not much," Lori said. "I think $1,000 per account and I think they had individual accounts. Let me check."

Lori excused himself and punched in some numbers on his telephone. He nodded his head a few times and took some notes. Bruce Moilanen had called Dec. 4, the Friday after Judy's death, and asked about the insurance. He had the papers filed by Dec. 16.

"How about marital problems?" Poupore asked.

"I don't know," Lori said. "Let me put you with Cheryl Houle. I know she worked with them on a loan."

Houle, it turned out, had called Judy Moilanen at work earlier in 1992 to ask her about one of Bruce's delinquent loan payments. Judy had been a co-signer.

"She told me she wasn't living with Bruce," Houle said. "She said his bills were his responsibility. When I dealt with Bruce, it was always, 'I'll pay tomorrow…It's in the mail…I'll be in to pay.'"

Not too long after that, Houle said, the Moilanens jointly applied for a $22,000 loan to buy a van. The request was denied.

She remembered being surprised that they had applied jointly, but passed it off to Judy just not wanting to be bothered with one of Bruce's problems in the earlier conversation. She figured Judy was looking for the quickest way off the telephone.

The credit union supplied the detectives with two files on the Moilanens, and Ball was scanning through them as they drove away. He found that Bruce had paid off a delinquent loan on a 1987 Subaru on Dec. 15. He paid with $2,346.71 in cash.

◆   ◆   ◆

A number of people had mentioned that Moilanen's North Country Claims Service was having some problems, likely involving a civil suit. Judy had alluded to something of that nature in her veiled conversations with friends.

Ball called the Gladstone Post, about 60 miles down U.S. 41 near Escanaba, to enlist help in the investigation. Trooper Jerry Racine was dispatched to the Citizens Insurance Company's main office in Escanaba to make inquiries. Racine was told by a Bernie Ramile that it had been 12 to 18 months since Moilanen had done any claims work for his company. The problem, Ramile explained, was that Moilanen simply could not get the work done in a timely manner.

"He told me his wife had been injured in an accident with a cement block," Ramile told Racine, "and he had to spend a lot of time with her."

"Any lawsuits or claims involving Mr. Moilanen?" Racine asked.

"None."

Racine thanked Ramile and drove to Delta County Circuit Court. He was to check past and present civil suits involving either Bruce Robert Moilanen or North Country Claims. No such suits existed.

Detectives had already been able to check counties closer to home. Whatever it was Judy Moilanen thought might have been hanging over their heads did not exist, at least in the form of a lawsuit.

◆   ◆   ◆

Bob Ball walked into his office Monday, Jan. 11, to a call from Gayle Lampinen. She had been getting calls from Moilanen at the rate of one every other day, both at home and at work. He was also popping in unannounced with more and more frequency.

"He called on Friday," she said, "and complained about all the money it was costing him to run that ad in the paper. He said he was trying to account for two hours of his time. I didn't know what he meant and I didn't ask."

"Any contact over the weekend?"

Ball did not yet have Cousineau's report, but Moilanen had been at the ski hill both Saturday and Sunday.

"I went out to my truck Saturday morning," she said, "and a bunch of clothes were on the front seat."

"Clothing?"

"Ski clothing and women's skirts."

"No notes?"

"No notes."

"We don't even know when he was there," she said. "He almost had to come into the driveway with his lights off. We never noticed any lights in the window or heard anyone at the door. The dogs were barking outside at about 8 o'clock Friday night, but we didn't think anything of it."

Gayle Lampinen seemed troubled.

"Det. Ball, Bruce has been coming into my office unannounced and then stopping off at the house like we're sure he did Friday night," she said. "He seems to be all over the place. We're also getting hang-up calls both at home and at our offices. Bruce is getting scary and we're both concerned for our welfare."

◆　　◆　　◆

Bob Ball received a call the next morning from a private investigator working for one of the insurance companies with policies on Judy's life. Payment was being held in abeyance dependent on the possibility of the beneficiary's involvement in the "accidental" death.

"The investigation is continuing," Ball said. "I'll call the company direct and bring them up to date. They may be able to help me too."

Ball jotted down the 800 number for SafeCo Insurance and contacted a representative named Norma Gerde.

"Judy had $20,000 in life insurance through Marquette General," Gerde informed him. "The policy has a double-indemnity clause in the event of accidental death so, in this case, it's worth $40,000. Bruce Moilanen is the beneficiary."

In this case, Ball was thinking, the death might not be accidental.

Ball was still bothered by the $7,200 check written to Judy that Moilanen cashed in the first couple of weeks after her death. His fingers were doing the walking. He dialed another 800 number, this one to Lincoln National Life, the carrier for Marquette General's tax-deferred annuity (TDA) program. A representative named Michael Bogart answered the call.

"Judy had $18,631.26 in her account," Bogart explained, "until a recent withdrawal was made under a loan provision we have in the program. They wanted to buy a van or a car, I forget which. The withdrawal was for $7,200."

Bingo.

◆   ◆   ◆

Bob Ball kept hearing about Bruce Moilanen and women. He could find no traces of an affair, but he thought maybe Moilanen might have struck up a reciprocal relationship with *somebody*. So far, as in the cases of Gayle Lampinen and Lee Anne Wysocki, it was a matter of Moilanen embarrassing himself with futile pursuits.

Ball had picked up on the name of a former Ontonagan living in Des Moines, Iowa. It was worth a call.

"I vaguely knew Judy from high school," she said, "and I don't think I've seen Bruce since I graduated in 1974. And he was *not* a boyfriend. Never."

Ball sighed. It had been worth a try. However, the woman was not done talking.

"I think it was spring of '92, though it might have been '91, when I got a call from out of the blue from Bruce Moilanen," she said. "He'd gotten my number from my mother. We talked a little bit about what we'd been up to since high school and I told him I was getting married and that my fiancé and I were buying a home."

"That was it?"

"No. Several days later, Bruce sent me a dozen red roses. I haven't heard from him since."

"Listen," Ball said, "I don't know how to couch this, but we've also heard rumors that Bruce was having an affair with your sister Priscilla."

"I don't have a sister named Priscilla."

◆   ◆   ◆

Bob Ball had taken the now-notorious Sweater Letter and forwarded it to Lt. James Steggell, a handwriting expert at the Michigan State Police Laboratory in Bridgeport. He had also sent copies of the "known" handwriting of both Bruce Moilanen and Judy Moilanen.

"The Sweater Letter," Steggell advised over the telephone, "was definitely not written by Judy Moilanen."

"What about Bruce?" Ball asked.

"I can't say for sure," Steggell said, "but I can't eliminate him either. There are similarities that suggest Bruce *could* have written it. Can you get me more samples of his handwriting?"

"No problem."

"One more thing," Steggell said. "I'm going to send this letter to the East Lansing lab. They have an electrostatic detector apparatus. We call it an ESDA."

Bob Ball knew what that was. It was a device that would pick up on indentations made by the writing on the prior page of the notepad.

"That might be helpful," Ball said.

◆　　　◆　　　◆

Ball as well as other detectives and troopers were, without success, scouring outdoor stores in the western part of the Upper Peninsula for any records of rifles purchased by Bruce Moilanen. They were, of course, particularly interested in a Savage 110 Model 30.

In the course of chasing dead-end non-leads on rifle purchases, Ball heard about a woman in Mass City who had reported a strange phone call at about 1 p.m. on Sunday, Jan. 17. The caller had identified himself as a State Police Sergeant. His questions seemed strange, so she called the Wakefield Post and asked for whatever sergeant was on duty.

Larry Schemansky was on duty at Wakefield and he had not called. Daniel Girard was on duty at Calumet and he had not called. Larry Wylie was on duty at Negaunee and he had not called. Ball knew that neither he nor Poupore had called.

Trooper John Raymond was dispatched to Mass City.

"This man identified himself as a State Police sergeant investigating the death of Judy Blake," the woman said. "She had another name I didn't catch. He kept asking if I had seen a silver-colored van parked near the intersection of M-38 and the Simar-Wasas Road."

"Had you?" Raymond asked.

"No, I hadn't," she said. "Then he started telling me about an autopsy report that said Judy had been shot at close range with a handgun. It seemed strange that a state policemen was telling me things like that."

Ball knew that Bruce had been at the ski hill that Sunday. He had been scheduled to arrive at the Blakes the day before, but did not show. He explained he was having trouble with his van. He got to Ontonagon at 10:30 and headed for the Porkies...with Elise.

Mary Ann Blake went to the ski resort and picked up Elise. The time was 12:15. Moilanen had been on his own at 1 p.m. Ball concluded that "Sgt." Bruce Moilanen had made the strange telephone call.

◆   ◆   ◆

Mary Saaranen, a Mass City resident, had seen Bruce Moilanen's advertisement in *The Daily Mining Gazette*. She called one of the telephone numbers in the ad, the one at the Blake residence. The woman who answered, presumably Mary Ann, took a message and said her son-in-law would return the call.

Moilanen called an hour later. He added Mary Saaranen's name to his alibi list. In spite of his insistence to the contrary, the police were, in fact, checking his list. Trooper Raymond went to the Saaranen residence to see what she had to say.

"I was driving home from the Elms Market," she said, "when I noticed a State Police car behind me. I remember he was behind me for quite awhile and I was getting nervous. I noticed a gray van near the intersection of the Simar-Wasas Road and M-38 and I saw somebody getting into it. It wasn't anybody I knew."

For his part, John Raymond knew who was driving the State Police squad car that had made her nervous. He had been the driver.

"What time was this?" he asked.

"About 5:30," she said.

Another alibi had gone awry.

◆   ◆   ◆

Bruce Moilanen was scheduled to return to work Jan. 18. Det. Sgt. Poupore called him at Marquette General on Jan. 19. He had asked for an extension of his leave of absence. He would not be back to work until Jan. 25.

"Maybe we can get him in for a polygraph this week," Poupore suggested to Ball.

They stopped at Moilanen's house on Jan. 19, but he was not home. They tried again the next morning, and he was home. He invited them in.

"We'd like you to come to the post this afternoon for an interview," Ball said.

"I'd like to," Moilanen said, "but I can't make it. I'm back at work on a new shift, 11 to 7. I have to be at the hospital at 11. I could do it tomorrow morning."

Ball and Poupore did not even exchange glances. They knew Moilanen did not have to be anywhere at 11 a.m., at least not at work.

"Listen, Bruce," Ball said, "we'd still like you to take a polygraph test..."

Moilanen interrupted.

"I'm on too much of an emotional roller coaster for that," he said. "I think I should wait until I calm down."

"Nerves and emotions aren't going to affect this test," Ball insisted. "You'll be familiar with all the questions before we even hook you up. You can even help us make up the questions."

"Hmmm," Moilanen said, "can we base the questions around the times and places on my alibi lists? Will I be asked if I was telling the truth about not being in the Turpeinen clear-cut that day?"

"Bruce," Ball said, "this isn't going to be a fishing expedition. We're trying to eliminate you as a suspect. You'll be tested basically on the issue of whether or not you killed your wife."

Moilanen was noncommittal, at best, but he did have something to offer that did little to pacify the detectives and what they really had in mind.

"I have another alibi list," he said. "I got some answers from my ad."

Ball and Poupore were frustrated when they left the house.

"He wants to be tested on everything *but* the relevant issue," Ball said. "Let's pull up over here and see where he goes. We know he doesn't have to be at work."

The investigators watched as Moilanen pulled out of the driveway a little after 11 a.m., driving his leased Pontiac Grand Prix. He drove downtown, parked and spent 20 minutes in an office building. The detectives lost him in traffic near Northern Michigan University, then found his car parked on an access ramp at Marquette General. Moments later, the car was gone. Unless he was on eight-minute shifts, he had not gone to Marquette General to work.

Ball and Poupore went into the hospital and contacted Patricia Blake, Moilanen's supervisor. She confirmed that Moilanen would not resume at the hospital until the following Monday.

"Why would he have been parked on that ramp?" Ball wondered.

"We found out that, in the past, he has used a couple of phones in the lithotripsy area," Blake said. "You can get into that area from that ramp. We've changed some keys in those areas, *because* Bruce has been using the phones, but maybe he has a key we don't know about."

Maybe he didn't, Ball thought. Maybe that was why he was parked for such a short period of time.

"While you're here," Blake suggested, "you should talk to Beth Heidtman. She's one of our nurses."

Beth Heidtman was a registered nurse on the day shift. She and her husband Gary, who worked for Upper Peninsula Power, lived just outside Marquette.

"I got five or six telephone calls from Moilanen over the course of a few months last spring," Heidtman said. "He'd always start by asking questions about work, but then he would try to turn to personal things."

Brashly, Moilanen was making these calls to her home.

"My husband was fully aware of these calls and he finally got fed up," Heidtman said. "He said, if this guy didn't stop calling, he was going to rip his face off. I don't think he said this to Bruce, but the calls stopped."

Beth Heidtman and her husband had also been rattled by the presence of strange vehicles lingering near their home during the middle part of December.

"We have no idea who was driving them," she said.

"If you see them again," Ball said, "try to get a description and license number."

Obviously, Moilanen was not easily daunted when it came to at least *trying* to establish a two-way relationship with a member of the opposite sex. Getting his face ripped off must not have been appealing, however.

◆　　　◆　　　◆

Lee Anne Wysocki's telephone rang at Marquette General and Bruce Moilanen was on the other end of the line. He told her he too was at work, calling from within the hospital. He was likely calling from inside the hospital during the stop he had made while Ball and Poupore had been following him. However, he was not at work.

"Can I use your phone at the house?" he asked. "It's like Grand Central Station around here."

There was also the fact that he was not supposed to be there, a minor detail.

"Fine," she said. "I'll call Stephanie and tell her to expect you."

Lee Anne arrived home a little later and Moilanen was sitting in her living room.

"The cops have been harassing me again," he said. "Two hours this morning. They even went to the store down in Mass where I bought a bottle of pop the day Judy was killed. He made them find a receipt."

Lee Anne had clicked into a listening mode and Moilanen was in a talking mode.

"I've been to see an attorney named Tom Casselman here in Marquette," he said. "He told me not to take the State Police polygraph test. He told me to take a private test downstate."

"Is Casselman your attorney?"

"I don't think I need one. This was just a free visit."

In truth, Moilanen had not even talked with Casselman. He had talked with Casselman's wife Rhonda, a private investigator working out of the attorney's office. A criminal justice major at Northern Michigan University, Mrs. Casselman was the first woman private investigator in Upper Michigan. Her husband kidding calls her Magnum U.P.

It was appropriate that Moilanen talk first with Mrs. Casselman, because she could address the pitfalls of being under investigation. That was her forte. Further, should Moilanen at some point hire Tom Casselman to be his attorney, Casselman's wife would be doing all the pre-trial investigation.

Rhonda Casselman's advice to Moilanen: "People who talk will be convicted."

Moilanen was doing everything he could to avoid talking to the cops, but now he was sitting with Lee Anne and the conversation got around to finances. He could not have known that her seeming eagerness to listen was not out of empathy.

"I think I can make it for three months without the money from Judy's life insurance," he said. "I've got one policy to live on and one in trust for Elise."

This was strange to Lee Anne. She thought she had heard about four or five policies by now, but maybe she was confusing them.

Lee Anne was also detecting paranoia of sorts.

"I'd really like to be able to use your telephone," he told her, "because Casselman warned me that the cops may have mine tapped."

They didn't.

After they talked for awhile, Moilanen got up to leave.

"You know, I don't think they think *I* did it," he said. "I think they think I *hired* someone to do it."

◆   ◆   ◆

Bruce Moilanen was scheduled for an interview the morning of Jan. 21, but the weather had come up bad. He called Poupore and said he could not make it because nursery school had been cancelled and Irene Janofski was not available. Poupore reset the interview for the next morning and then called Ms. Janofski.

"I'm available," she said. "He never called to ask."

Poupore had to concede that the weather was bad. The roads in the U.P. can become nearly impassable when the worst of winter storms hit, blowing snow across the highways and bringing visibility to close to zero. The detectives had encountered very few such days this winter, as their investigation took them on seeming interminable treks across the Western U.P. This was one of those days.

Ball, meanwhile, got on the telephone and called the Lutheran Brotherhood Insurance Company. Claims Examiner Kathy Sparks told him that Judy Moilanen had been insured for $60,000 and, no, there was no double indemnity for accidental death. Bruce was the beneficiary.

"No claim has been made yet," she said.

◆   ◆   ◆

Lo and behold, Bruce Moilanen was a profile in punctuality as he walked into the Michigan State Police Negaunee Post at 10 a.m. on Jan. 22. Det. Sgts. Ball and Poupore were actually anticipating another telephone call and another excuse.

"Maybe we could start by doing a little bit of work on this list of names you gave us…these two different lists," Ball suggested.

"This is kinda put more in order than what we originally had," Moilanen said. "This has the people who responded to the ad I ran. I had some others who saw my van but didn't remember what day, so they didn't do me two hoots worth of good."

The detectives went through Moilanen's newest list with meticulous detail. They talked about the truck from Laurium, an assortment of Makis, the two Johnsons, the note at Macy's, Mary Saaranen and seemingly half of the names in the Ontonagon County telephone directory, which weighs about as much as a comic book. Moilanen was stressing that Trooper Raymond and Ms. Saaranen had both seen him the afternoon in question.

"I agree with you that your van was out there on that Sunday," Ball said. "We have no problems with that whatsoever."

"Oh."

"What's puzzled us a little bit is why you're going to all this trouble to line up people who'd seen your van like from three in the afternoon."

"Because…"

"Let's say between 3 and 5. We're trying to establish your whereabouts, you know, for the whole afternoon."

Moilanen was obviously still thinking he had to be covered around 3 o'clock. He hemmed and hawed, as if little relevance could be found elsewhere.

"Then there's the morning time periods," Ball said. "There's no doubt in my mind you were right where you said you were. But we do have to cover this period in the early afternoon."

"Hmmm."

"That seems to be the blank portion here," Ball said, "like the missing piece of a puzzle, you might say."

"I didn't really ask that, I suppose," Moilanen said. "Maybe I should have put a broader spectrum on it."

They backed up to the morning hours and worked forward to that gap between when Moilanen went off on his own and when he had his near-collision with Wade Johnson.

"Okay," Ball said, "you saw Wade. It looks like 3 o'clock."

"It had to be way before 3," Moilanen insisted. "At 3, I was already back in Mass."

"The only thing is, you *couldn't* have had that incident with Wade until 3 o'clock," Ball said quietly. "I'll tell you why. You gave us that nice list and we went to it and it helped us generate some other interviews."

"Right."

"And," Ball said, "we've been able to determine that Wade didn't leave Mass until 20 minutes to 3. He said he had a good 15 to 20-minute run from there to where he saw you. So that makes it 3 o'clock."

"That's not feasible," Moilanen said. "Because there's no way I could have been in there, you know, seeing him, and then got back to the Elms at 3."

"Well, I'm saying you weren't back. Lori Johnson doesn't put you there at 3. She puts you there later than that."

"Uh, but…"

"That's why we're having a little trouble, you know?"

Alibis. Alibis. Alibis. Moilanen suggested maybe he would run another ad looking for people who had seen his van in Tank Creek during the gap in his alibis. That seemed a more reasonable alternative to what he considered the unreliability of a polygraph test.

"How do you think you'd do in a polygraph?" Ball asked. "Are you worried about it?"

"Yes, I'm…"

"You know it can't be used against you."

"If you fail the thing," Moilanen said, "it really makes you look bad."

"Well," Ball said, "if you didn't have anything to do with your wife's murder, 99.999 times out of a hundred this thing's going to clear you and we can get this thing moving for you. I would imagine you have some insurance money hangin' out there somewhere."

"Uh huh."

"I don't know how much is out there, but I'm sure you have a good track on it. At least, I would think you do. You know, this could be a motive, especially if there were financial problems and something happened to your wife."

"You start playing word games, looking at it like that," Moilanen said. "You take the amount of life insurance and stretch it over the fact that you have to raise a daughter for 18 years and it winds up being like $619 a month. The amount of money Judy would have made, were she still here, would have been $800,000. That's be pretty ridiculous."

Don Poupore stayed almost exclusively in the background during these sessions, taking notes and numbers. He was at a loss trying to figure where to start the math on this explanation. Ball too was pressing on the numbers, trying to get Moilanen to sort them out for him.

Moilanen did. He came up with $132,000 worth of insurance on his wife's life. Detectives were aware of one $75,000 policy with Northwestern Mutual that Moilanen had said was in a trust for Elise's education. That would account for part of the "shortfall" in money he said he had coming and available, but the detectives knew he was not disclosing all that was "out there."

Ball changed pace.

"You got anybody close you can confide in and get a little support from?"

"That's kinda been my problem through the whole thing," Moilanen said. "I'm kinda like the Lone Ranger, you know? What makes this whole thing a lot worse to bear is, of course, my wife and I just did everything together. I mean it was her and me did this, her and me hunted, her and me fished, whatever we did the other one...was there."

"You never separated?"

"No."

At one point, Ball and Moilanen got off on a 10-minute tangent talking about computer programs. It was a strange interlude, Moilanen eagerly explaining to the seemingly confused detective how one program or another worked and what it could do. Ball, for his part, knew Moilanen had a computer and he knew there might come a time, given a properly worded search warrant, when he might want to delve into whatever mysteries Moilanen's computer might contain. He had ulterior motives for being so interested.

Ball jolted the subject back onto track.

"The polygraph operator's gonna have to ask you if you killed your wife?"

"Right. I don't see that as being a problem."

"Did you *ever* think about killing your wife? Even in the past?"

"Never, never."

"Boy, Bruce," Ball said, "I'll tell you, the best thing for you is to take that thing. If you don't think you'd have a problem with a question like, 'Did I shoot my wife?' Seems like you'd be in like gold."

Once again, Ball twisted the conversation in a different direction, like he was tacking a sailboat into the wind. He kept trying to make headway.

"How about finances and bills?"

"My bills are about $1,200 a month more than I make right now without my wife's income."

"So that's gonna be a problem for ya..."

"Big time," Moilanen said. "To say the least."

"Let's get the test scheduled…"

"I don't want to sound like I'm hedging," Moilanen said, "but give me a couple of days to think it over."

The last 20 minutes of the interview was a tap-dance, Moilanen trying to tiptoe around a polygraph exam and the detectives trying to nail him down. They finally agreed to the week of Feb. 1 through Feb. 5, preferably early in the morning. They turned off the tape recorder at 12:07 after two hours of conversation.

"Now that we ain't got that thing running," Bruce Moilanen said, nodding toward the tape recorder, "maybe I can help you. You were having questions about your computer?"

◆   ◆   ◆

As agreeable as Moilanen could be when it came to discussing the complexities of computer programs, he was equally reticent to confront the complexities—and possible consequences—of a polygraph test. He was gone from the post less than an hour when he was on the telephone with Bob Ball.

"Monday's out," he said. "Can't do it Monday."

"That's fine," Ball said. "You said any time that week, so I'll set it up for later. Where you gonna be over the weekend? I'll call you."

"I'll be at the Blakes."

Ball set the date and time for Feb. 4 at 8 a.m. He called the Blake house and got Mary Ann, who dutifully wrote down the information and gave it to Moilanen…when he returned from another day on the ski slopes.

13

The Asset Letter

Bruce Moilanen had not been able to make the interview with the detectives on Jan. 21. That was the day the weather came up bad and nursery school had been cancelled and he had nowhere to take Elise. He had not, of course, bothered to check whether Irene Janofski was available.

In truth, he had other plans for that day. He had called Gayle Lampinen the day before and told her he was going to be at the hospital in Calumet the afternoon of the 21st to service some anesthesiologistic equipment. He said he was being paid on the side by some doctors from Marquette General.

At 3 p.m. on Jan. 21, Moilanen walked into Gayle Lampinen's office at Portage View Hospital. In spite of the horrendous weather, he had made the two-hour drive from Harvey to see her. There was no equipment to be serviced.

This four-hour round trip through what might have been the winter's worst storm produced only a brief visit. He handed Gayle a yellow envelope as he was leaving. She opened the envelope and pulled out a card. It had a cute cover picturing a little fellow with a whimsical smile standing next to a dog with a wagging tail.

If you need someone to listen,
I'm here!
If you need a little support,
I'm here!

If you need a pat on the back,
I'm here!

If she had sat at her desk and absorbed the cover for awhile, she probably would have thought it kind of warm and fuzzy, innocent and harmless.

She opened the card…

Naked mud wrestling
is also available on request
s/Bruce

She frowned. She reached back into the envelope and pulled out a two-page letter written on stationery with a bright strip of leaves and flowers across the top and bottom. It was dated Jan. 20.

Gayle:
I really don't know how to say what I feel. We've known each other for a couple of years now. And most of it has been pretty (for lack of a better word) shitty time in my life. Whenever I needed someone to talk to you are always willing to listen and for the most part tell me what you think, good, bad, or indifferent. We share many common interests maybe that's why I feel comfortable with you. "Comfortable," just what a beautiful woman wants to be called. I guess what I want to say is, I truly love you, not in the sense of throwing you in the sack and thrashing your bones, although any man who hasn't had that thought cross his mind is crazier than I am.
No, I just mean I hold your friendship very close to my heart. I will never be able to thank you enough for just being there. I just want you to know your (sic) one of the few people, "I would walk to hell on hot rocks for." If there is anything I can do for you or Paul please don't be afraid to ask. I will always cerrish (sic) the times we've had to just sit talk. And I

hope I haven't been a bother to you. I love you dearly. I'll be your friend and immoral (sic) supporter forever.

> *Year in, year out, in one ear & out the other.*
> *s/Love, Bruce*

Immoral supporter? Was that a Freudian slip or a slip of the pen or simply a brain cramp?

Gayle Lampinen was not at all bothered by being described as comfortable. She *was* bothered by the tone of both the card and the letter. She took the envelope and its contents home and showed them to Paul.

"I'm going to save it for Det. Ball," she said. "*You* may not want to read it."

She left it on the kitchen table. Paul read it.

In the course of the investigation, it would become known as The I Love You Letter.

◆   ◆   ◆

Bruce Moilanen had finally made it back to work, so to speak. He was due Jan. 25 at 11 a.m…and he was there.

For awhile.

Det. Sgt. Poupore contacted Pat Blake, Bruce's supervisor, a couple of days later to see how he was doing. He was startled by what he heard. Moilanen, according to Ms. Blake, disappeared after 5 p.m. and never returned. Ms. Blake promptly issued a written reprimand warning that the next such offense would result in his dismissal from Marquette General.

"I'm having trouble dealing with this," Moilanen told Ms. Blake, alluding to his return to work. "I just keep thinking about my wife. I was in the back stairwell crying."

Ms. Blake might have been more sympathetic if Moilanen had not been a problem employee *before* Judy's death. What's more, she had heard Moilanen paged during his absence and she knew the page would have been heard over the intercom system in the stairwell.

If, in fact, Moilanen had spent 2½ hours crying in the stairwell, he had ignored the pages.

◆   ◆   ◆

Meanwhile, The Sweater Letter had made its way to the State Police Crime Lab in East Lansing. It underwent an ESDA test for indented handwriting from the previous page. Lt. James Steggell called Bob Ball with the results.

The Sweater Letter's first words were *"These are."* The first two words on the previous page had been *"These sweaters."* The letter's author had had a very brief false start before getting into the meat of the very meaty letter.

"I've analyzed the handwriting in both The Sweater Letter and the indented writing over it," Steggell told Ball, "and the best I can say is that both were probably written by Bruce Moilanen. Judy did not write either."

◆   ◆   ◆

Lee Anne Wysocki returned to her apartment from work Jan. 26 and found a Fax machine, a $10 bill and a note from Moilanen, explaining that he had had to use the telephone. She was not pleased. She did not feel she had given him open-ended permission to use the telephone.

A couple of hours later, Moilanen was back to retrieve the Fax machine. He sat down briefly and turned the conversation toward the sexual proclivities of young people in this day and age. Lee Anne was uncomfortable with the discussion.

When Moilanen got up to leave, he bent over and whispered into her ear: "I got a card from a friend of mine in Houghton. She said, 'I'll be there for you, no matter what! Even for *that!*"

To Lee Anne Wysocki, there was no doubt what *that* meant.

When she related the incident to Don Poupore, he was wondering whether yet another woman existed—this one sexually involved with Moilanen—or whether this was simply another case of wishful thinking.

◆   ◆   ◆

Mid-afternoon on Feb. 3, Bruce Moilanen called the Calumet State Police Post. He was canceling his latest polygraph test.

"I'm on antidepressants," he explained. "Maybe we can reset it in about four weeks."

On the day Moilanen was supposed to have taken the test, Feb. 4, Ball and Poupore drove to Marquette General. He was actually back at work by then. Poupore called the operating room and asked if Moilanen could come to the lobby. Ten minutes later, a lethargic, almost dopey, Moilanen entered the lobby. As they talked, he swayed and rolled his eyes. He seemed on the verge of passing out.

"What's the matter, Bruce?" Poupore asked. "You look really tired."

"I'm taking an antidepressant called *Zoloft* and a sedative called *Seclium*," he said. "I'll be on them for four to six weeks. My doctors prescribed them because I just can't get any sleep without them."

Moilanen, it appeared, was veritably asleep on his feet. He excused himself and went back to work.

Ball was not impressed.

"Did you notice his eyes?" he asked Poupore on the way out. "His pupils were perfectly normal, neither constricted nor dilated. I think he was trying to deceive us."

"If he's like that down in the operating room," Poupore suggested, "they'd have to send him home."

"I suspect he's not like that in the operating room," Ball said. "Just in the lobby. Just for us."

Poupore called Pat Blake, who told him Moilanen had been three hours late for work. His excuse to her was that he was late because he had to get medication from his doctor. The ice was getting thinner at Marquette General for Bruce Moilanen.

"I think this medication may have made him a little too sleepy to safely do his work in the operating room," Poupore warned.

Funny thing, Poupore was told, Bruce did not seem at all dopey or sleepy back in the operating room. Tardiness was his only problem.

◆   ◆   ◆

One of Moilanen's businesses, the insurance adjustment business known as North Country Claims Service, seemed to be rather dormant. The detectives were trying to determine why. He had told the Lampinens he was selling the business, but there didn't seem to be any evidence of a transaction occurring. And much of what he was telling the Lampinens was deceiving, to say the least.

During the Jan. 22 interview, Ball asked about the claim business.

"What's gonna happen with the claims business," Moilanen said, "is it's gonna close because I don't have any time to do it. Back in June, they changed my schedule at the hospital and that almost took it right there."

"Okay."

"So what's gonna happen is North Country Claims Service is going out of business and it's gonna file bankruptcy."

Ball and Poupore got a different feel for Moilanen and North Country Claims Service when they visited Robert Goodwin at Goodwin Auto Repair in Skandia, a roadside stop 12 miles south of Marquette on U.S. 41. Goodwin had known Moilanen both through his auto repair shop as well as through his part-time work as an emergency medical technician, a job Moilanen also held for some time.

"As an EMT," Goodwin said, "I'm a first responder in this area. I'd occasionally run into Bruce and he'd come onto a scene like he was the only one who knew anything. He'd be telling everyone else what to do. I always thought he was an asshole."

Naturally, Goodwin would also run into Moilanen, the insurance adjuster, in his repair shop.

"It's been awhile since he's been around," Goodwin said, "but I remember how difficult he was to deal with. And he caused a conflict of interest in my mind. He was buying some of the wrecks he totaled and then later fixing them."

◆   ◆   ◆

Bob Ball called Gayle Lampinen Feb. 10 just to check in and learned of the I Love You Letter. He also learned that Moilanen's calls had picked up their pace to the point where they were an almost daily occurrence, usually at the office. The Lampinens now had an answering machine at home to screen calls.

"The latest," she said, "is that I got nine red roses and an unsigned card today while I was out of the office. There wasn't any name on it, but I recognized Bruce's handwriting."

"Have you sent him any cards or letters?"

"No."

"Have you called him?"

"No, but I've kept a log of *his* calls. He's been after us to go skiing with him. He even made a remark about picking me up and taking me skiing even if Paul doesn't want to go."

"How are you and Paul holding up?"

"We're nervous."

◆   ◆   ◆

Bob Ball was not about to give up on the polygraph test. He and Poupore stopped at the hospital Feb. 12, but Moilanen told them he was too busy to come to the lobby.

"Well, Bruce," Ball said, "I'm gonna call you early in the week to set this thing up."

"Fine."

Moilanen hung up.

"He said it would be fine," Ball said sarcastically.

"Sure," Poupore said.

Maybe a little heat would warm him up. With Ball and Poupore in one car and Det. Lt. Goad and Det. Sgt. Robin Sexton in another, they set up a surveillance for when Moilanen left Marquette General.

Moilanen knew immediately that he was being followed. He looked two of the detectives in the face as he left the parking lot. He went west to Lincoln Avenue, turned south and then quickly ducked into a side street. He disappeared into an apartment complex. Did he really think he could hide in *Marquette?*

Goad and Sexton, who weren't as familiar to Moilanen, parked a discreet distance from the Janofskis, who were watching Elise. The detectives watched as Moilanen drove past the house, as if to check for tails, before returning to pick up his daughter.

They had learned nothing from this surveillance. What they had done, basically, was launch a war of nerves.

◆   ◆   ◆

Ball and Poupore were curious about telephone calls Moilanen was making out of Marquette General. They contacted Brett Young, a clinical engineer with MGH. He told them it was possible to trace long distance tolls out of the hospital system. Ball gave him Gayle Lampinen's home and work numbers, both of which would have been toll calls from Marquette. Young was given no names or reasons, just the numbers to check.

Between June 1, 1992 and Jan. 29, 1993, Superior Telecom's summary listed 61 telephone calls from Marquette General to either Gayle's home number or her direct line at work.

Either Gayle Lampinen had a lot of friends at Marquette General or Bruce Moilanen was working very hard at being "just a friend" to The Sweater Lady.

◆   ◆   ◆

Bruce Moilanen knocked on Lee Anne Wysocki's door on Feb. 12. Lee Anne was not home. Her daughter Stephanie would not answer the knock.

Wysocki returned home to a bouquet of six red roses. It wouldn't have bothered her to know that another woman had gotten nine roses from Moilanen. It bothered her that she had gotten any at all.

She opened the card: *"Happy Valentine's Day...Perhaps someday we can be more than just friends...s/Bruce."*

When Ball and Poupore went to pick up the card, Wysocki produced her telephone bill as well. It contained two toll calls she didn't remember making. One was to a private investigator/polygraph operator downstate in Traverse City.

"What do you think?" Ball asked Poupore after they left.

"Maybe he wants a dress rehearsal," Poupore said.

They made three stops at Marquette flower shops. If Moilanen had sent flowers to two women, maybe they could learn of others.

The explanation they received at all three was the same: "If someone was sending flowers and paying cash, we wouldn't have the records in our computers. You're welcome to go through our receipts, but there are hundreds of them and they might not even list the name of the sender."

◆   ◆   ◆

Bruce Moilanen stopped at Portage View to see Gayle on Valentine's Day, which happened to be a Sunday. He had to make the one-hour drive from Ontonagon, where Elise was staying with the Blakes. He had told them he was skiing.

In the midst of the usual small talk, Moilanen probably told Gayle about his role in the rescue of a snowmobiler who had driven off a cliff in the Porcupine Mountains the night before. As a member of the Ski Patrol, he was a part of the effort in the cold and darkness that took until almost 11 p.m. He would surely avail himself of an opportunity to portray himself as a hero.

What's more, he had a revelation to make.

"I'm ready to get married again," he told her, "and start my life over."

He did not explain further. Perhaps he felt no further explanation was needed.

The Blakes, meanwhile, naturally assumed he was skiing on this Sunday. He was still not home when they returned from an evening church service, but he had said something about visiting relatives in Mass City after skiing.

When he finally arrived in Ontonagon at 11 p.m., Mary Ann asked him if it was still snowing in Mass City.

"It's been snowing all along over there," he said.

All along, he had been driving back to Ontonagon from Portage View in Hancock.

◆   ◆   ◆

Bob Ball was seemingly spending as much time at Marquette General as Bruce Moilanen, who supposedly worked there. Ball was there Feb. 18, three days after an occasion when Moilanen had called in sick and gone skiing and a day before he would call in sick again and go visit Gayle Lampinen…again.

Ball first visited with Roger Brooks, who told him that an investigator representing Safeco Insurance asked to review Judy's hospital file. Not her personnel file, but rather her patient file.

"He was particularly interested in the time when the chimney block fell on her head," Brooks said. "He wanted to see our records on the injury."

Ball smiled to himself. This private investigator was obviously not going to rely on the cops to get to the bottom of the circumstances surrounding Judy's death. It probably hadn't taken the guy too much digging to learn of the chimney block incident. It was much more questionable in hindsight than it had apparently been at the time.

"By the way," Brooks said, "you should probably visit Beth Heidtman again."

Bill Nemacheck, the administrator and Judy's former boss, was next on Ball's agenda. He was as much personal friend as boss.

"You know, in the weeks before Judy's death, she told me Bruce blamed himself so much for their financial problems that he told her he was having trouble facing her," Nemacheck said. "She was concerned that he might even consider committing suicide."

Nemacheck had a disbelieving look on his face.

"In retrospect," he said, "I think it was one of his ruses to try to get Judy to do what he wanted."

When last Ball had talked with Beth Heidtman, she had described personal telephone calls to her that Moilanen was trying to pass off as business calls. She described strange cars in her neighborhood. She also said the calls had stopped quite some time ago.

However, Moilanen's attention had surfaced again. Just two days earlier, she said, he had come up uncomfortably close to her in a hallway and put three candy hearts in her pocket.

"Read them," he whispered.

She walked away without removing them from her pocket, but she kept them in case Det. Ball happened to come around.

"Here they are," she said.

Ball looked at them.

"You're tops with me"
"I feel this way"
"Miss you"

"I'm getting very irritated with this situation," she said. "He follows me all over the hospital when I'm trying to work. My supervisor's told me they're trying to keep him busy on other projects, but it's getting to the point where I'm not comfortable coming to work."

Bruce Moilanen had created an adversary in Ms. Heidtman. And her husband was the man who threatened to rip his face off if he did not cease and desist, albeit the threat was not made to Moilanen himself. He might have been a bit more selective in his distribution of candy hearts.

"I can give you the names of other women who don't like working around Bruce Moilanen," Beth Heidtman concluded.

◆   ◆   ◆

One woman was, in a sense, stuck with him. Gayle Lampinen. She had agreed to string him along until it became unbearable. He was stretching tolerance to its limits.

He showed up Friday afternoon, Feb. 19, after calling in sick.

"I've told Marquette Generous that I'm only going to work until June 1," he told her, using his newly adopted pet term for his place of employment. "Then I'm going to be independently wealthy."

He talked for a little while and stared blankly for a little while.

"I went to see my psychiatrist last night," he said, "and I told him about our friendship."

His eyes glazed and he reached over and squeezed her hand, reaching up with his other arm as if to hug her. She tensed up and pushed him away.

"Bruce," she said, "that is *not* appropriate."

Moilanen was having problems with what was appropriate. He called and left a message on the Lampinens' answering machine the next night. He wanted them to go skiing with him. The number he left was the Blake residence in Ontonagon.

He called the Lampinens again the next morning and they declined his invitation. That night, there was a knock on their door. Moilanen had stopped to see them on his way home to Harvey.

◆   ◆   ◆

Bob Ball and Don Poupore, those nuisances, popped in unannounced at Moilanen's house on Feb. 25. Being somewhat of a master of unannounced visits, Moilanen was surely understanding. His van was running and he seemed anxious to leave…and not anxious to schedule a polygraph.

"I've got at least two more weeks on the medication," Moilanen told them.

"Bruce," Ball said, "are you going to stay on the medications as an excuse to avoid the polygraph test?"

"I wouldn't do that. I need them to sleep."

"This test is awful important to you," Ball said. "You'd be smart to get off them for a week just so you can take the test."

"That's a possibility."

"You know, Bruce," Ball said, "we have run across a number of people who think you killed your wife."

Ball said it like a buddy would share a confidence.

Moilanen did not ask what people thought he had killed his wife. He did not care to discuss the subject further. He excused himself and drove away.

Since his trash was sitting out in front, the detectives threw it into the car and they too drove away. All they found in the trash was trash, as they would on each of the three or four occasions they "pulled" garbage from in front of the house.

What they could not have known, but would know the next day, was that Moilanen had met with Pat Blake and told her he did not know what time he might be in on Feb. 26. He said he was going to the State Police Lab to take a polygraph test. He left the impression that he would get back to her on his availability to return.

Pat Blake never heard from Bruce Moilanen on Feb. 26.

Bruce Moilanen heard from Pat Blake when he returned to work Monday, March 1. She had his time cards in hand. He punched out after only seven hours on Feb. 24. He punched out for supper on Feb. 25 and never punched back in. He neither showed up nor called on Feb. 26.

Bruce Moilanen was suspended for three days, March 2 through March 4.

◆   ◆   ◆

Bruce Moilanen had been caught in a lie, both by Marquette General and the State Police. He had gotten a day off by giving each the impression he was occupied by the other.

The detectives were at loose ends as they chased loose ends.

Bob Ball had a question for Paul Lampinen, so he called him mid-afternoon. Moilanen had already called Lampinen *twice* that day, trying to arrange an outing at the Baraga casino.

"Det. Ball," Lampinen said, "I have to tell you we have some serious reservations about this arrangement."

He did not ask to get off the hook, so to speak, but the Lampinens were definitely wearing down.

Ball's Friday was brightened by a call from Lt. James Steggell, the handwriting expert. He could positively testify that Bruce Moilanen had written both the June 6, 1992 Sweater Letter and the Jan. 20, 1993 I Love You Letter.

"He attempted to disguise the June 6 letter," Steggell said, "but too many patterns are the same."

◆   ◆   ◆

Gayle Lampinen had been rejecting virtually all of Moilanen's suggested "dates," be they for lunch or skiing or going to the casino. She kept begging off because work was overwhelming her or she was going to be out of town or she was sorry but she had already made other plans.

Finally, he called and put her on the spot. The date was March 1.

"I'm off the next three days," he said. "What's best for you for lunch? Maybe I can make you feel better."

She sighed. She had broken a wrist the previous weekend when she fell from one of her horses. Moilanen, who did not mention *why* he was off the next three days, had worded his invitation so that it was difficult to decline.

"How about Wednesday?" she said. "I'll be pushed for time, so I'll drive my own car and meet you at The Library."

He still showed up at Lampinen's office at Portage View, sauntering into the office about 11 and regaling whoever would listen with a tale about how he was going to be independently wealthy by the time he was 40. He was almost 38.

Gayle could not understand so much time off after being off for so long and then out so frequently, but she remembered that Moilanen had told Paul that he had 11 weeks of vacation to burn.

Conversation at the luncheon stayed with small talk and dogs until Gayle leaned forward and asked with as much curiosity as she could muster: "Where *were* you when Judy was killed?"

Bruce switched to his mechanical, almost tape-recorded voice.

"I was in Uncle Ed's deer blind," he said. "The police have been talking to me and asking me questions that really aren't any of their business. They won't get complete answers from me."

"Bruce," she said, "they're only doing their jobs."

Lunch was about to end. The subject had become distasteful and Gayle had had the audacity to bring it up. She was getting into her car when Bruce handed her a card.

She opened it later.

I heard you've been lying in bed all day

Are you sick, or just hoping to get lucky?
Get well soon!

Bruce had added his own message:

"I'm sure God gave you parts much softer to land on."

Gayle Lampinen could not have known it at the time, but this hand-delivered correspondence was nothing like the envelope which waited in her mailbox at home in Chassell.

◆   ◆   ◆

Bruce Moilanen had written a nine-page letter in the early-morning hours of Feb. 28. He made the time clear in the very first sentence.

"It's now 3:40 a.m. and another night of no sleep."

Gayle never had to get to the bottom of a letter or note to know who wrote it, not if it was from Bruce. His penmanship was so distinctive it hardly required analysis to identify. His words would slash and slant their way across a page. The lower-case "G's" and "Y's" took on a life of their own, wrapping exaggeratedly under whatever word contained them and often obscuring the word below. The capital "G" in "Gayle" was a work of art with its strong vertical lines and triumphant and climactic curlicue.

As might be expected of a letter written at such an hour, it rambled through an assortment of subjects and a gamut of moods. It read as if Bruce sat down with a pen and pad and spewed forth with his thought of the moment. It went through a labyrinth to reach what, to him, was an upbeat conclusion. To Gayle, the conclusion would pile more queasiness on top of queasiness.

These were times when Bruce Moilanen was steeped in self-pity. No one understood him. He had no friends. The police were hounding him.

"Starting over, sometimes I think this will kill me or I'll kill me," he wrote. *"I don't know which will come first…Maybe I'm just a strange bird."*

Moilanen wrote of having so few good friends he could count them on the fingers of one hand and have fingers left over.

"I don't know if that puts you in good company, but it's a small group."

Gayle read through a lengthy and warm recollection of the years with Judy, the good out-weighing the bad. He even wrote about their sex life, which did not seem a particularly appropriate—that word again—subject to share. He conceded that he had occasionally flirted during the relationship, but insisted he had never done anything, his word, inappropriate.

"Well," he wrote, *"maybe with you I've gotten carried away on occasion."*

Anyone without insight into the "relationship" between Bruce Moilanen and Gayle Lampinen might have read this as a sort of mutual confession, shared in a personal moment for no one else to see.

The detectives who would later read the letter knew better. Gayle, of course, did too. *He* had gotten carried away on occasion and, a few pages later, was about to get carried away again.

Moilanen shifted into gear on the seventh page, where it started to become eerily reminiscent of The Sweater Letter purportedly written by Judy…

When we talked the other night I said I had too much at stake to gamble on a comittment (sic) that wasn't for keeps not to mention the emotional exposure. You've never asked and I've never offered, but my financial state is not that bad and I would hate to lose it to poor judgement (sic). This is between you and me and the fence post and this is not meant as bragging…You wonder how I take so much time off and why I'm thinking about going into dogs full time.

Well, I have approx. $387,000 dollars, an unfinished $82,000 house and a 324 acre farm and a couple of bills. Which makes my net worth about 1/2 million dollars and MGH pays me almost 30,000 a year for what I do. Talk about overpaid.

This was an interesting and rather optimistic assessment of his finances. Most of it depended upon accessing all of the life insurance benefits relating to Judy's death. And that number kept changing. He had admitted to $132,000 in policies in his Jan. 22 interview with Ball and Poupore and now a different and much-higher number was offered to Gayle.

So, if I ever decide to date again, maybe a couple of years down the road, you can introduce me to a 30-something girlfriend of yours who likes to work her butt off on a farm with her own horses and my dogs with no overhead and a small income and a young daughter to raise together. Prerequisites: 30-40, beautiful inside and out. Loves animals, driven to compete, willing to help raise a young daughter as her own. And a for keeps com-

mittment (sic). If in your travels you find someone who fits the job descrip-
tion give her my name. I'll let you know when I'm ready.

Moilanen did everything but add the postscript about not telling the "prospects" how unbelievably good he was in the sack.

Bruce Moilanen's "criteria" for this perfect woman did not represent an even vague attempt to disguise the identity of the actual woman he sought.

Gayle Lampinen.

In the investigation, this correspondence became known as The Asset Letter.

14

Guns and Dogs

Bruce Moilanen, suspended by Marquette General for the middle three days of the first week of March, was feeling quite domestic on Friday. Having advised Gayle Lampinen of his riches and his dream-woman, he demonstrated another dimension. He had taken yet another day off, telling Pat Blake he had to tend to legal matter. He spent the day in the kitchen.

When Gayle arrived home from work at about 4:40, Bruce pulled into the driveway directly behind her. He had either followed her or he had been waiting for her.

He had prepared quail for Gayle, another thoughtful gesture acknowledging her broken wrist. He brought her a roast quail dinner and raspberry pie and a box of rice. Paul got a serving too.

Dinner came with a note, as usual: *"Thought you might not be feeling domestic for a while so here's a little help."*

He waved good-bye, climbed in his van and drove to Ontonagon for the weekend.

◆   ◆   ◆

After spending three days on suspension and a fourth in his kitchen, Moilanen returned to work on Monday, March 8. He had a surprise for hospital personnel. He turned in his resignation effective June 1, 1993. He must have figured he would be cleared of suspicion by then and insurance dollars would be overflowing his many bank accounts.

Pat Blake had news for Bruce.

"The hospital administration," she said, "will accept this resignation...effective immediately."

Hospital officials had concluded that Bruce Moilanen had created so many problems and stirred up so much anxiety that he could not be placed in a "harmless" position. Heaven knows, Blake had tried to find a place to put him, to no avail. The influence of only one person had kept him employed at Marquette General as long as he had lasted.

Judy Blake Moilanen.

◆   ◆   ◆

Lee Anne Wysocki came home from work March 9 and Moilanen was sitting at her dining room table. Her daughter had lost her key, so the apartment had been left open. Moilanen apparently did not feel it inappropriate to walk in. He also seemed to have nothing to do and no where to go.

After a few minutes, he left.

Wysocki dialed the telephone and got Don Poupore. He and Ball were working in different directions at this point. Ball did most of the work in Ontonagon and the Houghton area, which were closer to the Calumet Post, and Poupore did most of the work in the Marquette area, which was closer to the Negaunee Post. Wysocki was on Poupore's turf...and she wanted him to know Moilanen had been on hers.

The conversation had barely begun and her door was opening and Moilanen was on his way back in. She excused herself and hung up. He sat down again at the kitchen table.

"Friday's the big day," he said. "I'm going downstate for a polygraph test."

"It's important that you do that," she assured him.

"By the way," he said, "did I tell you I'm not with Marquette Generous any more? I turned in my resignation for June 1, but Pat Blake was messing with my hours again. I said, 'Okay, it's effective now.' And I quit."

Don Poupore knew that Moilanen was not scheduled to take a polygraph test administered by the State Police. Maybe it had to do with that telephone call Bruce made from Wysocki's apartment to the private investigator in Traverse City.

Before Moilanen left, Lee Anne retrieved a *Marquette Mining Journal* and asked him if he had read the story on Judy's death. He looked surprised. He had not read it. He picked it up and read quietly for a few minutes.

He put it down.

"It sounds like they know who did it," he said.

◆   ◆   ◆

Investigators had decided to tweak their suspect, apply a little pressure and get him wondering what they knew. This was a period in which they were letting Moilanen run, somewhat like a hooked fish. They decided to let the media play a role in getting his attention.

Bob Ball worked with Jerry Kitzman, the Ontonagon County Sheriff, to produce a news release Kitzman would issue through his department.

The *Mining Journal* picked up the release and assigned reporter Greg Peterson to the story:

Mystery Shooting Believed a Murder

ONTONAGON—The shooting death of a Harvey woman last deer season is now believed to be a homicide rather than a hunting accident, police said.

Judy Moilanen, 35, was shot once in the chest Nov. 29 while walking her dogs near her parents' home in Ontonagon County.

"The shooting, which was originally thought to be accidental in nature, is now being investigated as a homicide," Ontonagon County Sheriff Jerry Kitzman said.

Police declined to say what changed their minds, what kind of weapon killed Moilanen, whether there's a suspect or a motive.

"Evaluation of the evidence and certain witness information has caused investigators to change the focus of the investigation," said Det. Lt. Richard Goad, who is in charge of state police detectives in the Upper Peninsula.

Several MSP detectives have been working on the case and last week additional manpower was added, Goad said.

Bruce Moilanen's attorney would later portray such tactics as harassment. Bob Ball preferred to call it an investigative technique.

◆   ◆   ◆

"Hello, beautiful," the voice said.

Gayle Lampinen cringed. It was Thursday and she was in her office. Bruce, who had visited her the day before, was now on the telephone. He asked her to pray for him the next day, because he was taking the long-awaited polygraph test.

"By the way," he said, "I was going to tell you how great your legs were yesterday, but there were too many people around."

Thank heavens, she thought to herself, there were a lot of people around.

Lee Anne Wysocki was not home that Thursday when he walked in and left a note asking her to pray for him as well. His note to her sounded like half the world was praying on his behalf.

Bruce Moilanen's destination was, in fact, Traverse City, a town of 15,000 on the Grand Traverse Bay in the northern part of the Lower Peninsula. He and Mike Niemi drove to Traverse City late Thursday for a test on Friday, March 12, with a private polygraphist named Robert Dufort.

Niemi was in the dark as to the details regarding the investigators' focus on Bruce. The Blake family had been informed back in December, but they had been asked not to involve anyone outside that innermost circle. The detectives did not want too many people having to act like they were unaware of what they were learning. Niemi, thus, could be himself, and it seemed he was taking Bruce at his word that he had nothing to do with Judy's death.

"I did well," Moilanen said after the test. "The test questions were good questions. I think this'll clear me."

Buoyed, Moilanen was home in time to call the Lampinens at 6:30 Saturday night. He wanted them to meet him at Gino's after a hockey game that night. They agreed to meet him. He made no mention of the polygraph test until Paul got up and went to the register to pay the tab.

"I took that polygraph at a police station down at the Traverse City Post," he said, reaching across and squeezing her hand. "Everything went well, hon. The examiner told me there was no way I could have been lying."

He smiled assuredly.

"That's the second one of these I've taken," he lied. "I'm not taking any more."

Moilanen also told the Janofskis, Elise's baby sitters, about the test. He exaggerated just a little more than a tad.

"I passed the test three times down there," he said. "They hooked me up and asked me maybe 8,000 questions. It was 8:50 Saturday night before I was done. I wouldn't want anyone to have to go through what I went through."

Bruce Moilanen must have talked himself into believing this private test would be acceptable to the State Police and that its results would set him free. His mood turned upbeat. He showed up at Portage View Hospital on Tuesday, March 16, in a truck Gayle had not previously seen, a blue Chevy S-10 pickup.

"I'm just out 'trolling' around," he explained.

Trolling around for that perfect woman? He made it sound so nonchalant, as though he was suddenly without a care in the world. He had not told Gayle he was no longer employed at Marquette General, but, of course, she knew anyway.

Gayle called Bob Ball when Moilanen left.

"Det. Ball," she said, "we're getting more and more concerned. What might Bruce do if he realizes we've been cooperating with the police? It's scary for us."

Bob Ball knew the Lampinens had gone far beyond what could reasonably have been expected. It would have been understandable if they had chosen not to involve themselves at all.

"Gayle," he said, "why don't you start screening your calls more tightly? I think it's time for you to start breaking connections with him."

◆   ◆   ◆

Conversations with Mary Ann Blake were never lengthy. She was a woman who called when she had something to say, or something to ask, and said it. She was not one to mince words. Mrs. Blake called Poupore just before Moilanen's Traverse City trip and told him about the upcoming polygraph test and also said she had heard Bruce was no longer employed by Marquette General.

"One more thing," she said. "Bruce called and told me that the police told him that his in-laws feel he did it."

She did not specify what "he did it" meant, but Poupore knew without asking. He also knew Moilanen was lying to his mother-in-law. He and Ball had told Moilanen that there were a "number of people" who thought he was involved in Judy's death. They mentioned no names.

◆   ◆   ◆

Detectives get the strangest of calls during investigations such as this, some helpful and some not. Don Poupore got a bizarre call from two cousins, one from downstate and one from Ontonagon, who had a run-in with Moilanen in the summer of either 1976 or 1977.

"Around the second cutting of hay season," one explained. "That would be August."

The cousins apparently siphoned gasoline out of the pumps at a chipping plant in the Mass City-Greenland area. They were driving away when the plant manager noticed what they were doing and jumped into a truck and chased them. He forced them off the road and started breaking the windows of their truck with a baseball bat.

They jumped out of their truck and the plant manager hit one on the leg before they overpowered him and started breaking *his* windows with the bat as he ran away.

About this time, they told Poupore, Bruce Moilanen drove by and then wheeled around and came at them. He pulled up alongside, pointed a steel-barreled .357 out the window of his truck and cocked the hammer.

"You're dead," he supposedly said.

One came up with a version that Moilanen ultimately pulled in the gun and drove away and the other said sheriff's deputies came along and broke up the altercation. Nothing, they said, ever came of the incident, though it sounded very much like they deserved to be arrested for stealing gas and assaulting the plant manager. One of them, Poupore learned later, *had* been arrested for the theft.

"I don't want to get involved with this Moilanen situation," one advised Poupore, "but I wanted you to be aware of this."

Poupore hung up and smiled to himself. He could not imagine what this had to do with anything he was investigating in the spring of 1993. It sounded to him like Bruce Moilanen might have been the hero of this little moment of drama. Maybe *that's* what these cousins were trying to tell him.

How could these cousins have known about a "Moilanen Situation" unless maybe Bruce had told them? And why in the world would they agree to be a party to trying to upgrade his image?

◆   ◆   ◆

Back in the Ontonagon area, Bob Ball was on another trek down Cherry Lane. He was checking and re-checking Jerry Schoch's guests, especially since John, the one from Iron River, had been called by someone from a telephone at Marquette General. *His* number showed up on the hospital's records. Little things like that bothered the detective. Ball remained relentless in his pursuit of Moilanen, but he could not take a chance he was either after the wrong man or that maybe another man was involved.

Another thing bothered him about Schoch's guests. One who supposedly arrived after John supposedly left for Iron River had apparently lied. John had said this late-arriving guest was the one who came and got him out of the woods.

"I lied," the late-arrival explained, "because I knew John was on some sort of probation and I didn't think he was supposed to have a gun."

The so-called late-arrival had actually spent the night Saturday. The story stood about the people from Iron River leaving before noon.

Ball was also trying to account for the men Marsha LaFernier and her children had seen in mid-afternoon. He questioned her further and learned that she had made three or four trips out of her driveway that day, including one around 10 a.m. to go into bible school. She *might* have seen the men that trip, but it still did not mesh with the men coming out of the woods around 9.

Finally, it struck him. He called Iron River and asked John if he changed his watch when he came to Ontonagon.

"No," John said, puzzled.

"Thank you," Ball said.

Iron River was on Central Standard Time. When John checked his watch and saw 9 o'clock, it was 10 in Ontonagon on Eastern Standard Time. Iron River, ironically, was east of Ontonagon.

◆   ◆   ◆

Bruce Moilanen was continuing to press Gayle Lampinen, but suddenly the response was growing chilly. He made four telephone calls through the middle of March, far less than normal, once getting rejected on a dinner invitation and later getting a cool reaction to a suggestion that Gayle set him up with a girlfriend.

The Lampinens were ready to get out of Dodge, so to speak, and let law enforcement take over.

When Gayle came out of work March 26, she found two Teddy bears and a card on the front seat of her truck. She didn't even have to look to see whom it was from. The card was computer-generated and ended with the message: "Sometimes, I miss your voice 'un-bear-ably'"

Moilanen was back on the prowl, presumably thinking a Teddy bear or two would irresistibly thaw the chill that had come upon the relationship. He showed up at the Lampinens' house March 28 and at Portage View March 29, neither time invited. And neither time was he warmly received, to say the least.

"Marquette Generous gave me the day off today," he said on the 29th, brightening. "It's my birthday."

He was clinging, undoubtedly for appearance sake, to the job he did not have.

Two letters were postmarked March 30, one from Bruce to Gayle and the other from Gayle to Bruce. It was the first correspondence of any kind from her to him and the first time she had initiated contact since she called Nov. 30, 1992 to express condolences at Judy's death. It was also her last correspondence to Bruce Moilanen.

For his part, Bruce was writing to try to smooth over whatever had gone wrong. He blamed the Teddy bears.

"Since the week of Judy's funeral," he lamented, *"not one of our so-called friends has stopped by or so much as called…to see if I'm still alive, its like I have developed AIDS or something. It seems my only contact with anyone is at work & then it's only because we have to communicate*
"I want to apologize & say I'm sorry. I make some foolish decisions right now. I really don't know why. The bear thing was a poor idea in retrospect & I'm sorry…"

Moilanen got off onto a tangent about training dogs and horses and how there is always room for improvement.

"There ain't no 10s," he said. *"Short of you that is."*

Gayle Lampinen, meanwhile, was packing up those Teddy bears and writing a note to go with them…

Dear Bruce,
These bears need to go to your daughter Elise. I cannot accept them or anything else from you.
Everyone needs someone to talk to at difficult times in their life, especially when they're going through hard times. I was this person for you, but from here on out you need to figure out your life on your own. Not with Paul or I. Paul and I have our own life and I can no longer be this person for you.
Please do not contact me in any way.

Good-Bye and Good Luck
to You and Elise
s/Gayle

◆   ◆   ◆

Two "old friends" Bruce Moilanen could have done without were missing him. He had not been visited by Det. Sgts. Ball and Poupore since Feb. 25. He might have thought their investigation had cooled off, but the reality was that he had made himself increasingly difficult to contact. He was not working and his answering machine protected him at home.

Ball and Poupore were waiting for him outside his house on April 1. They could be patient. They had all day. They wanted him to take *their* polygraph test. Eventually, Moilanen backed out of his long driveway in his Pontiac Grand Prix and headed toward Marquette. They followed him, keeping a distance.

"He was driving around real slow," Ball said later. "He stopped at McDonalds several times. He seemed like a zombie."

Moilanen finally saw the detectives and ducked down a side street. The detectives swung around in a U-turn and doubled back. They caught him and waved him over. For the first time since the investigation began, the detectives encountered an agitated Moilanen. The veneer of calm had been chipped away.

"I heard you took a test?" Ball said. "Why didn't you tell us?"

"I didn't see any need to inform you."

"How did you do?"

"I passed."

"You got a problem with us doing our job?" Ball asked.

"The only problem I have is you going around telling relatives Judy and I had marital problems or financial problems. That's not true."

"I didn't make it up," Ball said. "Judy told her friends and they told us. We're not spreading any rumors."

Moilanen didn't have a comeback.

"I just want to get this thing over with," he said.

"Let's go down the street to the Big Boy," Ball suggested, "and see if we can get this monkey off our back."

Detectives and suspect drove down the street to the Big Boy Restaurant and took a booth in a quiet area off to the side of the sunroom. They ordered coffee.

"I was given the polygraph in Traverse City by Robert Dufort," Moilanen said. "He said I didn't lie. I didn't do it."

"Fine," Ball said. "Do you have any problems with us contacting Dufort?"

"No."

"You know he won't give us any information without a signed release from you."

"I'll call him," Moilanen said.

"I'll save you the expense," Ball said. "I'll call him and come out to your place with an acceptable form."

"Okay."

"We still want you to take our test."

"Okay, but I'm not comfortable with Vern Peterson doing it. I know him from when I worked there."

"We'll make arrangements. When's good?"

"Not next week," Moilanen said. "Elise is off for Easter vacation. I have to baby sit. The following week, April 12 through 16, should be okay."

"Bruce," Ball said, "is there anything you've told us you want to change? Anything that wasn't true, maybe?"

"Nothing."

"You've disclosed all your weapons?"

"I maybe missed one," he said. "I bought my father a 30-30 deer rifle years ago. It might be in my name, but I've never had it in my possession."

Ball and Poupore knew that was not the weapon they sought. Moilanen probably knew it too, though he could feel he had appeased them with a morsel of something.

They prepared to leave and Moilanen sighed.

"I wish this whole thing hadn't started," he said.

Bruce Moilanen had been snappy and angry when he jumped out of the car after stopping in the street. He seemed resigned and maybe even whipped as he got back into his car in the Big Boy parking lot.

◆   ◆   ◆

As resolute as the detectives had been, they might have had less to do with Bruce Moilanen's frame of mind than Gayle Lampinen did. He had gotten her note...and the Teddy bears. And, in spite of her admonitions, he wrote her a response.

Postmarked April 1, Moilanen's last letter to The Sweater Lady arrived at her desk at Portage View Hospital in a plain white business envelope with her name on a mailing label. The contents were obviously computer-generated, neatly justified at both the left and right margins.

"This may seem impersonal," he wrote, *"but I felt if you recognized my handwriting you may not read what I had to say."*

Bruce was taking full blame for whatever had happened between them. In a sense, this may have been the most pathetic of all his "love" letters to this woman, because it represented hopeless resignation.

Maybe I'm the biggest fool believing that a married woman and a widowed man could be the best of friends.

Time and again, the letter stressed that all he wanted to be was friends. It had never crossed his mind that they might be any more than that. Deepest apologies if he ever left a contrary expression.

Your (sic) the most beautiful person I've had the privilege to know. And the best friend I've ever had.

Of course, Bruce had not completely surrendered any notion that this relationship could never be rekindled...on some level, at least. He enclosed a self-addressed, stamped envelope.

Gayle Lampinen was troubled by how Bruce might react to her termination of their friendship. She called Bob Ball to express her concerns.

Ball notified State Troopers at the L'Anse and Calumet Posts, the two closest to the Lampinens' Chassell home, as well as the Houghton County Sheriff and Hancock City Police. He asked that they be quick to respond in case the Lampinens called for assistance. He also called a state parole agent who lived down the street and asked him to be watchful for Moilanen's vehicle.

A couple of days later, an exasperated Gayle Lampinen was again on the telephone.

"Bruce called Paul today," she said, "and asked him if he wanted to go out to lunch. Paul said it was as if nothing had happened."

Paul declined.

◆   ◆   ◆

Bob Ball and Don Poupore were not having much luck getting back in touch with Moilanen after their April 1 conversation in the Big Boy Restaurant. They wanted to get their hands on the results of the polygraph test in Traverse City and they wanted to get their hands on Moilanen to arrange for their own examination. He was not answering his telephone and he was not answering his door, if, in fact, he was at home when they attempted to visit.

Finally, they decided their best bet was to set up surveillance in front of his house. On Tuesday, April 6, they pulled up at 8:55 a.m. and waited. Moilanen's Grand Prix was in the driveway. He came out at 10:30 and the detectives pulled up behind him.

"How about Thursday for the test?" Ball asked. "We have an operator available."

"I told you this week's out," Moilanen said. "I'm baby sitting all week. Next week's fine."

"Okay," Ball said, "we also have an opening April 23. How about that?"

"Fine. What time?"

"Be at the lab at 11 a.m."

Moilanen had opened the garage door to reveal a vehicle the detectives had not previously seen. It was a 1989 Chevy S-10 with an extended cab. It had "Guns and Dogs" written across the bug shield on the front.

"You sure you passed that test down in Traverse City?" Ball asked.

"The guy told me I did," Moilanen responded. "I don't know why he'd tell me I'd passed if I didn't."

"We talked to Dufort and put together a release form," Ball said, reaching into his pocket.

Moilanen carefully read the form and then shook his head.

"I really hate to renege on you guys like this," he said, "but I'd rather just go in and take your test. I got no trouble with that."

They went back and forth on the issue of Dufort's test results and Moilanen finally relented and signed the form.

"We'll see you in a couple of weeks," Ball said.

Ball and Poupore were on their way back to Marquette along U.S. 41. Lake Superior was on their right side and, at one point, they passed the Marquette Branch Prison on the left.

"I'd sure like to move Bruce down the street a little ways, huh?" Ball mused.

"Yeh," Poupore said. "He sure seems nonchalant about our polygraph test."

"If he's so damned confident about it," Ball said, "why didn't he take it months ago and get it out of the way?"

Poupore sighed.

"I wonder what excuse he'll come up with this time."

◆   ◆   ◆

Two days later, Bob Ball got a message that Robert Dufort had called. He had gotten the release form signed by Moilanen and he was willing to discuss the test results.

"It was strange," Dufort said. "I came out to the lobby to get Bruce and he was so sound asleep it was almost like he was unconscious."

"Huh?"

"I couldn't stir him," Dufort said. "I even kicked him in the foot... hard. I couldn't rouse him."

"What'd you do?" Ball asked.

"I left him sleeping there in the lobby."

"How long?"

"Maybe an hour. I finally heard him stirring and got him into my office for the test."

"What'd he say?"

"He said he'd been on some antidepressants," Dufort recalled, "but he'd been off them for a week."

"How'd the questioning go?"

"He wanted me to stay with questions about where he'd been."

"You didn't ask whether he'd shot his wife?"

"I got that in."

Dufort ran through a list of what he thought were the most pertinent, from Ball's standpoint, questions and answers...

That Sunday, Nov. 29, do you know for sure if anyone deliberately shot Judy? Answer: No.

Did you plan with anyone to cause Judy Moilanen's death? Answer: No.

That Sunday afternoon between 12 noon and 5 p.m., were you within one-half mile of the area of your wife's shooting? Answer: No.

Are you now withholding any information about your knowledge of the cause of Judy Moilanen's shooting death? Answer: No.

Last Nov. 29, did you personally shoot Judy? Answer: No.

"Those are some questions we'd like to ask him," Ball said. "He passed, huh?"

"I didn't tell him he passed."

"You *didn't?* He said you did."

"It was inconclusive."

15

The Tyrant

Det. Lt. Chuck Allen was "imported" from the Bridgeport State Police Post near Saginaw in the Lower Peninsula. Bruce Moilanen had insisted all along that he did not want to be tested by Vern Peterson, the regular polygraphist in Marquette, claiming an overblown conflict of interest. He claimed he had known Peterson well when he worked as a dispatcher at Negaunee. Thus, Allen made the 355-mile drive to administer the *scheduled* test.

The question, as Ball and Allen reviewed the tack they would take the morning of April 23, was whether the drive had been for naught. Moilanen had been scheduled for polygraph tests on previous occasions and always found an excuse to beg off.

Indeed, 11 o'clock came and went and Moilanen neither showed up nor called. Ball was antsy.

"This," Ball had said the night before, "is probably going to be our last interview with Bruce Moilanen. *If* he shows, we've got him on our turf, in our facility. We've got to flush him out."

They had assembled six pages of discrepancies and lies he had told during the course of the investigation to detectives, family and what few friends he seemed to have. They had, for example, come up with three different versions of the chimney block incident. Moilanen did not even know that The Marble Man had found the bullet and that he had inadvertently established his ownership of a Savage 110 rifle. They could even hit him with their awareness of his fixation with Gayle Lampinen, and how she had helped them.

First of all, they could only hope he showed up.

At 11:30, Bruce Moilanen walked into the Marquette State Police lab. He was finally going to submit to a polygraph test. Allen explained the process and left him alone to read the Miranda rights form. When Allen returned, he re-read him his right to remain silent and have an attorney present. Moilanen, arrogant and cocky as always, waived his rights and signed the form. Allen hooked him up to the machine. Ball settled into a nearby room and took notes as he watched on a television monitor.

Allen started with basic information, asking Moilanen if his health was good, if he was on medications and if he was getting enough sleep.

"Now, Bruce," Allen said, "I want you to run through what you did on Nov. 29, 1992. Start with the morning and go through your day. Give me your account."

Moilanen went from morning to night, detail-by-detail. Ball, sitting in the nearby room, had heard it before. The story still had that gap where detectives were being asked to accept that Moilanen was where he said he was and not waiting in the woods along Cherry Lane. Moilanen finished and Allen fidgeted with his equipment.

"Now," he said, "I'm going to go over some things with you."

The detective worked his way into the test itself, a blend of innocuous questions and accusatory questions. As he went along, he would lay out a tidbit or two on discrepancies between what Moilanen had said and what the investigation uncovered. He had thoroughly digested the police reports Ball had sent him two weeks before his trip to Marquette.

"The polygraph is a great tool," Ball had said earlier. "It puts the subject under stress."

This subject remained calm, at least outwardly calm. Ball could not know what the charts were saying, but Moilanen was stubbornly sticking to his insistence that he was hunting elsewhere when his wife had been shot.

"Damn," Ball muttered to himself. "This is like pulling teeth."

Allen mixed in questions about Moilanen's whereabouts with the tough questions…

Did you kill your wife? Answer: No.

Were you the person holding the gun that shot the bullet that killed your wife? Answer: No.

Allen was trained in both verbal and non-verbal communication. He was looking for anger or sorrow. He was looking for a red face or crying, waiting for a raised voice or maybe even an emotional outburst. Moilanen remained stoic.

At one point, Allen reached into a folder and slid a sheet of paper across the table in front of Moilanen. It was The Sweater Letter.

"That letter," Ball had told Allen, "will speak for itself."

It did. Moilanen's eyes brimmed with tears. He turned sullen.

"We've got him," Ball thought to himself, clenching his fist and leaning closer to the monitor.

Allen was reading his charts, letting the silence grow.

"Bruce," he said, "I can't pass you on this examination. I think you shot your wife."

Moilanen was quiet. He made no attempt at denial.

Ball was nervous. Moilanen was not under arrest. He was afraid he would jump up and say, "I've had enough of this. I'm outta here." If he bolted at this point, the case was flimsy at best. They would have to have a summit conference to decide where to go from here. They could hardly get a conviction by marching a parade of suspicious people who dislike Moilanen in front of a jury. They could still neither place him at the scene nor, with certainty, place the weapon in his possession. Ball's palms were sweating and his mouth was dry.

Moilanen didn't bolt.

Allen changed directions. He had not brought up the gun…and wouldn't. The strategy was to hope Moilanen would incriminate himself by revealing the weapon he had listed on his loan application's asset list. Allen would tweak him with the bullet.

"Did they find a bullet, do you know?" Allen said.

"Fragments," Moilanen said. Incongruously, he chuckled. "All they found were fragments."

"They've got the bullet...all of it."

"They do?"

Allen took off his glasses and leaned across the table, his voice taking on a sympathetic tone.

"Bruce, was this deliberate," Allen asked, "or an accident?"

"I probably shouldn't say without an attorney."

"I won't make you," Allen said. "You don't have to say anything. I'm not going to twist your arm. If you want to get an attorney in here, get one."

"Yeh, okay."

"Well?"

"I'll go ahead," Moilanen said. "It wasn't deliberate."

He had regained his composure after the brief welling of tears when he saw The Sweater Letter. He was matter-of-fact again, as though he was talking to an officer giving him a speeding ticket.

"You just panicked and ran?"

"Yeh."

"I'm going to get Bob Ball in here. You know he's going to want to talk to you."

"Yeh."

Allen turned as he was leaving the room.

"Bruce," he said, "you want to get an attorney in here, call him. Get him over here and we'll get this thing out in the open."

"Yeh."

Ball and Allen crossed paths in the hallway. Allen's interrogation began at 11:39 and now it was close to 4 p.m. Allen had taken a couple of breaks, but Moilanen had stubbornly stayed in his chair. He was offered soft drinks or water and snacks, but he declined. He was offered the use of rest room facilities, again declining. He was still sitting in the same chair when Ball walked in. He had decided not to bother calling an attorney.

The polygraph test could not be tape-recorded, but Ball's interview could. Allen scrambled through the post for a tape-recorder. He found one and set it up, but the batteries were dead. He found another but it wasn't set up properly. Of all the electronic gadgetry in a police crime lab, the most basic figured to be a tape-recorder and Allen was having nothing but trouble. As remarkable as it may seem, given the circumstances, only portions of the ensuing conversation ended up on tape.

Ball, unaware of the veritable keystone kops routine over setting up a tape-recorder, plunged ahead with his interview. He walked in with his case file, which was about the size of a metropolitan telephone directory, and stood in front of Moilanen.

"Bruce," he said, "there's no surprise here for me today. Myself and Don, we knew you did this. We've assembled a lot of evidence. We knew you were involved in your wife's death. We just don't know all the reasons why."

Ball sat down and delivered a recitation of what he and Poupore and other investigators had uncovered, such as the discrepancy in the time he ran into Wade Johnson, the abundance of insurance on Judy's life…and his fixation with other women. He spread the letters to Gayle on the table in front of him. Gayle was not a part of the original game plan, but, as Ball later recalled, Chuck Allen's mention of her name seemed to be the crusher that cut Moilanen's legs out from under him.

Moilanen did not acknowledge the letters spread in front of them, keeping his head up as though disinterested. Ball could see that the eyes were stealing peeks, however. He kept talking.

"For another thing, we know about that chimney block incident and a lot of people don't think that was an accident," Ball said. "There were also financial and marital problems you denied to me."

Bob Ball was doing most of the talking. He was not getting any eye contact from Moilanen, who sat listening. He knew there was no excuse for what Moilanen had done, but he was trying to give him reasons. He wanted to stir a response.

"She was domineering, wasn't she? She threatened to leave and take your property away? She backed you into a corner?"

Moilanen was nodding his head.

"Bruce, you shot your wife, didn't you?"

No answer.

"You shot her, didn't you?"

"I did," Moilanen said, "but it wasn't for Gayle."

"Why, Bruce? Why?"

"She's been threatening to leave for 2½ years. And she was going to take half of everything I had."

"That was it, huh?"

"She was a tyrant at work and a tyrant at home," Moilanen said.

"Hmmm."

"She was so involved in work. She'd be gone 12, 16 hours a day. I'd be left home to take care of Elise and I'd end up doing most of the cooking. She couldn't cook very good anyway."

Ball had heard lame excuses for murder, but Moilanen had literally cooked up a dandy. Her co-workers, for example, regarded *her* with nothing but affection and *him* with nothing but distaste. If there was a tyrant in the household, it was not Judy.

"I had to ruin everybody's lives," Moilanen was saying.

"You did ruin some."

"Whose life do you feel worse about?"

"Well, I feel sorriest for Elise."

"Taking Judy's life wasn't right, Bruce. We can't forgive that. Do you feel remorse over this?"

"I guess guilt and remorse are the same thing."

"Why didn't you go the divorce route?"

"Yeh, but, like I said, I'd have lost what little I have," Moilanen said. "Either way, I'd lose what I had."

"That was a big concern?" Ball asked. "Losing half of what you had?"

"Yeh."

Ball paused. This guy had killed his wife over losing half of what little he claimed he had. And he had thought he could pass it off as a hunting accident and walk away with what he considered "independent wealth" from life insurance policies.

"Looking each other in the eye here," Ball said, "if you had it to do over, do you think you could take her life?"

"Not after all the misery it's brought on."

"What went through your mind that night after you went back to the Blakes' house?"

"Just stood in the backyard and waited for her to come back."

"But you knew she wasn't coming," Ball said. "And you stood in the backyard?"

"Yeh, by the tree. I did the same thing the next morning. For about an hour. I stood there waiting for her to come back."

"Do you think the Blakes suspected anything that night?"

"No," Moilanen said. "They never have."

Ball sighed. The strength of that family astounded him. For almost 4½ months, they had kept their terrible secret inside. They had managed to spend weekend after weekend with their daughter's murderer under their roof without giving him an inkling of what they knew.

"What did you do that night?"

"I didn't sleep. I sat in the rocking chair all night. And the following day. I couldn't sleep for the first three days."

"Did you realize this thing wasn't gonna fly as a hunting accident in those first few days?"

"I don't think so."

"Did you think it could happen without being questioned?"

"Everything's gonna be investigated."

"Why did you do it?" Ball said, asking a question that never would be satisfactorily answered. "Were things that bad between you and Judy? I'm just talking in your mind. They were that bad you were willing to take the risk?"

"I guess."

Not much of an answer, Ball thought.

"How long before the shit hits the proverbial fan?" Moilanen asked.

"Real quick," Ball said. "It's at the point where we couldn't wait any longer. Even if you wouldn't have come in here today, the plans were laid. We even had concern for you. I mean you're talking to Gayle in one of your letters here and you made referral to taking your own life. We had some real concern that things were coming to a head."

"Can I spend Saturday and Sunday with my daughter?"

"I don't see how we're gonna be able to allow that."

"Give me a break. Give me Saturday and Sunday with her. You know I'm not going anywhere."

"How do I know that?"

"I'll be here Monday. I'll come right up to the post."

"We'll have a heart to heart here," Ball said, "and you give me some reasons to trust you. Tell me about the gun."

"The gun?" Moilanen said. "The gun is history."

"How did 'history' happen?"

"I destroyed it with a torch."

"What happened to the parts?"

"They're in…would be the Ford River."

Ball had taken a course called SCAN, short for Scientific Content Analysis. He did not pick up on "would be" until later, when he was reading the tape transcription. Moilanen had not said the parts *were* in the Ford River.

The Ford River enters Green Bay just south of Escanaba, a city on the other side of the Upper Peninsula from Marquette. Moilanen explained that he threw the bits and pieces of the gun off the upstream side of the bridge. He assumed the metal parts sank and the stock floated out into the bay.

Interestingly, Moilanen maintained he had disposed of the piece-meal weapon en route to the city of Green Bay with Elise for last minute shopping the week before Christmas. This was *after* detectives had searched his house and confiscated all the weapons they had found…and all the weapons Moilanen said he possessed.

"What type of gun?" Ball asked.

"A 30-06."

"Model?"

"Savage," said Moilanen.

Bingo, thought Ball.

"Where did you park the car?" Ball said. "Did you lie to us about the Turpeinen clear-cut?"

"No, I never went in there. I parked at the Lukkari property plant."

"How long did it take you to walk back to the van?"

"I don't know. I ran."

"What time did you pull the trigger?"

"No idea."

"You must have some idea."

"Quarter after 2. Somewhere around there."

"How did you know she would be there?"

"I didn't."

"You thought there was a good chance?"

"A possibility," Moilanen said. "Walking the dogs."

"How long did you wait?"

"Awhile. And then I heard her coming with the dogs."

"Did she see you?"

"No. She went by and I couldn't do it."

"She went by once?"

"I couldn't do it."

"Why?"

"Just couldn't do it."

"Did the dogs detect you?"

"No."

"So what happened then?"

"She went off to Nieminen's field and she was gone for awhile. Then she was coming back."

"And…"

"And I couldn't do it again."

"Go on…"

"Finally," Moilanen said, "I just…pointed and closed my eyes and pulled the trigger."

"Did you see what happened?"

"No. Didn't even look."

Ball started to talk, but Moilanen interrupted him.

"By the way, you guys got your information wrong."

"What do you mean by that?" Ball asked.

"You guys thought she was shot in the back…and she wasn't."

"Why do you say that?"

"I talked to the medical examiner."

"Bruce, when you get our reports, you'll see they're very clear about where we think she was shot," Ball said. "Yes, the medical examiner did have a different opinion than we had. You'll see that when you get those reports."

Ball mused to himself that it was nice of Moilanen to confirm for him what had actually happened. Moilanen was also cooperative when Ball asked him to mark a sketch for him, indicating with an "X" where he had been positioned when he fired the shot. He had been 50 yards away when he pulled the trigger, shooting from east to west. The maple tree with the graze mark was perfectly aligned.

"What about the shell casing?"

"I don't remember. I ran for awhile and then I might've ejected it."

Ball went over Moilanen's itinerary for the remainder of that fateful day. There had been, according to Moilanen, no panic. He said he drove out of the area at a normal speed and proceeded to set up what he called a "smoke screen." He realized that the police might not immediately accept the premise that it was a hunting accident.

The Savage 110, the mysterious and missing weapon, was still a concern to Ball. When Dan Castle found the bullet, he remarked that he had always been able to find bullets in criminal investigations…but *never* the gun. Killers cannot find the bullets to hide them, but they can hide their guns. There may be no more perfect place to hide a murder weapon than Michigan's Upper Peninsula, with its hundreds of lakes and rivers and miles of dense wilderness. *Airplanes* have disappeared into that wilderness, never to be found.

"Where did you buy the gun?"

"Out of an ad in the Action Shopper."

"Did you know the person you bought it from?"

"Wouldn't know him from Adam. I met him in the parking lot at the Holiday Gas Station."

"What'd it cost you?"

"I paid him $150. It was in pretty rough shape."

Once again, Moilanen asked if he could have the weekend free. He even invited Ball to stay with him at his house. Ball would rather crawl in with a hibernating bear. He was being a "good cop" though, explaining that the prosecuting attorney would have to make such decisions."

"What I'm going to have to do, for the time being," Ball said, feigning an apologetic tone, "is put you in custody. We'll deal with it from there."

◆   ◆   ◆

Det. Sgt. Don Poupore was not a part of either the polygraph test or the subsequent interview at the Marquette lab. He was participating in a search of Moilanen's home in Harvey. Ball had obtained a warrant and the search was taking place while Moilanen was occupied by Allen and Ball...assuming he had shown.

The task force involved in the search, one lieutenant, three sergeants and two troopers, assembled at 11:30 at the Trudell Plumbing and Heating Company next door.

At exactly 12:01, Poupore knocked at the door leading into the enclosed breezeway between Moilanen's house and the attached garage.

"State Police," he said, "We have a search warrant. Open the door."

He got no response. He knocked three more times with no response before moving to the front door. Again, no response. He went around to the patio, where the chimney block had "accidentally" fallen on Judy Moilanen's head. No response. He tried the back door to the breezeway. No response. After one more try at the patio door, he returned to the breezeway's back door. He turned the knob and walked in.

"State Police," he said. "We have a search warrant."

The officers went to their assigned areas in the single-story house. They covered the basement, the main floor and the dusty attic. Specifically, they were looking for a 30-caliber firearm, financial records and documents and a personal computer with accompanying files or disks.

Poupore himself found 110 live shells in a 39-ounce Hills Brothers coffee can in the basement. Interestingly, not one was a 30-caliber bullet. He remembered thinking Moilanen was probably consciously trying to misdirect them regarding the types of weapons he owned.

The first item seized, by Poupore, was the Leading Edge computer, serial number 01335874, from the computer table in the breezeway. This was the house's office area. This was where Moilanen obviously did whatever business he happened to be in at the time.

A total of 44 items were seized and marked, all of them packed into Poupore's automobile to be transported to the Negaunee Post for storage.

At 3:55 p.m., the house was locked and officers drove away. They were headed for the home of Wiljo Moilanen, Bruce's father. He lived in Trenary, a community maybe 40 miles down U.S. 41 from Harvey.

"We're investigating your daughter-in-law's death," Poupore explained. "Bruce told us he gave you a 30-30 as a present and we'd just like to check it out."

"Bruce gave me the rifle," Moilanen said, "but I think my daughter Joanne has it."

Wiljo Moilanen had no problem with the police searching his residence. He signed the consent form and invited them in.

"I actually thought you'd be here sooner," he said.

Officers found no rifles at Wiljo's house.

Det. Lt. Goad, meanwhile, had driven back to Marquette to Menard's Hardware Store, where Joanne Moilanen was working. Joanne signed the consent form and Goad called Poupore on the car radio to let him know they could enter her house. Wiljo Moilanen accompanied officers into the house.

They did, indeed, find the 30-30 Winchester Model 94 weapon Bruce had bought his father a few years ago. For all these detectives knew at the time, they could have had the murder weapon in their hands.

◆　　　◆　　　◆

Don Poupore drove back to Marquette, getting there at 9 p.m. Bob Ball was waiting for him.

"Bruce confessed," Ball said. "He's in custody."

Poupore smiled. It was not a time for elation. It was a time for satisfaction, perhaps, but much work was left to be done. An arrest was not the same as a conviction. Bruce Moilanen could be helpful, if he so chose.

Ball, having heard of Allen's problems with the tape recorders, wanted to tape a confession from beginning to end, but Moilanen refused. He was having an understandable change in attitude since he had experienced the reality of being placed under arrest.

Still, Ball was being considerate. He wanted Moilanen to show him where he had thrown the rifle in the Ford River and the drive to Escanaba would take them through Harvey. He offered to stop at Moilanen's house on the way.

"I know you want see Elise," Ball said, "so I'll call the baby sitters and have them bring her over to the house. We can stop for a few minutes on the way to Escanaba."

Elise and the Janofskis were there when Ball and Poupore arrived with their prisoner. For all of his fuss about seeing his daughter, Moilanen immediately went about tending to his dogs. He fed them and made a couple of telephone calls to arrange for their care. If he was feeling emotional, he was not showing it.

Finally, he and Elise went into a bedroom for a few minutes alone. It may or may not have registered with him that this could be the last time he would be able to embrace her. More likely, it didn't occur to him at the time.

For their part, detectives were expecting to see tears shed. They didn't.

"That's just Bruce," Ball said later to Poupore.

Moilanen wrote a note giving the Janofskis permission to keep Elise overnight and specifying that David and Yvonne Blake, her "guardians" according to his note, would pick her up the next day.

Ball and Poupore put their prisoner in the back seat and backed out of the driveway.

"How far is it from here to the Ford River?" Ball asked.

"The other side of Escanaba."

"Miles?"

"Maybe eight, 10 miles past Escanaba," Moilanen said. "I don't know."

"Now that's not a wild goose chase you're sending us on, right?"

"No."

"'Cause that's a pretty rough river there and we'll be putting divers in there," Ball said. "We don't want to risk anybody. If that's not the truth."

Ball and Poupore were in the front seat and Moilanen was in the back. Escanaba was 66 miles away and the Ford River was a little beyond. They arrived at the river and they were halfway across the span when Moilanen told them to stop. He gestured to a spot on the rail on the right, or upstream, side.

"There," he said. "Right there."

"You sure?" Ball said.

"I'm sure."

They did not get back to Marquette until the early morning hours of April 24, when he was booked into jail for the first time in his life.

◆　　　◆　　　◆

Bruce Moilanen was on his way back to Ontonagon Saturday morning. He was in the back seat of Poupore's car and Ball followed in his. As they neared Ontonagon, they passed a couple of the sites where Moilanen's van had supposedly been parked Nov. 29, 1992.

One of those sites was at Lukkari's Cement Bulk Plant on M-38, just a little to the east of Cherry Lane. Moilanen had said he hid the van in the parking lot before making the trek through the woods to the scene of the killing.

"Show me where you parked your van," Poupore said.

"You've gone by it," Moilanen said.

"I have?" Poupore said, turning his car around.

"In there," Moilanen said.

Moilanen did not point to the Lukkari parking lot, but rather to the Gitche Gumee Oil storage plant next door.

"Over there."

Moilanen had parked to the south of the fuel pumps, the side out of sight from M-38. The only chance he was taking would have been that someone had come to the fuel pumps that afternoon. Detectives checked Gitche Gumee's records and no one was there during the time Moilanen's van would have been parked.

Don Poupore pulled out of the parking lot and continued west toward the Ontonagon County Jail, which awaited the arrival of its most notorious occupant in all the years since James Kirk Paul set up housekeeping on the banks of the Ontonagon River. The community was abuzz over the news.

◆   ◆   ◆

Bob Ball would later express astonishment that Bruce Moilanen had broken down and confessed to the murder of his wife.

Ball knew Dale and Mary Ann Blake were in Arizona so he called David in Ontonagon to update the family on the development. David, reserved by nature, hardly expressed surprise.

"We really believe in the power of prayer," he said, "and a lot of people were praying."

16

Haunting the Jailhouse

Bruce Robert Moilanen's new home was bigger than the one he had in Harvey. In fact, it had five "bedrooms," so to speak. That these five bedrooms were also known as cells caused him great dismay. He checked into—or was checked into—the Ontonagon County Jail the Saturday morning after the failed polygraph test and the ensuing confession in Marquette.

Ontonagon County had a new sheriff, who would be Moilanen's keeper. Jerry Kitzman, previously sheriff from 1976 through 1988, was back in office after defeating Tom Corda in the November, 1992 election. He was a ramrod straight man given to wearing western boots. He could be garrulous and friendly, but he also brooked no nonsense. His new "tenant" would test his tolerance.

The jail is part of the Sheriff's Department facility, which was built in 1967. To the frustration of Kitzman, it has no "high risk" cell for prisoners who present special dangers to either themselves or others. This would be a cell without bars, glass, electrical outlets or anything else a prisoner could utilize in a suicide attempt. Kitzman, who had taken over as sheriff January 1, 1993, had a cell, which already had a television monitor, he wanted to convert to that purpose, but was unable to get the county to approve the expenditure.

Moilanen was placed in a cell at the rear corner of the facility. It had a metal bunk, shower and toilet. Two locked doors barred his path to the outside world. It seemed a sensible place for him to be.

However, two days after Moilanen was brought to Ontonagon, Kitzman glanced at a television monitor and noticed the prisoner was completely under the blankets in his bunk. Instinct told him that something was wrong. He grabbed the keys and headed for the cell-block.

When Kitzman opened the door, Moilanen was still. The sheriff rushed to the bunk and threw back the blanket. Moilanen had tied one end of the sheet around his neck and the other to his feet. He had tightened the noose around his neck by straightening his legs. Kitzman recalled that he was semi-conscious.

"What the hell are you doing?" Kitzman growled.

Kitzman was angry. He is tall and strong and now his hands were ripping the sheet from around Moilanen's neck. He slammed the prisoner against the wall to jar him out of his stupor.

Bruce Moilanen said nothing.

Kitzman grabbed the sheets and blankets and stormed out of the cell. Something would have to be done about accommodations for *this* prisoner.

◆   ◆   ◆

David Blake's telephone rang at 7:30 that Monday evening. The voice was not one he longed to hear. It was broken and sobbing.

"I tried to hang myself," Bruce Moilanen said. "They got here too soon."

"Don't do that," David said. "The hell you're going through now is nothing compared to next."

"David, I don't know if I'll ever be able to explain how or why it happened," Moilanen said quietly. "I just went nuts."

A devoutly religious man, David had faith that allowed him to see things at both a higher and a deeper level than most humans could imagine given the trauma of the conversation.

"God will forgive you," he said, "if you have true repentance in your heart."

Moilanen sobbed indecipherable words.

"Bruce," David continued, "you could have a much more fulfilling life in prison if you repented and you lived your life for God than you ever had out. You…you could even have a perfect relationship with Judy in heaven."

David was spilling his heart out to a person a lesser man would have hated, but Moilanen came back defensively.

"Judy's been threatening to leave me and take Elise for 2½ years," Moilanen said. "She told me the courts would give Elise to her because she made more money. I couldn't stand it. Judy's a very two-sided person. She had a bad side none of *you* ever saw. Det. Ball will tell you about her bad side."

Of course, the only time Bob Ball heard there was a bad side to Judy was during Moilanen's confession. If the detective seemed at all receptive or even agreeable, it was because he wanted to listen to Moilanen…not debate with him.

For his part, David knew the two-sided person was on the other end of the telephone line. When he was growing up, six years younger than Judy and eight younger than Bruce, he saw Moilanen as sort of a "bonus brother" who would hunt with him and fish with him. When he grew up and became more perceptive, he came to realize there was a dark side to his brother-in-law.

Like Ball, David was not going to debate with Moilanen.

"Did you give Judy reason to want to leave?" David asked.

"Never," Moilanen responded.

"Does that make what you did right?"

"I just went nuts," Moilanen repeated.

And leave it to David Blake to be caring.

"Bruce," he asked, "are your dogs being taken care of?"

"My sister has them," Moilanen said. "David, I want to tell you I love Elise. Can I talk to her?"

David handed the telephone to a three-year-old who did not understand.

◆   ◆   ◆

Bruce Moilanen called again the next night.

"I don't know what to say to you," whispered David Blake, his patience and nerves running close to empty.

"Let me talk to Elise," Moilanen said.

"No, Bruce, we're not going to do this every day," David said. "Besides, she's very fussy tonight."

"Does she miss her Dad?" Moilanen asked.

"Yes," David said. "And her Mom."

◆   ◆   ◆

Lee Ann Wysocki was shocked, frightened and angry. She was on the telephone with the State Police. She had just hung up after getting a call from Bruce Moilanen.

"This really sucks," she told the dispatcher. "I cannot believe he called me. Where is he? I thought he was in jail."

"Hang on," the dispatcher said. "Let me make a quick call and get back to you."

Wysocki had a right to be scared. She had cooperated with police and Moilanen knew it. She did not know where the call originated. For all she knew, Moilanen had gotten out on bail and was around the corner from her apartment.

The telephone rang and she jumped.

It was the State Police.

"Moilanen's in the Ontonagon County Jail," the voice said. "He has access to a telephone there."

The call itself had been vintage Moilanen. He asked if she and her daughter Stephanie wanted to move into his empty house and share it with his sister.

"*His* empty house," she thought ruefully. In her mind, it was *Judy's* empty house.

No thanks, she said. She could not wait to get off the telephone.

◆   ◆   ◆

Irene Janofski was equally shocked when her telephone rang the same evening and Bruce Moilanen was on the other end. She did not feel as vulnerable as Lee Ann, but this was no conversation she cared to have.

Bruce, though, was, in her words, business as usual.

"I'm thinking of moving Elise back to Marquette," he said. "Would you baby-sit for her?"

"I'll, I'll…have to check…with John," she stuttered.

She hung up as quickly as she could without worrying about politeness.

Moilanen, from jail, had launched a very annoying campaign. Elise was in more than excellent hands with David and Yvonne Blake, but David had had the nerve to tell him he could not talk to his daughter. He would fight for telephone visitation rights and he would, almost perversely, fight to get Elise placed with *his* family.

◆   ◆   ◆

Bruce Moilanen wanted a visitor. Of likely more importance to him, he needed someone to retrieve some things for him. He called Mike Niemi and asked him if he would bring a suit and a briefcase with things such as a notepad, calculator, stamps and envelopes. Also, please, a picture of Elise.

Niemi had other business as well on this depressing occasion. Moilanen had leased his Pontiac Grand Prix from Courtesy Chevrolet, where Niemi worked. Niemi had voluntary repossession papers to be signed.

This visit would be difficult for Mike. Months later, he would lament the loss not only of a cousin he loved, but also the loss of a friend…Bruce Moilanen. The friend had been lost through betrayal. Moilanen had been jailed for a week when Niemi came to visit with the things he had requested.

"Bruce," Mike said almost plaintively, "how did this situation happen?"

"I just snapped," Moilanen said. "I must be crazy, because only crazy people do what I did. Someday…I'll explain the whole thing."

"Why not divorce?" Mike said. "We could all live with divorce and still be friends."

"We were having financial problems…"

"We were all there for you if you had financial problems. You knew that. I don't understand what you did."

"Things have been bad between us for 2½ years. I thought about divorce, but Gayle talked me out of it."

This was a lie, of course. Gayle Lampinen had been a more than patient listener, but she never adopted the role of adviser. What's more, at this point, Niemi likely had never even heard the name "Gayle."

It grew quiet for a moment. Mike was almost at a loss for words and Bruce had momentarily retreated inside himself, crying.

"You know," he sobbed, "I'll be 65 before I see my daughter again? Elise will be in her thirties."

The conversation moved slowly through 45 minutes, Moilanen at one point asking if Mike had heard about his attempted suicide. All these references to "snapping" and "crazy" and "suicide" led Mike Niemi to conclude that Moilanen was building up to a defense based on insanity.

Mike Niemi got up to leave, but Moilanen stopped him.

"Next time you come," he asked, "could you bring me a television?"

◆   ◆   ◆

Fred Neville was a salesman and dog trainer who lived in Green Bay. His hobby, if training dogs can be called a hobby, had brought him and his wife Sue together with Bruce and Judy Moilanen. They knew about Judy's death and they remained cordial with Bruce. Friends asked them why and they invariably said because they had liked Judy so much.

When Bruce was charged with Judy's murder, the Nevilles were not surprised. Sue, for one, had never believed that the chimney block incident had been an accident.

Fred was home alone one day in mid-May when he heard a telephone ring. It was the children's line, but he picked it up anyway. He was shocked. Bruce Moilanen was on the line.

"What's the story?" Fred challenged.

Moilanen could not have been more nonchalant if he had been walking a dog.

"I never should have been arrested," he said. "We have a green prosecuting attorney here that doesn't know what she's doing. The police have nothing on me. They talk about some one-hour-and-15-minute gap I can't account for, but I have 18 witnesses who can vouch for where I was."

"They must have had good reason to charge you," Neville said.

"My bond's been reduced to $100,000," Moilanen said. "I'll be out before too long."

"Fine," Neville said. "Just don't call here again."

Neville hung up, called Judy's brother Jerry in Shawano and told him of the call. Jerry hung up and called his mother in Ontonagon. Mary Ann hung up and drove immediately to the courthouse, where she knew Bob Ball had business.

"I just got a call that Bruce's bond has been lowered to $100,000," she said. "He called the Nevilles and told them he is getting out."

Det. Sgt. Ball did not have to check with anyone. He knew Bruce Moilanen's bond would stay at $1 million. The prisoner was not going anywhere. Moilanen had other ideas.

◆   ◆   ◆

Moilanen's fingers were still working the telephone from jail. He made a couple of arrangements with his family, one borderline understandable and the other borderline bizarre.

The borderline understandable arrangement was that he wanted to raise funds for his legal defense. He was charged with first degree-premeditated murder. He had hired Tom Casselman as his attorney, and he was not a Kmart Blue-Light Special attorney.

Casselman's office was located in the Savings Bank Building at the corner of Front and Washington in Marquette. It was a long, narrow building constructed of redstone and brick with marble pillars in front and a three-sided clock tower overlooking both the harbor and downtown. Casselman's suite, which he shared with his wife Rhonda, the private investigator, was modest but comfortable.

An Ontonagon man, faced with divorce, called Casselman's office to inquire as to representation. He had not really thought about cost.

"They told me they could make an appointment," he recalled, "but they told me to bring a $5,000 retainer with me."

He hung up. He did not have $5,000 in property for an attorney to protect.

Moilanen had his freedom to protect.

Irene Janofski, the baby-sitter, noticed an advertisement in the Marquette newspaper for an auction. The address, in Harvey, was familiar. The Blakes were camping in the area and Irene was able to find Mary Ann.

Together, Mary Ann Blake and Irene Janofski drove to the Moilanen house to see what this auction was all about. They were flabbergasted. Things belonging to Bruce, Judy and Elise were all to be auctioned off to raise defense funds. Selling Bruce's possessions was understandable, but selling Judy and Elise's possessions was an exercise in the outrageous.

"What are you doing?" Mary Ann demanded. "These are my daughter's things…my granddaughter's things."

Judy's jewelry was to be auctioned as were crystal sets Mary Ann herself had given to her daughter. The stir they created stunned the auctioneer, who had been brought in by the Moilanen family.

"Do you know," Irene demanded of bewildered customers, "that this auction is to raise legal expenses for a man who killed his wife?"

There was not as much to auction off when Mary Ann and Irene were finished taking items belonging to Judy or Elise. And no one was left to bid anyway. Potential customers had disappeared into their cars and headed away down U.S. 41.

The bizarre got more bizarre. Moilanen ordered a marker for his wife's grave, or at least he had a relative order a marker for his wife's grave. The Blakes had already taken care of this saddest of details, but Moilanen had a different idea.

One side of the marker said:

Judy Blake Moilanen
Beloved Wife of Bruce
Oct. 16, 1957-Nov. 29, 1992

And the other said:

Bruce Robert Moilanen,
March 29, 1955-

The man had balls of marble. The marker was in place on Judy Blake Moilanen's gravesite. Once again, the Blakes were furious about the audacity of what this man was manipulating from his jail cell. The marker was gone before the day ended.

◆   ◆   ◆

The Ontonagon jail has one unique cell. It is next to where the duty officer sits manning the telephone and scanning the television monitors. A window made of unbreakable glass separates the cell from the duty officer...and the main room where business is conducted by the sheriff's staff. The prisoner is always in sight in that cell.

This cell was not without its drawbacks. For one thing, only one locked door stands between the prisoner and escape. For another, the prisoner can see and hear everything that is going on. Only one room in the facility, a lounge in the back, is beyond the prisoner's hearing.

Moilanen was moved to that cell. He became a glowering, almost eerie presence. Nothing could transpire without his knowledge unless the conversants adjourned to the lounge at the back of the building. He so unnerved the deputies that they came to eagerly await his departure.

What Bruce Moilanen had in mind was making their wishes come true...on his terms.

◆   ◆   ◆

July 31, 1993 was a Saturday. The heat was stifling. Ontonagon has extremes in the summer as well as the winter. Many of the residents, in fact, pack up camping gear and set up housekeeping at the Township Park on Lake Superior to escape the heat.

This was also a Saturday when the Ontonagon County Fair was in progress in Greenland, a community 12 miles away down M-38. Tom Cousineau, the DARE officer, was at a sheriff's department booth at the fair, distributing literature on drug abuse and answering questions. He was sweating under his brown dress uniform.

Sheriff Kitzman was in the office that morning talking to Dale Rantala, the youngest member of the force. Rantala was the duty officer and he was talking with Kitzman about the fair and the drug abuse prevention program.

"Well, Dale," Kitzman said, "I'll be out at the fair if anything comes up. You can get me on the radio."

Rantala nodded his head. He looked through the window as Kitzman was going out the door. Moilanen had been listening, but he quickly looked away. His Saturday morning chore was to clean his cell. Because of the heat, he was allowed to wear shorts.

Twenty minutes passed. Rantala knew Kitzman would be in Greenland by then. Moilanen also knew the sheriff would be in Greenland...and maybe away from his radio.

Rantala heard a tap on the glass.

"I'm done," Moilanen said. "My trash is ready."

The prisoner was standing with a grocery bag in his arms. His cell was neat.

"Okay," Rantala said.

The deputy opened the door and reached out. Moilanen whipped a bowl out from under the bag and threw a concoction his eyes. It was later determined to be a mixture of salt, pepper and soap shavings. Startled, Rantala covered his eyes with his hands and tried to wipe the mess away to no avail. He could not see.

Moilanen bolted past him. Rantala had not been armed, nor were there any firearms in the office itself. The prisoner did not stop to look around. He burst through the front door to freedom. Moilanen was now an escapee rather than a prisoner.

Rantala literally groped his way to the radio to alert anyone who might be listening to Moilanen's escape. He broadcast a description of what the escapee was wearing, unknowing that Moilanen had put on two pairs of shorts and two T-shirts. He shed his outer shorts and T-shirt as soon as he was out of sight of the department offices. The ploy would not be of much help in Ontonagon, where everyone knew what he looked like, but it might be effective if he was able to get as far away as he hoped he might be heading.

Bill Burgess, the village man of many hats, was resting in his recliner when he heard Rantala's broadcast. He noted that it was 1:40 p.m. Burgess, being a special deputy as well as seemingly everything else but mayor, grabbed the telephone. He punched in the sheriff's department number. Rantala, his eyes burning, was crying.

"I need help," Rantala said. "Moilanen's escaped."

"What can I do?" Burgess asked.

"Maybe you can find the sheriff," Rantala sobbed. "He was headed for the fair."

Burgess was on his way to Greenland down M-38 when he noticed Kitzman's squad car at the courthouse. The sheriff was just coming out the door when Burgess wheeled into the parking lot with his tires screeching. Unfortunately for Moilanen's travel plans, the sheriff was far from Greenland. He had stopped at the Ontonagon County Court-house to run an errand. He was three minutes away.

"Moilanen's escaped," Burgess called.

"What?" asked the incredulous Kitzman.

"He threw something in Dale's face," Burgess said. "Blinded him."

Tim Guzek, the Ontonagon Village Police Chief, heard the alert. Unfortunately for Moilanen's travel plans, Guzek was two minutes away.

Moilanen was also the "victim" of what was likely an erroneous assumption. Sitting where he sat, he knew the department's problem with understaffing. If Rantala was in the office and Cousineau was at the fair, he likely concluded that the County of Ontonagon did not have a deputy on the road. Cousineau, on this occasion, was on special duty. Deputy Terry Dove was on the road…only minutes away.

◆   ◆   ◆

Police radios were now crackling and a remarkable number of Ontonagons were eavesdropping. It's one of those diversions that make a small town unique and special.

David Blake was delivering fuel oil that Saturday afternoon, which seems to have been a peculiar chore given the time of year and the weather. He made the deliveries and went back to help at the station. They were a little short-handed because his parents were in Lower Michigan, but Saturdays are usually a little slower anyway.

He was pumping oil when a neighbor came bursting into the yard.

"Dave," he yelled, "Bruce has escaped."

David had a dumbfounded look on his face, a disbelieving look.

"He's what?" he asked, his jaw dropping.

"I just heard it on the scanner."

David's mind was churning. What could Bruce Moilanen have in mind? Would he be going after Elise? Would he head for the woods? What might be his frame of mind?

David knew his folks were out of town, and he also knew that Yvonne was preparing to play the organ at a wedding. Elise was home with a baby sitter. If Moilanen was headed in that direction, she may as well be home alone.

There was no time to go for the car. David jumped into his orange and white Blake Oil truck and headed for his house. It was only a few blocks away, but he didn't know how long Moilanen had been out. His heart was pounding.

David Blake needn't have worried. By the time he got to his house, it was surrounded by protective neighbors who had reacted to Rantala's alert. Bruce Moilanen could not have gotten near David's house, if, indeed, that had been his intent,

There is an expression heard with some frequency in this village and it was certainly appropriate on this occasion.

Only in Ontonagon.

◆   ◆   ◆

Bob Ball, the man most responsible for Moilanen being jailed in the first place, was in no position to be helpful. His sister was visiting from

New York and he had taken her three children, ages 6 to 11, on what he called an adventure.

Ball and the children were more than a mile from his house, hiking down a ravine toward a river valley. They were enjoying their walk through nature, but the heat was starting to get to the 6-year-old. Ball ended up with the youngster on his back.

Suddenly, his beeper went off. He started heading back toward the house. His beeper went off again and again, several different telephone numbers appearing on the display, including the Ontonagon County Sheriff's Department.

Something bad was happening, but he couldn't have imagined what.

◆   ◆   ◆

Kitzman decided that Moilanen's options, in terms of direction, were very limited. The main street and the river were south and west, so that was no way to go. Residential neighborhoods, where he might easily be sighted, were to the north and east. His best bet was to chance a couple of blocks of neighborhood directly north and get to the shore of Lake Superior, where he could skirt the main part of town and then duck inland into the woods before he got to the busy Township Park.

What's more, Kitzman's suspicions were confirmed by an inmate who told officers that Moilanen had gone north on Houghton Street.

"What do you want me to do?" Burgess radioed.

"Go to seven-oh," Kitzman said, using the radio terminology for the department office. And then he had another thought. "Never mind, set up a post at Paul Bunyan Avenue and Seventh Street. I think we have him in a vee. Let's see if we can make it smaller."

They positioned their cars so they could see if Moilanen tried to cross a street. Strategically placed, four cars could monitor more than half of the streets in the direction they suspected the escapee went. He could hardly move without being spotted.

Just as a neighbor came out of her house and asked him if he was having car trouble, Burgess noticed a figure running along Lakeshore where Paul Bunyan dead-ended at the lake.

"I think I've got him," Burgess radioed. "I've got a man running down Lakeshore toward the park."

Guzek drove up behind Burgess on Paul Bunyan and took a right on Seventh toward the lake. Kitzman was coming up Lakeshore and Dove was on his way.

"You're closest, Timmy," Kitzman said. "Go get him. I'm right behind you."

Guzek spotted the escapee. Moilanen was wearing tight shorts and a T-shirt, obviously unarmed. Rantala could not have known for sure when he broadcast his alert, but Guzek could see that he was not going to encounter the danger of a gunfight. The nature of the capture would likely have changed dramatically and dangerously if Moilanen had been able to escape with a firearm.

When Guzek pulled up, Moilanen was yelling.

"Shoot me, Tim," he screamed. "Shoot me."

Guzek did not even bother to pull his gun. Moilanen was not going anywhere. Kitzman pulled up and Moilanen's plea was more urgent.

"Shoot me," he yelled. "Don't take me back. Shoot me, Jerry."

Kitzman tackled him, cuffed him and stuck him in the back of the patrol car. Moilanen's freedom had lasted 25 minutes. That was about how long it took Dale Rantala to get his vision back. All Moilanen got for his escapade, outside of exercise, was a lacerated forehead from Kitzman's tackle. "Freedom" ended up being an escorted trip to the hospital.

By the time Bob Ball and his sister's kids got out of the woods, Bruce Moilanen was back in his cell.

◆   ◆   ◆

Jerry Kitzman now established another new rule, another rule tailored to the special problems Moilanen seemed to create. No deputy could enter the cell for any reason unless an armed deputy was outside.

Bruce Moilanen had unsuccessfully attempted suicide and he had successfully escaped, albeit for a rather short period of time. He was far from a model prisoner.

Thwarted twice and under constant scrutiny, he settled into place. He sat gloomily in his cell and either watched the television above the duty officer or read magazines. His favorite magazines were almost predictable.

Guns and hunting.

17

Muddy Waters

Bob Ball thought Bruce Moilanen was lying about cutting up the Savage 110 and throwing the pieces into the Ford River. He suspected the rifle was history, but that it had not been thrown off a bridge south of Escanaba. It could easily have been disposed of on the day Judy was shot, thus lessening the danger, from Moilanen's perspective, that investigators or even family might run across it.

Why would a suspected murder weapon, one Moilanen thought he had been careful to hide, be kept around until he went on a shopping trip to Green Bay in mid-December?

Still, Ball could not take a chance that the pieces of that rifle *weren't* in the Ford River.

Don Poupore and a team of five divers went to the bridge on April 26, the Monday after Moilanen had been arrested. The dive master was Bruce Dykehouse, a sergeant at the Petoskey State Police Post in the far north of the Lower Peninsula. Three of the five divers, in fact, had made the trip from the Lower Peninsula.

If the gun *was* in the Ford River, the State Police wanted to maximize their chances of finding it.

Trooper Carl Stutzner was the first in the water and he fought the strong current for 20 minutes before surfacing and shaking his head.

"We've gotta work from a boat," he said. "It's just too rough down there."

A Department of Natural Resources boat arrived about an hour later, giving divers a platform from which to work. They searched for two hours and found a metal rod, pop bottles and even nails, but nothing resembling a chopped up Savage 110.

"Visibility is good down there," one of the divers explained. "We're just not finding what we're looking for."

Poupore knew it was a longshot, but he went to the closest residence and asked if the couple had noticed anyone stopping to throw anything off the bridge. It was starting to sound like the "Ode to Billy Joe." As he suspected, they didn't really pay much attention to traffic on the bridge.

"Do you know when it froze over?" Poupore asked.

"Not until sometime in January," they said.

Divers came back a couple of weeks later to try again, this time concentrating on the downstream side of the bridge. Again, they had no luck.

Ball and Poupore desperately wanted to get their hands on even a chunk of that gun, but fate—and maybe Moilanen—were not cooperating. They had had their last shot at the suspect himself. He now had an attorney and they would see him only in court.

◆   ◆   ◆

Tom Casselman was quite familiar to Upper Peninsula law enforcement officials, and not just because he battled them so doggedly from the defense table. He taught criminal law at Northern Michigan University and many troopers and deputies had been through his course.

There came a time, in fact, when he and his wife Rhonda were on their way to the family hunting camp near Grand Marais when two of his erstwhile students pulled him over. He thought his 1973 Cadillac had been on cruise control at 57 miles per hour in what was a 55 mile-per-hour zone.

"What's the hurry?" a trooper asked.

"There isn't any," Casselman said. "I was going 57."

"We had you at 67."

"I don't think so," Casselman said, "but what about our bargain?"

Casselman laughed as he was telling the story. He would greet each of his classes on Day One with the proposition that he would make them better investigators if they would remember him should the time come when they pulled him over for a traffic violation.

"You give me a stern warning, right? Raise your hands if we have a deal."

Invariably, all the hands would go up. Now he had two of his former students telling him they caught him on radar going 67. He was incensed.

Rather than simply pay the fine, Casselman sought experts in radar and insisted on going to trial. The case went to trial in Sault Ste. Marie, 170 miles east of Marquette where the Upper Peninsula snuggles up against Canada. The proceedings took 12 hours and Casselman, the defendant, relished them, because he was taking his time with a trap he would spring.

"We're out of here," he said to Rhonda. "We're going home because they can't find us guilty."

"Huh?" said the prosecutorial team.

The Casselmans' investigation had uncovered the fact that the arresting officers were working with expired radar certification. They could not legally operate the equipment on the day they ticketed Casselman. The ticket was dismissed.

All of the papers involved in the case—the ticket, subpoenas and even the expired radar certification—are framed in Casselman's office. He had not gone to all the time and expense to avoid what would likely have been a $35 fine at the time, but rather to prove a point.

Tom Casselman's students could learn their lessons in the classroom…or on the job.

◆　　◆　　◆

Mike Niemi, Judy's cousin, had loyally supported Moilanen for all of the months since the shooting. He had refused to believe that Bruce could have been involved. His brother Gary had actually called Ball to complain.

Of course, Mike and Gary had had no reason to be suspicious. Detectives had chosen to limit the number of people who were aware of why Moilanen had become the focus of their investigation. It was a blow when the Niemis learned that Bruce Moilanen had badly betrayed their trust and played on their sympathies.

Mike Niemi had one question when Bob Ball walked into his office at Courtesy Chevrolet in Ontonagon four days after the confession.

"Was Judy shot with a muzzle-loader?" Niemi asked.

"No, Mike," Ball said. "She was shot with a 30-caliber rifle."

Niemi was relieved. Moilanen had given him that muzzle-loader for Christmas. It had been nagging at him that perhaps his Christmas present was the weapon that had killed his cousin.

"What weapons did he have with him that weekend?" Ball asked.

"All I saw was the old 33 Winchester," Niemi said, "but he said he had a muzzle-loader in the van."

Niemi paused as if in contemplation.

"In retrospect," he said, "Bruce could have had anything in that other gun case…including the murder weapon."

"Did Bruce talk about Judy's death?" Ball wondered.

Mike Niemi was one individual with whom Moilanen figured to have been comfortable talking. The Blakes had remained friendly throughout their ordeal, but they were not out-going, conversational people by nature. And there had to be subtle undercurrents of tension when Moilanen was at the Blake home.

"Numerous times," Niemi said. "Bruce would bring it up and come up with various scenarios about how this happened or that happened. It was always a hunting accident."

Moilanen, it seemed, had even made a rather sick joke once when he was complaining about the investigation.

"Why would I kill my wife?" he said. "We wouldn't have her to drive deer for us anymore."

Ball was curious about the March 11 trip to Traverse City and, indeed, it turned out to be a curious trip. Moilanen shopped for trucks all the way down and, finally, on the way back, actually traded the van he was driving along with $1,200 for the Chevy S-10 pickup. This was the van he had been in the process of buying, and so dearly wanted, that Thanksgiving weekend just a few months earlier.

In the midst of all that shopping, he managed to take Robert Dufort's polygraph test.

◆   ◆   ◆

Bob Ball had gotten his lesson in computer technology from Moilanen himself, but he wanted to have an expert help him with his exploration of the Leading Edge computer confiscated in the search of April 23.

Only one thing of interest to Ball was found on the disks.

A will. Bruce Moilanen's will.

He was leaving $15,000 to Gayle and Paul Lampinen.

◆   ◆   ◆

In his confession, Moilanen purported to have bought the Savage 110 through an advertisement in the Action Shopper. If he had not been truthful as to the rifle's destination, maybe he had been about its origin.

Det. Lt. Richard Goad contacted the newspaper, sat down and went through the issues from July through December of 1991. He was looking for an advertisement for a rifle fitting the description of a Savage. He found no such listing.

However, the asset list that included the Savage was not submitted with the First National Bank loan application until April of 1992.

Goad would return to check later issues.

◆   ◆   ◆

When Ball learned Moilanen had called the Nevilles in Green Bay from his jail cell, he was quickly on the telephone. He knew Moilanen's bond had not been reduced, but maybe the Nevilles knew some things he did not know. They had apparently been good friends of the Moilanens through their mutual interest in dogs.

Fred Neville, a salesman, was out of town, but Sue was in.

"We do have our mutual interest in dogs," Sue explained, "but we were friendly with them more because we liked Judy. We've had bad feelings about this from the beginning, because we never really believed the falling chimney block was an accident."

Moilanen's mid-December trip to Green Bay had supposedly been made to both Christmas shop and visit the Nevilles. He had not caught up with the Nevilles and never explained why. Sue did.

"Fred was in North Carolina on business," Sue said. "I told Bruce I had a sick relative in Eau Claire. I didn't want to be alone with Bruce in my home when Fred was away."

Fred Neville was still away a couple of days later when Ball called again.

"What bothered you so much about Bruce?" Ball asked.

"He is a liar and he's arrogant," Sue Neville said. "I can't think of any redeeming qualities he has. We've known them for eight years and I can't think of anyone in the dog training field who likes Bruce Moilanen."

"So you haven't had much contact with him since Judy was killed?"

"He's called a few times and he showed up once here uninvited. He's talked about Judy's death a couple of times, but even that's kinda bothered me. He's never once said he missed her."

"Did he say anything about our investigation?"

"Never mentioned it," Sue said. "The only thing I remember was once when he said he didn't think he really wanted to know who was responsible."

What a coincidence, Ball was thinking. He definitely did not want *us* to know who was responsible.

◆   ◆   ◆

One dog, Streak, had returned to the Blake home the day of the shooting. The others hadn't. They remained in the woods until Mary Ann Blake blew the dog whistle.

Why?

Fred Neville, the dog trainer, provided some insight when Ball finally got him on the telephone.

"Moilanen's dogs were so well-trained," Neville said, "he could have given a blast on his whistle or a 'hup' and the dogs would stay in place for an hour or more."

It had seemed unlikely to Ball that the dogs were unaware of Moilanen's presence. After all, these were hunting dogs. They were trained to be the eyes, ears and nose of the hunter. They may have been carefree on their walk with Judy Moilanen, but they would not have been oblivious to their surroundings.

Ed Niemi, Judy's uncle, shed further light in a later conversation.

"Bruce did a demonstration for me once when we were going for a walk into my blind down in the Flintsteel River valley," Niemi said. "We were walking through the woods and he said, 'Watch this.' He gave the dogs a signal and they froze. We kept on going all the way down to the blind. We were there for awhile and, when we came back up the trail, they were still there. Bruce did not say a word. We walked right past them and walked all the way to the van before he blew his whistle. They came running."

Between Neville's knowledge of dogs and Ed Niemi's personal experience with Moilanen's dogs, Ball had a better idea of what he *thought* had transpired in the woods along Cherry Lane. The disciplined dogs, *his* dogs, stayed in place and Streak, the Blake's dog, raced home.

"Bruce's reaction following Judy's death didn't seem appropriate to me," Neville was saying. "He wanted to run a full-page memorial ad in Spaniel Magazine and he wanted to set up a memorial trophy. What really struck me was that he wanted to have her death *announced* at an event in Pennsylvania."

Fred Neville did not seem to think too highly of Bruce Moilanen.

"Bruce," he said, "is an asshole."

◆   ◆   ◆

Bob Ball was convinced the gun was not in the Ford River, nor that Moilanen had chopped it up into little pieces. Bruce, through his alibi list, *had* established that he had been at Ed Niemi's blind later that Sunday afternoon.

Had he disposed of the gun in that area?

On May 24, a search party gathered near the intersection of the Simar-Wasas Road and M-38. Ed Niemi and his sons Mike and Gary were there as well as Deputy Tom Cousineau, DNR officer Jackie Strauch, Trooper John Raymond, Ball, Poupore and two handlers with explosive-sniffing and tracking dogs. They fanned out and searched along the path down to the blind without luck.

Their intention was to search the Flintsteel River, but muddy waters made it impossible. Recent rains had raised the water level and the currents were churning as the river made its way to Lake Superior.

Other areas were also marked, such as a branch of the Ontonagon River near Tank Creek, a beaver pond near the intersection of M-26 and M-38 and even the pond back in the woods along Cherry Lane.

Bob Ball felt secure with the case, but there was no feeling of complacency. Not with the weapon missing.

◆   ◆   ◆

It was late spring before Ball got the autopsy report from Dr. Hugo Castilla, the medical examiner. It contained Castilla's conclusion that the bullet had entered behind the left armpit and exited in the upper right chest. This conclusion ran counter to what Ball and Lt. Ray Kenny determined, as well as Bruce Moilanen's account.

"Dr. Castilla," Ball asked, "could you review your findings for me?"

"My opinion," Castilla said, "was based partly on my own observations and partly on what deputies told me."

Castilla listed a number of points he considered, the first of which was the piece of tissue protruding from the wound over the right breast.

"Did you know that I examined and photographed Judy's body at the morgue the night she was killed?" Ball asked.

"No," Castilla said. "I didn't know that."

"I pulled that piece of tissue out when I was moving her shirt to photograph the wound."

"No one told me that."

Ball would normally have been at the autopsy, where he would have had an opportunity to explain this seeming incongruity before it made its way into an autopsy report. Unfortunately, police business forced him to be in Gogebic County that day. Even Bob Ball cannot be in two places at once.

"You do indicate you feel this was a close-range shot," Ball said, "and I agree with that."

"Because of the damage," Castilla said.

"Right."

Ball and Kenny had come to that conclusion from the trajectory as well, the bullet leaving the body at a higher point than it entered. Ball left Castilla and drove to Cherry Lane, where he entered woods now lush with new growth. It seemed a different world than it had been that dreary November night.

Standing where the body had been found, he stepped off the 37 feet to the maple tree and then measured the height of the graze mark from the ground. The bullet had glanced off the tree 14 to 17 inches higher than it had been when it passed through Judy's body.

Given this trajectory, Ball walked in a straight line to the opposite direction across the path and through the underbrush on the east side of the trail. The line of trajectory would hit the ground 108 feet from the victim, considerably closer than the 50 yards estimated by Moil-anen. He found a small stump 82 feet from the body.

"This," he wrote in his report, "would provide both concealment and a gun rest for the shooter."

◆   ◆   ◆

The preliminary hearing was on July 6, 1993 in the Ontonagon County District Court. In spite of his confession, Moilanen had entered a plea of innocent. Thomas Casselman, his attorney, would argue that the confession was obtained under duress created by the intensity of the investigation. The prosecution, he felt, had little more than the confession.

Elizabeth Paczesny, 27, would represent the people in opposition to Casselman, a 53-year-old from Marquette who had been voted by his peers the best defense attorney in the U.P. in a 1992 *Marquette Mining Journal* survey. Anyone who thought this exercise would be a walkover, a mere formality, for the prosecution did not know the pugnacious Casselman. Anyone who thought the youthful prosecutor would be a pushover for the veteran defense attorney did not know the determined Paczesny.

Casselman already had them shaking their heads in the Ontonagon County Courthouse. These were the mild summer months and he would often make the two-hour trip from Marquette on a motorcycle, wearing leathers and helmet. He would disappear into a men's room and come out in suit and tie.

In reality, Casselman likely made that two-hour trip just a little bit more quickly on his motorcycle, maybe a lot more quickly. He was an adventurous individual, given to speed and daring, the more outrageous the better. One of his goals, on his 1,000cc Ninja, was to travel on an arrow-straight stretch of road between Shingleton and Seney, two U.P. hamlets east of Marquette, in 10 minutes. Be advised that they are 25 miles apart, meaning he would have to average 150 miles per hour and likely peak at 180. He had made the trip in 11½ minutes. A dragonfly almost tore his helmet off on one such excursion, but he remains undeterred.

Casselman had always been a goal-oriented person and not many of his ambitions escaped him, except one big one. He came out of the University of Michigan Law School determined to incarcerate people rather than defend them. He wanted to be an agent with the Federal Bureau of Investigation. The problem was that he was 5-foot-6 and he needed to be 5-foot-8 to meet minimum height restrictions.

Undaunted, he did everything imaginable to overcome that two-inch barrier, just short of hanging by his thumbs with his ankles weighted. Unbelievably, on the day of his FBI physical examination, he measured 5-foot-8…or close enough. He still flunked…because he was color-blind. He argued this point for two years, actually trying to create "reasonable doubt" that he really was color-blind. Juries could be swayed by reasonable doubt, but not the FBI.

Casselman decided he would go ahead and become an attorney.

Those were the days of the war in Vietnam, but Casselman was 25, short and color-blind. He knew he was not going to be drafted, so he chose an altruistic manner of beginning his law career. Born and raised in the Detroit area, he went north and took a position with Upper Peninsula Legal Services. He represented indigent clients over hundreds of square miles between Grand Marais on the east and Baraga on the west.

When he decided to get into private practice, he resisted the temptation to return downstate in pursuit of higher compensation. He loved the forests and rolling hills and lakes and he had come to value lifestyle above dollars. What's more, no U.P. courtroom was strange to him. Cases had taken him throughout the peninsula. He settled in to practice criminal and family law out of Marquette, for he had become a Yooper.

◆   ◆   ◆

Casselman's trip to the preliminary hearing was almost normal, in as much as he rode in the family car with Rhonda. A striking blond who would add a touch of glamour to the court proceedings, she had been doing the investigating to prepare the case, interviewing prosecution witnesses and seeking defense witnesses.

However, both Casselmans had been frustrated by the person who figured to be most cooperative...their client. Moilanen had ignored Mrs. Casselman's advice that he *not* chirp to the cops and now he wasn't chirping to anyone, even his attorney. He was withdrawn and moody, never offering as much as a "good morning" or "good evening."

"I'm done," he told them. "I'm cooked. I'm gone."

For his part, Casselman was not one to press his clients on guilt or innocence. He had built up the tough veneer that allows defense attorneys to wage war with the prosecution regardless of their own suspicions, be they confirmed or not by their clients.

Casselman, in fact, tells the story of a client who had been arrested for drunk driving on a New Year's Eve. The client's account was that he had consumed a couple of beers in a saloon before leaving for home, only to roll his car into a ditch maybe 100 yards from his house. Shaken, he walked unhurt to his house and proceeded to drink tequila until police officers arrived later to investigate. They noted his inebriated condition and arrested him.

"What do you want me to tell you?" the client asked the attorney. "The truth? Or what I told the cops?"

"The story you told the cops," Casselman said firmly. "That's the story I have to work with."

Casselman knew the story Moilanen told the cops, but he was not getting much help from his client on what happened April 23...or anything else that might be of help.

Paczesny awaited this exasperated attorney on the morning of July 6, knowing what she *had* to do and wondering what he *would* do. Casselman, as is always the case, had the advantage of knowing what the prosecution had on hand, but the prosecution would be getting its first taste of how the defense would respond. Paczesny was unaware of how uncooperative Moilanen had been with the Casselmans.

Bruce Moilanen, wearing a navy blue suit and maroon tie, sat next to his attorney with Rhonda Casselman next to him.

With Judge Anders B. Tingstad Jr. presiding, the hearing began at 10:17 a.m. and the first witness was a very nervous Mary Ann Blake, Moilanen's mother-in-law. Paczesny led her through a heart-wrenching account of finding her daughter's body in the woods behind Cherry Lane. The courtroom was quiet throughout her testimony. Casselman too was quiet. He could hardly object to a woman making such painful recollections.

When he rose to cross-examine, it quickly became obvious one direction the defense was heading. Casselman was trying to shake her on her recollection of time, exactly when Judy Moilanen must have left the house. He questioned her at length, in fact, on precisely when her casserole came out of the oven.

"Is it fair to say you don't remember looking at the clock?" he asked.

"No," she said, "it's not fair to say that I don't remember looking at the clock, because I apparently must have if I knew it was time to take the casserole out."

Casselman was less aggressive with Mrs. Blake than he would be with later witnesses, but he was still too abrasive for her tastes. She would grow to passionately dislike the defense attorney, an emotion almost foreign to her gentle nature.

Bruce Moilanen had been, in those weekend visits, hammering her with the necessity of sticking to that "2 o'clock story" on Judy's departure from her house that Sunday afternoon.

"It was *your* story?" Casselman said. "The 2 o'clock story?"

"He apparently called it a story," Mrs. Blake said. "I didn't call it a story."

David Blake testified that he thought it strange that Moilanen came into the hospital and, upon being told she had been shot to death, wanted to know if she was wearing orange.

"You do put emphasis on that?" Casselman said.

"I thought it was strange," David said firmly.

"Hindsight, sir," Casselman said. "Do you put emphasis on it in hindsight or do you put emphasis on it at the time?"

"At the time, I thought it was strange."

At one point in David's testimony, he asked to refer to notes he had written to himself after the two occasions when Moilanen called him from the Ontonagon County Jail. By the time he finished testifying, Casselman had the notes in his hands. David wanted them back.

"Sir, my notes?" David asked.

Tingstad: "Does Mr. Casselman still have your notes?"

Casselman: "I'm sorry?"

Tingstad: "Do you still have the witness's notes?"

Casselman: "Yes, I do have the witness's notes."

Tingstad: "He'd like to have them back."

Casselman: "Well, that's a matter for the court to decide."

Tingstad: "All right. Have you had a chance to read them?"

Casselman: "I've had a chance to read them."

Tingstad: "Okay, then give them to…"

Paczesny: "I never had a chance to read them."

Tingstad: "Give him his notes back. He may not want to let you read them."

Casselman: "I want a copy of these notes and I want this made an exhibit for this preliminary exam."

Casselman's insistence on entering David Blake's notes seemed strange. These were the conversations where Moilanen had admitted his guilt to the victim's brother. If anything, they seemed damning to the defense.

Mike Niemi, Bill Dorvinen, Deputy Cousineau and Bill Burgess followed David Blake to the stand. And then it was time for Dr. Hugo Castilla, the medical examiner.

"I thought the bullet would come from the back and exit in the anterior portion of the chest," Castilla testified.

"I'm assuming you mean…" Paczesny said.

"…A piece of, what I thought and confirmed later, of tissue was hanging out from the inside of the wound," Castilla said. "I took it as a clue that that piece of tissue was pushed out, from inside out, as the bullet came out."

Paczesny presented the supposition that the tissue had fallen out when Judy's shirt had been pulled away and asked if Castilla's opinion would be changed.

"Yes," he said. "It would make my finding equivocal."

Casselman largely ignored the issue of the tissue and concentrated on the time of death, which was listed on the death certificate as 3 p.m. Castilla testified that it could be five hours in either direction.

In looking at the death certificate, Casselman noted that Castilla's name was typewritten rather than signed.

"Is that customary?"

"No," Castilla said.

Paczesny: "Dr. Castilla, did you fill this death certificate out?"

"Probably I did, yes."

Castilla was obviously not a strong witness, but the prosecution could hardly present a case without the medical examiner. Paczesny would have to do her best with him, particularly should the case come to trial.

Det. Lt. Ray Kenny, the microscopist who examined the bullet, had also had considerable experience dealing with entrance and exit wounds. He was also a longtime friend of Casselman and, on the occasion of a divorce, a client as well, but they were adversaries in this courtroom. Casselman argued vehemently that Kenny was not an expert on entrance and exit wounds.

"It would be just as if Mrs. Blake, Mary, suggested what was the entrance and the exit wound," Casselman said. "It is not relevant to the court's proceedings to have someone give an opinion in an area in which it requires an expert. For example, the prosecutor began these statements with Dr. Castilla, suggesting that the doctor was mistaken in his expert opinion. That is an expert. This gentleman is not…"

Tingstad over-ruled the objection and allowed Kenny to give his opinion as a layman. And Kenny *was* just a bit more knowledgeable in these areas than Mary Ann Blake, but Casselman's main weapon was obviously going to be the creation of doubt. This type of statement might play well in front of a jury.

When Casselman started dealing with Kenny's expertise, the examination of the bullet, he planted the thought that the bullet had hit the tree *before* striking Judy.

"Would that support the theory of accident?" Casselman asked.

"I don't have an opinion on that," Kenny said.

He did, of course, but that would open another debate about entrance and exit wounds. In this case, the entrance wound was not consistent in form with a bullet that had already been damaged by a ricochet off a tree. Casselman undoubtedly knew that too, but he was still building on reasonable doubt. It was a matter of whether he was constructing a house of cards or a skyscraper.

Det. Sgt. Bob Ball was called to the witness stand at 4:32 p.m. Paczesny led him through a recitation of his background, including seminars with pathologists and the investigation of violent crimes.

One of the seminars he attended was conducted by Dr. Werner Spitz, a world-renowned pathologist from Wayne County, covering the Detroit Metropolitan area. Casselman, whose research material included Spitz's book "Medical-Legal Investigation of Death," had been at that same seminar with his wife.

None of this, in Casselman's mind, made either himself...or the detective...an expert in the field of forensic pathology. He rose to object.

"If the purpose of the prosecution is to now make this officer a forensic pathologist...because he eats with the President, sleeps with the President, discusses things with the President, does not make him President. I object."

Paczesny and Tingstad jockeyed back and forth and finally Tingstad said: "Where are we going with this?"

"That's my objection," Casselman said.

"That you're now going to elect Det. Ball President?" Tingstad mused.

The attorneys were called to the bench and a compromise was reached. Ball, like Kenny, could give his lay opinion on entrance and exit wounds.

When it came to the protruding tissue, Casselman was on his feet again: "Am I to understand, Detective, that before the medical examiner got to examine this person, you played medical examiner?"

"Well," Ball said casually, "I don't know if you would term it that. I played investigator."

These men, Casselman and Ball, would have one clash after another, Casselman driving and twisting with his questions and Ball calm almost to the point of irritating his antagonist.

Ball was examined by Paczesny for one hour and 40 minutes, including intermittent objections and *voir dires* from Casselman.

When she finished, Tingstad asked if it was appropriate to break for dinner.

"Hell no," Casselman said. "I want to finish this right now. I want to talk to this detective this minute, your Honor."

Casselman pressed Ball on the length of the investigation, the elimination of other suspects, the grilling of Moilanen's associates and the pressure applied to Moilanen himself. He began to touch on the complicity of persons such as the Janofskis.

"Did you have his friends reporting to you?" Casselman asked.

"I can't say that I learned that he had any friends," Ball said.

Casselman worked his way around to the lack of footprints at the scene of the crime, at least the fact that investigators found no footprints at the scene.

"Should we deduce that there were, but you were incompetent?" Casselman said. "Or should we deduce that there were, but none were retrievable?"

"I would not say we were incompetent," Ball said.

"Or shall we deduce that there were none?"

"I don't think you can deduce that there were none," Ball said. "It's just like there's lots of fingerprints on that table up there, but I'm willing to bet you can't see them. There could be latent footprints, you might say, like latent fingerprints."

Casselman's cross-examination went for more than an hour before he thanked Ball and started to sit down.

"Can I add one thing?" Ball asked.

"No," Casselman said. "I have no idea what it is, so you can't."

Paczesny moved that Bruce Moilanen be bound over for trial on one count of premeditated first degree murder and one count of possessing a firearm in the act of committing a felony.

Casselman asked that Tingstad exclude the statements Moilanen made to Chuck Allen and Bob Ball on April 23, suggesting insufficient evidence existed without it.

"In fact," he said, "there is only evidence of accident…of ricochet…of indetermination."

Paczesny's first statement was brief, her response was lengthy.

Concluding, she said: "…It didn't change what he stated to the detective, that he shot his wife. Not the first time he caught her in his sights, not the second time did he do it, but the third time. We clearly believe that Bruce Moilanen carried the Savage rifle—he said he did—that he used to shoot his wife."

Casselman stood and looked at Ball.

"Detective," he said, "after exhaustive searching and after every kind of look-see from the legitimate house search to the legitimate garbage search, what do you have to corroborate what you've finally got? I haven't been able to corroborate anything. I don't have a gun. I don't have a shell that matches a bullet. I have some bullshit. About 50 per cent of what he told me I don't believe. The only things I do believe end the search and end the inquiry so I believe them. From Day One, always the husband."

Casselman had done an interesting job of interjecting *his* thoughts into the closed mouth of Det. Ball. He addressed the court as though *he* was Ball, sarcastically denigrating his own case. If Moilanen is a liar, he was suggesting, why believe some of what he said and disbelieve other statements? Why believe the confession and disbelieve the rifle's disposition? This was another case of an argument that might play better before a jury than before Judge Anders B. Tingstad Jr.

After Tingstad took a 20-minute break, he returned to the courtroom with his judgment.

"The difficulty in this case comes from the nature of the death," Tingstad said. "Had Mrs. Moilanen been found in the City of Detroit or, you know, some more developed area with a gunshot wound, the question of an accidental, lesser occurrence would not have arisen to make this difficult."

Tingstad concluded that evidence showed that the bullet hit Judy Moilanen and then the tree, eliminating an accidental ricochet. He noted Moilanen's misstatement of the amount of life insurance to David Blake, failure to disclose the Savage to Mike Niemi or, for that matter, to the investigators and uncanny recall of his whereabouts that Sunday for all but the time that mattered most. He even cited Moilanen's "Is she dead?" response when Niemi told him something serious had happened.

"I'm going to bind the defendant over on both counts," Tingstad said. "The felony firearm count is relatively simple. If we find probable cause on the first one, the second one naturally follows."

"Is the court finding premeditation and deliberation?" Casselman asked.

"Yes," Tingstad said. "I am."

◆   ◆   ◆

Tom Casselman's determined demeanor and dogged questioning had not won over the judge, not that he really expected it would. He knew the case was not going to be whisked away at any preliminary hearing. However, as he and Rhonda and the defendant filed into the law library, which served as sort of combination detention cell-office, Moilanen was eyeing his attorney and his wife with interest he had not previously shown.

"You really do care, don't you?" Moilanen said rhetorically. "You're really trying."

"I've been trying since Day One," Casselman said.

Henceforth, Bruce Moilanen would cooperate with his attorney. He would even say "good morning."

◆   ◆   ◆

Bob Ball did not have to go through the rigors of the preliminary examination to realize the lack of a weapon could be a problem. He had scheduled five dives for the next morning, once again headed by Sgt. Bruce Dykehouse with four troopers from all over the state.

"I think we'll start concentrating on the Flintsteel River," Ball said. "We have two possible locations where it goes under the old M-38 and new M-38 bridges and another near Ed Niemi's deer blind. That's about three-quarters of a mile north of the Simar-Wasas intersection with M-38."

Nothing was found, even though the water level was down and the bottom was not nearly as murky as it had been. They had no luck at the beaver pond on the other side of M-38 nor on the East Branch of the Ontonagon River near the Tank Creek area.

Ball knew he was grasping at straws. All of the divers in the State of Michigan could search all of the lakes, ponds, streams and rivers in the Western U.P. for the rest of their lives and not find that rifle, even if it *was* there. For all Ball knew, it could be tucked under a rotting log.

One thing he did not believe, and never would believe, was that the Savage 110 was chopped up at the bottom of the Ford River.

18

Action Shopper

Bruce Moilanen, being somewhat fanatical about insurance, wanted to make sure he could account for his possessions in the event his house burned down…or maybe in the event he left glowing ashes next to the woodpile. To this end, he had gone through the house with a camcorder and videotaped all of its contents.

Bob Ball was sitting with the videotape on the VCR, watching Moilanen's "home" movies.

Moilanen went all through the house, but Ball paid closest attention when a firearm was being taped and described. This was part of his continuing search for further evidence of the presence of a Savage 110. He had no more luck with the videotape than the divers had had in the Firesteel River or beaver pond.

One part of the tape struck him as peculiar. Moilanen was filming a wall filled with trophy heads of game he had shot. Ball knew the wall. He knew a lot of that house like the back of his hand. A beautiful framed picture of Bruce and Judy on their wedding day was on that wall.

Bruce Moilanen skipped past that picture as if it had no significance whatsoever. The date on the recording was 1-22-91.

◆   ◆   ◆

Det. Lt. Richard Goad was still "shopping" the Action Shopper, looking for a party who had sold a Savage 110. It was late summer of 1993 when the telephone rang at the Ishpeming home of Jon Lyle. He had to be surprised at the staying power of an advertisement in the Action Shopper.

"Were you selling a Savage 110?" Goad asked.

"I was," Lyle said, surprised at the call. "I sold it quite awhile ago."

Bob Ball made the trip to Ishpeming, a community west of Marquette. Lyle had a copy of the ad.

For Sale: 30-06 with scope for only $180. Call JON after 7:30 PM.

"I got it new and used it for a few years," Lyle said, "and sold it when I needed some money."

"You remember the person you sold it to?"

"I don't remember the name right off hand, but I'm sure I would recognize the guy. He knew a lot about guns, I remember. The stock wasn't in very good shape because I'd gotten into a scrap with a bear. I took $150 for it."

Leave it to Bruce, Ball thought, to pay $150 to a guy asking $180 and then list it on an asset sheet for $300.

"Can you describe the guy who bought it?"

Lyle's description was reasonably close, so Ball showed him a picture of Moilanen.

"I think that's the guy," Lyle said. "I'd know for sure if I saw him in person."

"I can arrange that," Ball said.

Moilanen had a brief court appearance upcoming. Lyle drove to Ontonagon and met Ball at the courthouse. Ball sat in his place at the prosecutor's table and Lyle sat behind him. When the proceedings ended, Ball turned to Lyle. The young man had a half-smile on his face and he was shaking his head. He knew by now the crime allegedly committed with the gun he had sold.

"No question," he said. "He's the guy that bought the gun. The hair stood up on the back of my neck when I saw him."

Bingo.

The trouble with bingo is that they check the numbers. Something about this manner of identifying a subject would become a problem.

Ball thought he was safe since it was not a matter of a victim identifying the perpetrator at a crime scene. The defense would argue to the contrary.

The defense's position might have been weakened at about this time, because this was when Moilanen made his short-lived escape from the Ontonagon County Jail. Unfortunately, the escape was technically a separate crime and could not be used in the trial for premeditated first-degree murder. Beth Paczesny knew the escape was not admissible, but she had hopes for Jon Lyle's very positive identification of Bruce Moilanen as the man who bought his Savage 110.

◆   ◆   ◆

The Casselmans, meanwhile, were finally making headway with a suddenly cooperative client. While Tom busied himself on other cases and other clients, Rhonda researched, investigated and interviewed persons from both Moilanen's alibi lists and the prosecution's witness list.

This was a most interesting couple, which took the team approach to preparing for trial. The Casselmans also took the team approach to life, which they lived as few others could even imagine. Rhonda's sons, Andy, 19, and Troy, 17, were very much a part of this team approach to life.

On one particularly adventurous occasion, the entire family flew unguided into an isolated peninsula in the Hudson Bay area to hunt caribou. They were startled when a herd of caribou so large it sounded like a 747 taking off thundered past a short distance away. Young Andy got the first shot and brought down one of the animals from a distance of more than 600 yards.

This was a family that had mountaineered in the Grand Teton, mountain-climbed in Switzerland, traveled in Egypt just days before Desert Storm, rubber-rafted down the Salmon River in Idaho and sailed in the Virgin Islands. Tom and Rhonda even tried skydiving…once.

Certified dive-masters in three different disciplines, the Casselmans were engaged in an on-going search for $3 million in gold coins purported to be at the bottom of Lake Michigan not far from Escanaba. The French were trying to "end run" the bullion to the Rebels during the Civil War when they were caught by a Federal gunboat, dumping three steel chests overboard to keep them from falling into Union hands.

While a stern and almost vicious presence in a courtroom, Tom Casselman could be an entertaining and convivial companion when it came to telling countless stories over countless hours away from the challenges tossed his way by the justice system.

◆   ◆   ◆

The admissibility of Bruce Moilanen's April 23 confession was also a continuing subject of debate. This would be resolved, however, at a proceeding scheduled for Sept. 23. A Walker Hearing is used by the State of Michigan to determine whether a confession can be used at trial by the prosecution.

Bob Ball's testimony covered most of the same ground covered in the preliminary hearing. He detailed the investigation from its inception, building to having probable cause, which he hardly needed, to justify subjecting the spouse to a polygraph test.

The difference between the preliminary hearing and the Walker Hearing was that Chuck Allen was there to address his role in the interview process. Specifically, he was pressed on having adequately advised Moilanen of his rights. He testified to his thoroughness in making the Miranda Rights understandable before he started, as well as to his willingness to halt the interview when Moilanen later balked and asked about having an attorney present. Allen had played it by the book.

Since the detectives committed no procedural flaws, the prosecution could use the confession. The trial jury would hear Bob Ball and Chuck Allen testify as to what Bruce Moilanen told them on April 23, 1993. This was a victory.

◆　　◆　　◆

Tom Casselman, at the preliminary hearing, had complained that lay opinions prevailed over Dr. Hugo Castilla's "expert" opinion of entrance and exit wounds. Paczesny and Ball knew they had to address that situation at trial or Casselman would (or could) have the jury totally bamboozled.

Ball sent photographs of the two bullet wounds and the jacket Judy was wearing to Dr. Stephen Cohle, a forensic pathologist at the Blodgett Memorial Medical Center downstate in Grand Rapids. Cohle had done 3,500 autopsies, between 300 and 350 on gunshot wounds.

"In my opinion," Cohle wrote in a letter to Ball, "the entry wound is in the chest and the exit wound is in the back. The reason for this is that the chest wound is round and regular and the back wound is irregular."

Ball sent the report—and the bill—to Beth Paczesny.

◆　　◆　　◆

Beth Paczesny was now getting more involved in the case. The preliminary hearing was over and the trial was on the horizon. At her young age, she was surprisingly well-versed in legal ramifications but Bob Ball was light years ahead of her when it came to investigation.

They were sitting in the Marquette office of John Evans, an agent with Northwestern Mutual Life Insurance. They were about to have a very enlightening interview, regarding, among other things, the timing of insurance purchases in the Moilanen household…and who set them up.

In April and May of 1991, Moilanen met three times with Evans to negotiate $75,000 in life insurance on him and his wife. A double-indemnity clause was attached to both policies in the event of accidental death.

"Who suggested that?" Ball asked.

"Bruce," Evans said. "I never push that benefit."

"Was Judy a part of this?"

"I went to their house in June," Evans said, "to do a closing on the policies. Judy was there."

"These policies were tied to a trust for Elise?"

"There was never any talk of that."

Ball looked at Paczesny. These $75,000 policies had been tied by Moilanen into a trust for Elise in his Jan. 22 interview. Another lie.

"Then there were the corporate policies," Evans said. "Bruce set these up a month later. These were $70,000 policies on himself and Judy to protect investors in Big Creek Kennels. There was no accidental death benefit on these."

Ball and Paczesny knew that the only "investors" in Big Creek Kennels were Bruce and Judy Moilanen. In the event of accidental death, the $75,000 policy would be worth $150,000 and combine with the corporate policy to create a $220,000 benefit to the survivor of such a tragedy. Neither had to remind the other that all of this insurance was accumulated just months before the chimney block incident and the fire in the basement in the fall of 1991. And Judy had little to do with the purchase of these policies.

Ball and Paczesny were about to come up with a real bingo.

"I thought it rather unusual during the summer of 1992," Evans said, "when Bruce's policy lapsed and Judy's stayed current."

"Huh?" Ball said.

"I tried to call Bruce," Evans said, "but I always got the answering machine."

"Was Judy's current when she died?" Ball asked.

"It was," Evans said. "Bruce came into the office a few days after she died and reinstated his. He wanted the beneficiary to be a trust for Elise."

Bob Ball wanted to know who had made the payments keeping Judy current while Bruce's policy had lapsed. He got his answer.

Bruce Moilanen.

◆   ◆   ◆

Financial problems, which Moilanen insisted did not exist, could manifest themselves in different ways. They can be caused by excessive spending or diminished earnings. Or both.

On the spending side, the Moilanens were obviously not extravagant people. They did not party and they did not seem to travel. They lived in a nice home, but they had the amenities of what might be called a normal household. Moilanen did have this penchant for changing and upgrading vehicles more often than most would deem economically sensible.

Problems, thus, might be found in the income side of the equation. Don Poupore submitted a search warrant to Marquette General Hospital, asking for the Moilanens' W-2 forms for 1991 and 1992. Moilanen himself complained at one point that the hospital had cut back on overtime, incongruously complaining in his confession about the hours his wife had worked.

When Poupore got the W-2 forms, he saw that Moilanen's pay had dropped only slightly from $22,953.25 in 1991 to $21,834.80 in 1992. Judy was obviously the big breadwinner in the family, but her pay dropped from $38,207.34 to $28,381.93.

But what about those other businesses?

Det. Lt. Goad asked for the Moilanens' tax returns for those years, as well as returns for Big Creek Kennels Inc., Big Creek Incorporated and North Country Claim Service. None of those companies existed on the tax rolls, but the Moilanens' joint adjusted income dropped from $56,068 to $44,624. The disparity in the total income either reflected income from the other businesses or tax deductions or both.

Of course, through no fault of Judy's, neither worked in December of 1992.

◆   ◆   ◆

Bruce Moilanen had been doing business with Lutheran Brotherhood Insurance since 1985, when he purchased a $61,000 policy on himself with a $40,000 spouse rider on Judy. His policy contained an automatic cost of living increase.

He had to deal with a new agent, Ogden Johnson, when he called Lutheran Brotherhood on July 17, 1989. He wanted to purchase $25,000 in life insurance on his infant daughter, listing him and Judy as beneficiaries. Ball was intrigued when Johnson told him about $25,000 in life insurance on an infant, but he became more intrigued when he started learning about the summer of 1991.

"By July of '91," Johnson explained, "Bruce's coverage was $74,000. He wanted Judy's spouse rider increased to $80,000 and his coverage increased to $80,000 as well. He told me he wanted the increases to cover the home mortgage as well as Elise's educational expenses."

Johnson said there was a slight delay in putting the new policies into effect because he had forgotten that Lutheran Brotherhood allows increases only in $10,000 increments. Bruce's policy had to be increased to $84,000.

"Was Judy aware of the new coverages?" Ball asked.

"Bruce made all the requests," Johnson said, "but Judy had to sign the forms."

"The increases would have been in effect Sept. 23, 1991?"

"No question," Johnson said.

Johnson did not know the significance of that date. In the months leading up to Sept. 23, 1991, Bruce Moilanen's dealings with North-western Mutual and Lutheran Brotherhood had increased life insurance coverage on Judy, including the one double-indemnity policy, from $40,000 to $300,000 with those companies alone. It was on that date in September of 1991 that the chimney block "accidentally" fell from the roof and landed on Judy Moilanen's head.

◆ ◆ ◆

Beth Paczesny called Bob Ball on Oct. 11, 1993. Tom Casselman, Moilanen's attorney, had sent her a letter listing 29 possible alibi witnesses for the defense.

"You've accounted for 25 of them in your reports," she said. "None of them account for his whereabouts during that gap."

"Who are the new ones?"

"One of them is Bruce's mother."

Ball was on his way to Ontonagon County again. It mattered not that 25 of the 29 witnesses would be harmless to the prosecution. He could not take any chances on the other four. It was not as much a matter of insuring a conviction as insuring fairness.

What if one of them clearly remembers seeing Bruce Moilanen at between 2 and 2:15? Ball thought it virtually impossible, but he had to know.

Two of the possible witnesses, Chet Maki and Lucy Peterson, had been driving together when they saw a gray van as they were nearing the Firesteel River not far from the intersection of Simar-Wasas Road and M-38.

"I saw the ad in the paper," Maki said, "but I don't know what day it was. I just know it was during deer season."

Lucy Peterson's response was the same.

Sigrid Miilu Moravich lived south of Mass City toward Rousseau, a "community" that seems to consist of a ramshackle bar and little else. She saw a van parked along M-38 on a couple of occasions, including the day of the shooting, but paid so little attention she could not even recall its color much less its make.

"I remember the day," she said, "because I went to Watersmeet to play bingo with Huldah Moilanen."

So, Ball thought, the other two possible witnesses were also in the same vehicle. And one of them was Bruce's mother Huldah.

"What time would that have been?" Ball wondered.

"I had to pick Huldah up by 1," she said, "because we were in Watersmeet for 'Early, Early Bird Bingo.' It starts at 3."

"Central Time?"

"Yes," Moravich said. "That's 2 our time."

"You sure you got the day right?"

"Yes, because Huldah called me after we got home all upset because Judy'd been shot."

Ball later measured the distance to the Watersmeet casino at 58.4 miles. Unless Sigrid Miilu Moravich was hell on wheels, they had to leave a little before one to be in Watersmeet in time for Early, Early Bird Bingo. And M-38 was only minutes away, so they would have cleared that area by a little after 1. Moilanen's mother and her bingo buddy could not even account for the most critical of times.

Still, he drove to Mass City and found Huldah Moilanen getting into her car.

"Mr. Casselman has your name on an alibi list," Ball said. "Can you give me a few minutes?"

"I don't care to talk about it," Mrs. Moilanen snapped.

"Can you tell me if you saw Bruce that day?"

"I saw his van at M-38 and Simar-Wasas."

"Can you tell me the time?"

"Between 2 and 3," Mrs. Moilanen said.

"You were with Mrs. Miilu?"

"Yes. We were going to bingo."

"Mrs. Miilu puts the time at approximately 1."

"She gets the time mixed up," Mrs. Moilanen said. "We never go to Early Bird Bingo."

Mrs. Moilanen was already in her car and now she was backing out of the driveway. Ball watched her drive away. Bruce had one witness who would insist she saw his van between 2 and 3.

His mother.

◆   ◆   ◆

Bob Ball and Det. Sgt. Dave Johnson pulled up at Moilanen's house in Harvey on the afternoon of Oct. 29, 1993, exactly 11 months after Judy's shooting death. They served a search warrant on 19-year-old Don Doyle, Moilanen's nephew, who was in the driveway when they arrived.

"Go ahead," Doyle said, "I'm not taking sides on this. I'm not backing up Bruce. You guys do what you need to do."

What Ball needed to do was to see for himself what could or maybe could not have happened on Sept. 23, 1991. The chimney block incident troubled him *before* he learned how much Judy's life insurance had been increased late that summer. A boost from $40,000 to $300,000 was almost too dramatic to be coincidental.

Ball and Johnson, a detective with the Marquette crime lab, occupied themselves taking videotapes and measurements while they awaited the arrival of Beth Paczesny and Trooper Don Brown. Paczesny and Brown were purchasing two chimney blocks from Wick's Building Supply.

Hauling the blocks out of the trunk was a chore. Ball measured them at 21½ inches by 16¾ inches by 7½ inches. They weighed 85 pounds each. They compared them with a block lying on Moilanen's property to ascertain they were dealing with the same size and weight. They were.

From pictures filed with Moilanen's insurance claim for damages to his patio in 1991, they were able to determine that the block hit Judy 65 inches from the wall of the house. They ran a rope parallel to the wall to mark where the block had fallen.

And then Trooper Brown hauled the two blocks up onto the roof.

Ball wanted to see what it took to cause one of these blocks to fall. Brown placed one of the blocks at the edge of the roof and jumped up and down to create vibration. It did not budge. Ball climbed up on the roof and, in an almost comical scene, he and Brown both jumped up and down next to the block. Again, it did not move as much as a fraction of an inch.

All the while they were doing this, they were describing what they were doing and Johnson was videotaping the experiment.

They weren't done jumping. They put the second block on top of the first in case one would slip off the other. They jumped up and down and neither moved. One block was then placed so that it extended eight inches over the roofline, hardly a place where a block would sensibly be left, but even then it did not move when they jumped next to it.

"One of these blocks," Ball announced for the sake of the video-taped account, "will not slip off these shingles."

The experiment told them that the chimney block incident could not have been an accident.

Ball went back down the ladder and Brown stayed on the roof. He slid one of the blocks until gravity caused it to fall. He did it again and then lugged both blocks back to the roof. He did it a third time, Ball all the while measuring the distance of impact from the wall. The blocks hit the ground 52, 50 and 51 inches from the wall.

"Give that last one a shove," Ball called, "and see where it lands."

Brown shoved the brick and it tumbled toward the ground. It hit dead center on the rope, 65 inches from the wall.

◆   ◆   ◆

Pre-trial motions were scheduled for the following Tuesday, Nov. 2, and Tom Casselman was attempting to suppress anything involved with the chimney block incident from the upcoming trial. The paramedics, investigating trooper, Mary Ann Blake and Det. Sgt. Ball were all to testify.

The prosecutorial team would come out of this hearing feeling as though *it* had been hit by an 85-pound block. Paczesny's questioning of Ball lasted until Casselman rose to object as the detective started to relate the encounter with Donald Doyle in the driveway.

"May I see the warrant, if such exists, Your Honor?" Casselman asked.

It would seem a nuisance request, since the investigators would surely have tended to such housekeeping.

"I have a copy of the warrant," Ball said.

"Please provide it," Judge Roy Gotham said.

"I have received a copy of what appears to be a search warrant," Casselman said. "It is unsigned by any judge or magistrate. It is undated. I wonder if there is one that has been signed and dated."

"This is the service copy," Ball said. "There is a signed copy."

Det. Sgt. Don Poupore left the room to find the original. When Poupore returned, Casselman looked at the warrant. His eyebrows arched noticeably and he handed the warrant to Ball.

"Is there a signature?" he demanded.

Ball looked.

"There's not a signature," he conceded.

"The magistrate never signed the search warrant?" Casselman said.

"That's correct," Ball said.

The affidavit had been signed, but the search warrant had not. It was an oversight, of course, but an oversight that could not be overlooked.

"I must conclude," Gotham said, "that the search, or experiment, if you will, was not conducted pursuant to warrant."

Thus, Gotham could not issue a ruling relating to the admissibility of The Chimney Block Incident. It would have to be argued in a hearing within the trial itself, with the jury out of the room.

Det. Ball and Company returned to Moilanen's Harvey home the next day to do a recreation of the recreation…with all signatures properly in place.

19

The Bulldog and the Puppy

Beth Paczesny felt confident on the eve of the trial. The date was Nov. 29, 1993, exactly one year from the day Judy Blake Moilanen had been shot in the woods along Cherry Lane. She looked out from a friend's kitchen across a yard blanketed by snow, deep woods crowding the edge of the clearing. It was not far from Cherry Lane, either geographically or topographically.

"I just wonder if we would be where we are right now," she said wistfully, "if we had had this much snow a year ago today. Bruce could not have gotten in and out of Cherry Lane without leaving tracks."

Not only that, footing would have been bad even with snowshoes. And speed would have been impossible.

Unfortunately for Judy, Ms. Paczesny—or some other prosecutor—might ultimately have been trying the same person, only on a different date with different circumstances. If it was not a gunshot or a chimney block or a fire in the basement, heaven knows what Bruce Moilanen's mind might have contrived.

Unfortunately for Judy, only Judy could have saved Judy. Only Judy could have recognized all those red flags that seemed so obvious in hindsight. She had confided superficially in others, but kept so much to herself. And she was too blinded by love and stubbornness or both to see the dark side of her husband.

The absolute worst had happened and now it was Beth Paczesny's job to present this case to a jury and get this man incarcerated for the remainder of his life. She had the Mikkola conviction behind her, but that had been a rather cut-and-dried case. The man had virtually plunked himself into the laps of law enforcement, getting arrested for drunken driving in the victim's car. He veritably had blood on his hands.

The Moilanen case was vastly different in terms of community perception. This was a victim ripped from the heart of Ontonagon, the only daughter of one of the village's most respected families. This was God and motherhood and apple pie, all that is good, wiped away by an act only one person in the world could possibly begin to understand.

Paczesny insisted she felt more confident on the eve of this trial than she had on the eve of the Mikkola trial, yet she had tinges of concern she did not suppress.

"If I don't get this conviction," she said, "I don't know if I'll be able to walk the streets of Ontonagon."

It was a relatively solid case, but it was hardly a gimme. The suspected weapon could be linked with Bruce Moilanen, but it could not be placed in his hands. It could be proved where he wasn't, but not where he was. The chimney block incident was still to be debated, in terms of how it might be used in the trial. The jury could, figuratively speaking, be manipulated into enough confusion to hang itself rather than the defendant.

Darkening this cloud of uncertainty was Casselman's presence at the defense table. Rumors were rampant about how Casselman was being paid for his services, especially since the investigation had uncovered the shakiness of Moilanen's financial dealings. Months ago, Moilanen himself had told Lee Anne Wysocki that the attorney he wanted would cost him $25,000.

Regardless, Casselman came to the trial with a reputation for being a calculating, controlling defense attorney. If this man could not get Moilanen off the hook, no one could. He was glib and smooth, but also abrasive and accusing. He had a commanding, demanding quality to his voice.

In 1992, when a *Marquette Mining Journal* survey identified him as the best defense attorney in the U.P., he had been asked about cross-examination: "It's an art form. I don't think you can be taught. I build a box out of which they can't escape. I ask 20 questions. Four are relevant. There is no escape, except the one I want."

Casselman was surely cocky, as well as annoying to prosecution witnesses and victims' families. However, his style worked.

Paczesny was far from glib, but she was earnest and sincere. She was so good-hearted and good-natured that she couldn't raise a threatening voice in the face of an accused murderer. She would seem almost apologetic at times when Casselman was climbing the heights of arrogance. What she *could* do was relentlessly pound on the pages and pages of facts she had in hand.

Their physical presence was also a study in stark contrasts, Casselman short, 5-foot-6, and wiry and Paczesny about the same height, sturdy and big-boned. They both dressed conservatively and wore their hair neatly trimmed, but Tom Casselman had the intense look of a bulldog and Beth Paczesny had the carefree look of a puppy.

While it was only natural that onlookers should be comparing the styles and appearances of the attorneys, Beth Paczesny knew where the real battle lines would be drawn. They would not be drawn between her and Tom Casselman, but rather between Det. Sgt. Bob Ball and Tom Casselman.

◆   ◆   ◆

Obviously, jury selection would be a problem. The case did not get the national attention of the Menendezes or O.J. Simpson, but the area media gave it considerable play. What's more, it was "covered" via word of mouth in the aisles of Pat's and Fraki's, in the booths at Syl's and Wagar's and on the stools at the Shamrock and Doc's.

Very few people in Ontonagon County were unaware of Judy Blake Moilanen's death and the twisted machinations of the man alleged to have murdered her.

Thus, the attorneys were faced with the chore of finding 14 people in Ontonagon County, two alternates included, without pre-determined ideas on what happened down Cherry Lane that November Sunday in 1992. As it turned out, eight of the 14 jurors were from the South End of the county and only four were from Ontonagon itself. Rumors (and facts) did not have quite the circulation in places such as Ewen and Trout Creek as they did in Ontonagon.

◆　　◆　　◆

The Ontonagon County Courthouse is one of the newest structures in a town with very few new buildings. The origin of many homes is listed as "cir: 1900," meaning they were built in the first few years after the fire that razed the entire town in 1896. The old red brick courthouse still stands on the same block with the Ontonagon County Jail, but the new one is on the outskirts of town on M-38. It is an austere brick edifice, two stories high, obviously built for function rather than old-fashioned picture-postcard aesthetics.

Cherry Lane was six-10ths of a mile from the new courthouse.

Neither the parking lot nor the courtroom could handle the mob scene the morning of Nov. 30. In search of 14 unbiased jurors, 120 people had been summoned to Judge Roy Gotham's Circuit Court.

To the left, facing the bench, were four pews behind the prosecution and, to the right, were five pews behind the defense. Only 54 people could be comfortably seated. On the morning of Nov. 30, Undersheriff John Gravier was checking jurors' names from a podium in the hallway and deputies were trying to find a way to get them seated. Folding chairs were hauled from all over the courthouse. Pews were jammed, aisles were jammed and prospective jurors overflowed into the hallway, craning their necks to hear as Judge Gotham took the bench.

Each day the Blake family filled the second pew on the prosecution's side with friends and relatives in the pew behind them. No one from

Moilanen's family set foot in the courtroom throughout the proceedings.

Judge Gotham's nine predecessors as Circuit Court judges looked down from the wall behind him, some of the faces stern and some friendly. One of them was Merv Griffith's ex-father-in-law. A bust of Oliver Wendell Holmes was off to one side, just below an antique pendulum clock that at some point in its life stopped at 2:32.

Gotham himself could present a face both stern and friendly, depending on what was happening in front of him. He was built along the lines of Casselman, about the same height and only slightly stockier. Perched on the bench, he had the presence of a hawk surveying what was below him. He did not miss much, but he may or may not have known that his wife was the president of Bruce Moilanen's graduating class at Ontonagon High School.

The jury box, to the left of the courtroom, was empty.

"I won't get picked," one prospective juror said as she entered the room. "I know the family."

"We *all* know the family," corrected another.

They had come wearing a motley range of attire, from a very few coats and ties to a man with ragged jeans and a Dirty Dick's Saloon jacket, from high heels and dresses to battered sneakers and sweatshirts. It was an icy day and outerwear was scattered through the District Courtroom across the hall.

Moilanen came in through a side door from the law library, limping in his shackles. Deputies joked that he had been limping since the day he was arrested, except the one day he got free and had a chance to run. And deputies were all over the place, both in and out of uniform.

"What a great day to rob a bank," laughed a bystander. "All the cops are here."

In this county for this trial, *most* available cops were in the courthouse. One officer, Ontonagon native Tom Rosemurgy, had been borrowed from the Calumet force for security duty. Death threats had been received and, while the reality of such danger was uncharacteristic to the area, they had to be taken seriously because of the intensity of interest in the case and the proliferation of firearms in the population. Metal-detecting wands scanned spectators as they entered the court-room.

Once jury selection got underway, it seemed Casselman's plan was to dismiss 30ish-looking women with children who could most directly empathize with the victim. The judge dismissed two postal workers who argued that they were about to enter their busiest period at work. Ontonagon's mayor, Kurt Giesau, was excused.

During Gotham's *voir dire,* he asked one of Moilanen's contempo-raries from Mass City if she would be biased for or against him.

"Possibly," she said. "I didn't really like him as a child. We didn't get along."

Gotham kept running into familial, though often remote, relation-ships to either the Blakes or the Moilanens.

"Her grandma's sister somehow."

"Bruce is the brother to my aunt that was married to my uncle, and they were divorced."

"One of the witnesses is my mother-in-law."

"One of the witnesses was my son's landlord on Cherry Lane."

"One of the jurors is my boyfriend's grandma."

Paczesny's approach was warm and interested. On more than one occasion, she asked prospective jurors if they had gotten their buck. Her interest was more in placing an intelligent jury rather than one with a particular demographic profile, because she would be presenting a complicated case she knew Casselman would try to twist into a plate of spaghetti.

Casselman, working from a podium in front of Gotham, asked one prospective juror if he could see him.

"Well, how tall do I appear to be?" he asked.

"Not too tall."

"I don't appear to be very tall?"

"Five-eight," the prospective juror responded, smiling.

"Look at me with your thumb and your finger, about an inch?"

"Yes."

"Things don't always appear to be what they are, agree?"

In his way, Casselman was pressing the point of illusion…what was real vs. what seemed to be real. He was twisting perception before evidence was even presented.

"Do you have the ability," he asked another juror, "to discern between the truth and baloney?"

"I think so, definitely."

"No matter how thin you slice it, it's still baloney, right?"

Casselman also pressed prospective jurors on whether they had ever made statements they regretted, which they would like to retract. He tried to characterize how a person "whipped, beat and broken" would respond. He was setting up the jury for how he would portray Moilanen's confession.

By the middle of the second day, they seemed to be getting close. Only one prospective juror had been dismissed at the most recent break. At 2:24 on Dec. 1, both prosecution and defense were satisfied.

Eight men and six women were selected, the women ranging in age from 42 to 62. Forty two prospective jurors had been dismissed, 29 by Gotham, eight by Casselman and five by Paczesny. Inwardly, the defense attorney had hoped that this process would be interminably difficult, and thus give him cause to move for a change of venue. He could see early on in the proceedings that a jury would be seated, albeit not easily, and Gotham would never go for such a motion.

However, if Casselman's goal had been to keep thirty-something women from the jury box, he had succeeded. For that matter, only two of the men were below 40. One was a 22-year-old from Bruce Crossing who looked like he was on an outing with his aunts, uncles and grandparents.

The trial, the People vs. Bruce Robert Moilanen, would begin Dec. 2.

◆   ◆   ◆

Beth Paczesny's opening remarks detailed the background of Judy and Bruce Moilanen's relationship, building to the day, she said, that Judy's trust in Bruce got her killed. She talked of how investigators built their case from that day until the day Moilanen was arrested.

With as firm a voice as she could muster, she debunked Moilanen's alibis.

"The only person near him at 2 o'clock, the time of the murder, was Judy Moilanen," Paczesny said, "and she's dead."

Gayle Lampinen's name was introduced to the jury.

"She will tell you about what is called The Sweater Letter," Paczesny said. "Now The Sweater Letter is a letter that she found in a box of sweaters that the defendant gave to her...sweaters and clothes of his dead wife."

Paczesny talked about the confession and Lee Anne Wysocki and the Savage 110 and the insurance policies, which ultimately totaled $321,000. She suggested the defense could not attack either the facts or the law, so she predicted it would instead attack the police.

She did not mention the chimney block incident and she did not mention Jon Lyle's identification of Moilanen as the man who bought the Savage, because she could not. Those issues and their admissibility would later be argued with the jury out of the room.

"Ladies and gentlemen," she said, "don't let him get away with murder."

Casselman's opening remarks were briefer, as if he wished to imply that the prosecution's case was so weak it was hardly worthy of lengthy comment.

"The prosecutor, the lady, must prove beyond a reasonable doubt that he is not innocent," he said, "and they will not because they cannot. There is a tragedy, there was an accident and a young woman is dead by a hunter's bullet."

The jury heard from Casselman about the pressures that built upon Moilanen through the months of intense investigation.

"In 1604 in Salem, Mass.," he said, "they had these kinds of things. They were called then, and I'm serious, witch-hunts."

During jury selection, Casselman had asked numerous jurors if they had ever said anything they were sorry they said, that wasn't true, that they wanted to retract. Bruce Moilanen, he said, made just such a statement. Carefully, Casselman did not call that statement a confession.

"The evidence," he said, "will show there is no evidence but for that screwed up statement."

Just as she had been at the preliminary hearing, Mary Ann Blake was the first witness. She once again had to relive that painful experience, delivering riveting testimony that had handkerchiefs out throughout the room.

"I saw her lying on the ground," she said, choking back sobs, "and I could see she was not alive."

When she was asked about the defendant, she noticeably hardened. His tears and his grief had obviously grown repugnant to her and she recalled the time shortly after Judy's death that he lamented that he had maybe $45,000 in life insurance…not even enough to pay the mortgage.

"Did he ask what time Judy left to walk the dogs?" Paczesny asked gently.

"Yes, he asked me many times what time she left," Mary Ann said. "I always said I don't know for sure and he always said, 'Let's stick to the 2 o'clock story.'"

If Mary Ann hardened when asked about the defendant, she stiffened defensively when Casselman stood to cross-examine her. He had a job to do, but she did not like how he did it. In truth, she likely would have felt the same way about anyone in his shoes.

Casselman did not press her on time quite as hard as he did at the preliminary hearing, but he went through the chronology of church, casserole, going to her office and Jerry's family leaving for Shawano.

He asked if she had seen Streak leave with Judy and her dogs. He was trying to confuse her, but Mary Ann was not to be confused.

Mary Ann Blake was questioned at length about the weekends when Moilanen and Elise visited Ontonagon, about how her attitude toward him changed as the investigation progressed but how she had disguised her feelings. His thinly veiled suggestion was that Moilanen was welcomed only so that she could conspire with the police to implicate him. He might have pressed the point just a bit too far.

"Many a time," she said, "I didn't know if I dared go to bed at night, because I was concerned what Bruce might do to all of us. But as long as Elise was in my home, at least I knew what was happening to her at that point, at that time."

Moilanen did not know of the Blakes' suspicions. He ate at their table. He slept in their house. He was veritably sleeping with the enemy, so to speak.

"As long as he thought I knew nothing," Mary Ann said firmly, "he would continue to bring my granddaughter to my house. From Day One, she was my biggest concern."

Mary Ann was doing little, through this segment of her testimony, to establish guilt on the part of the defendant, but she was piling up sympathy points. Paczesny picked up on the theme, asking whether Bruce ever asked if the family was suspicious.

"Not ever at our house," Mary Ann recalled. "He did call me at work one day and said, 'Those guys think that you think I did it.' I said what guys and he said, 'The detectives.' I changed the subject. I didn't answer. I didn't want him to know…because he would immediately have stopped coming over and probably forbid us to see Elise."

Casselman took one more brief shot, but Mary Ann simply would not weaken. Every response seemed to work in his client's disfavor.

"I've known Bruce for 16 or 17 years," Mary Ann said, "and I knew he was always looking out for No. 1. Himself."

Tom Casselman had no more questions of this witness. Beth Paczesny had to be a very happy prosecutor, because her first witness had put on a star performance.

◆   ◆   ◆

Jerry Blake, Judy's brother, was the person who could most closely pinpoint the time Judy had left to walk the dogs. He testified that she was at the house at 1:15 when he went into the sauna and gone at 1:30 when he came out.

Jerry was quite sure when he and his family had left for Wisconsin and he was quite surprised that Judy had not gotten back to say good-bye. He testified with such clarity that jurors could almost see Streak bounding across the yard as the family was climbing into the car.

Of course, Paczesny also asked him about Moilanen's light-hearted Christmas morning telephone call to Gayle Lampinen, which he described as strange.

"I was very surprised that he would make that phone call so soon after my sister had died," Jerry said in response to a question from Casselman. "It just bothered me."

"What is it you want us to believe about the phone call?" Casselman asked.

"The significance is that I felt he should still be in mourning," Jerry said, "especially the first Christmas after my sister passed away. He should be mourning that and not making phone calls to someone else."

◆   ◆   ◆

Bill Dorvinen, the neighbor, played a brief and painful role in the drama along Cherry Lane that afternoon. It was he who had accompanied Mary Ann on that anxious walk that came to such an anguished conclusion.

Dorvinen's testimony was essentially a narrative, but Casselman picked up on his recollection rolling the body over. He was trying to establish whether *rigor mortis* had set in, a key element in establishing the time of death, and time of death would be a key element in Casselman's plan of attack.

"Was the person stiff?" Casselman asked.

"I know when I rolled her over, her arm came back to the ground. I can't say that she was stiff or..."

"I recognize it as not a particularly pleasant thing but I need to know that, sir."

"At the time," Dorvinen said, "I didn't pay much attention to it."

◆   ◆   ◆

Deputy Tom Cousineau could also testify only to what he saw at the scene, namely dog tracks, and what he did not see, namely any sign of a human other than the victim having been in the area.

Casselman pressed Cousineau on his role in the investigation, at one point implying that Det. Sgt. Bob Ball had essentially taken over the case and put Cousineau, the original investigating officer, in a subordinate role.

Cousineau conceded that he thought he had a hunting accident on his hands when he arrived at the scene, but that his original conclusion was short-lived. He began to suspect Moilanen at first when the husband insisted on viewing his wife's body and then when he noted the defendant's behavior after he left the morgue.

"It was more of sobbing without tears to me," Cousineau testified, "if you want to call it sobbing."

Later that evening, Cousineau was to relay his observation to Det. Sgt. Bob Ball.

◆   ◆   ◆

Bill Burgess had arrived at the scene in his role as an EMT and switched roles to medical examiner's investigator at the morgue.

Tom Casselman was now getting to witnesses he could use to attack Bob Ball. He grilled Burgess on why he allowed Ball into the morgue on that Sunday evening when the medical examiner, Dr. Hugo Castilla, was not due until the next day. He grilled Burgess on how the body was treated, how it was clothed, how much of the clothing was removed. Why? By whom?

Burgess, an affable sort, was not rattled by Casselman's questioning. He insisted standard procedures had been followed. Casselman might have wondered how standard procedures were established, events such as this being rare to the point of non-existence in Ontonagon County. If he did, he didn't ask.

Instead, the defense attorney switched directions and started stroking the witness. He was asking about *rigor mortis* and lividity and building Burgess up to be knowledgeable far beyond his expertise or experience. He was trying to elicit testimony as to precise time of death.

Paczesny was on her feet: "Your Honor, I'm going to object. I think this is getting beyond the scope of this witness."

In one of those ironic twists that make trials so interesting, Casselman asked for and received permission to question the prosecution's witness and establish his credentials as an expert witness. And the prosecution set about to discredit him as an expert.

After all of the jockeying back and forth, which filled most of what remained of Day One, Judge Roy Gotham ruled that Burgess could not render an opinion relating to the time of death.

Tom Casselman, who had railed at Ball's "inexpert" testimony at the preliminary hearing, had almost gotten away with eliciting "inexpert" testimony on the defendant's behalf on the first day of the trial…from a prosecution witness.

Burgess was finished testifying. And the trial's first day was also finished, coming to an end, from the prosecution's standpoint, with a very close call.

◆   ◆   ◆

The prosecution was also a bit apprehensive about upcoming testimony early in Day Two…Dec. 3. Dr. Hugo Castilla was the second witness on the docket, following Dr. Steven Gervae. The prosecution was not comfortable with Castilla as a witness, but it could hardly omit the medical examiner's testimony.

Gervae had been with the body all of five minutes at the morgue. His role was to pronounce the body dead of a gunshot wound, which he said entered in the right front and exited in the left rear. To him, it was cut and dried. No question.

Casselman, of course, had questions. After his pronouncement, had the doctor left Bill Burgess with any instructions?

"I instructed Mr. Burgess not to disrobe the body."

Burgess had already testified that he *did* disrobe the body…under the direction of Det. Sgt. Bob Ball.

Dr. Hugo Castilla was next. He was somewhat of a Jonathon Winters-lookalike with a heavy accent. He was renowned as a whiz of a pathologist, but detectives cringed when he became involved in a potential criminal case as a medical examiner. For better or worse, he rarely dealt with gunshot wounds.

"The wound in the chest was showing this piece of tissue hanging out from it," Castilla said. "It is logic that the bullet when it came out, you know, dragged this piece of tissue with it."

That initial thought was on the autopsy report, along with 3 p.m. as approximate time of death, approximate being a pivotal word. He talked of lividity in the area of the left shoulder as well as *rigor mortis,* but conceded he had established time of death more from talking with investigators such as Tom Cousineau.

"What did you see when you went into the morgue?" Casselman asked. "What was the condition of the person?"

He had this distant way of asking questions. He would stare off in some remote direction as he posed the question, his voice very deliberate and under control. He would turn at the end of his question and face the witness, as if just realizing that person even existed.

"In a cart," Castilla said.

"On a cart?"

"Partially dressed and with the chest exposed."

"Stripped?"

"No," Castilla said. "I believe not."

"Who was present?"

"Mr. Cousineau, Mr. Burgess and me."

"Not Det. Ball?"

"No."

"Did the deputy say to you, 'Doctor, I need to know what time this person was actually slain?'"

"No."

"Did he appear to want to know?"

"Well, not from me probably," Castilla said.

Time of death was of tremendous importance to Casselman and he had the pathologist who did the autopsy in front of him.

"You've heard of that thing called an alibi where somebody needs to say for a certain reason they were at Point X instead of Point Y?" the attorney asked.

"No."

"Never heard of that?"

Casselman was taken aback.

"I don't think it's a medical term," Castilla said.

Casselman would ask a multitude of questions to camouflage what he really had in mind. Using this technique, he led Castilla to testify that the time of death was between 3 and 5 on the afternoon of Nov. 29, 1992. Moilanen, of course, had alibis for that time period.

Gotham declared a brief recess, but the proceedings were delayed when Castilla could not be found after the break. The judge took the opportunity to inquire as to Casselman's health, since the attorney had a bad cold and came to court wearing a scarf. Casselman said he could continue and Castilla eventually made his way back to the witness stand.

Casselman moved to the area of entrance and exit wounds, realizing Castilla had originally concluded that the entrance had been from the back. The piece of tissue protruding from the chest had caused him to form that opinion.

"You changed your mind because the police told you they had done something to the body, correct?" Casselman asked. He had this way of coloring questions by punctuating them with words such as correct, true and right. It was his way of answering his own questions.

"Yes, but…"

"What is it that they told you?"

"They told me he was pulling clothes from the bullet hole, you know, this piece of tissue came up."

"Who?"

"I think it was the detective."

"Do you see him in the room?"

"No."

"You don't see him?"

Ball, of course, was sitting directly in front of the witness.

"Was it a deputy sheriff with a brown uniform, sir, who told you that he had removed the clothing and the flesh came out?"

"No, the deputy."

"Who told you?"

"The detective."

"Well, do you see him in the room?"

"Yes."

"Where is he?"

"In front of me."

"Is it usual procedure…that detectives go to the morgue and probe wounds before you do?"

Castilla started with "usually not" and ended up with "never" before Casselman was finished with a flurry of questions. Never…in 25 years.

Paczesny came back and tried to work with time of death, but did not seem to make any headway. She was content with leaving the issue of entrance and exit as it stood.

Judge Gotham intervened on the question of establishing a more precise time of death. The issue was so clouded now and Castilla had been so confused by Casselman's questioning that Gotham could not even sort things out. At one point, Castilla said it might have been between 5 and 6.

Judy Moilanen's body had been found a few minutes after 5, already very dead.

◆　　　◆　　　◆

The next witnesses would go much further toward establishing time of death than did the medical examiner. Jerry Schoch and Marie Lyons had heard a shot between 2 and 2:15. These witnesses presented an interesting contrast, one a robust and rough-hewn young man and the other a fragile but feisty elderly woman.

Schoch took the stand and Paczesny asked him what he had been doing that afternoon.

"Just screwing around the house," Schoch said.

He testified that he was outside washing windows at approximately 2 o'clock when he heard a shot from the woods across Cherry Lane from his house. At that same moment, Marie Lyons was hitchhiking down M-38.

"I was going to the Candlelight," she said from the witness stand. "There was a party for Russell Reid, a birthday party. You know

Johnny Reid from here? His father. It was his 90th birthday or something like that."

Ms. Lyons was so tiny she could barely be seen in the witness stand. Next to her, Casselman would have looked like Kareem Abdul-Jabbar. Neither attorney really knew what might come out when she piped up in her squeaky voice.

"Everything was so quiet, and all of the sudden the gunshot," she told Paczesny. "Then I thought I was wearing a light tan coat and that was a bad color to be wearing during hunting season."

Marie Lyons set the time at 2:10 to 2:15.

"You were hitchhiking?" Casselman asked.

"I was going to a party," she said.

"Had you had anything to drink, Ms. Lyons?"

"I wasn't drinking then," she said emphatically, "because I was on medication." She brightened. "But I didn't want to miss a party."

◆   ◆   ◆

Anyone wondering what might have been going on during recesses and lunch breaks in the law library, the defense team's headquarters in the courthouse, might have been surprised to learn that the seemingly dour defense attorney often captivated both his client and the ever-present bailiff with stories.

And Tom Casselman, the adventurer, had stories to tell. He had shared them at various times with Roy Gotham, Beth Paczesny and Bob Ball as well.

"Did I tell you about hunting wild boar with a spear in Tennessee? No? You don't *throw* the spear. Bulls, bears and boars will run at you when they are enraged. You step aside and stick the spear where you'd normally shoot them."

Casselman's friend Mike Gierke, a deputy sheriff from Escanaba, was with him on this trip, as was Rhonda, of course. Their guide had heard of this outrageous method of hunting and he had invited friends,

Deliverance-type hill people, to watch. Everyone was in trees, but the hunter himself.

"I stuck the spear and it broke off as the boar went by," Casselman continued. "Now I had a two-foot stick in my hand and 300 pounds of pissed off boar turning to come at me. I yelled at Mike to toss me his jackknife."

Dogs were barking and the natives were yelping from the trees as the boar charged over and over again, each time Casselman stepping to the side and taking a thrust at his very angry adversary's under-belly. Rhonda had brought a tape-recorder, which now contains 34 minutes of veritable cacophony.

"I don't know how many runs he made, but I was into him up to my elbow before I finally brought him down. My jacket saved me, because his tusks had torn it to shreds."

Onlookers spilled out of the trees wide-eyed with wonderment at having watching a slight 50-plus-year-old attorney kill a 300-pound boar with a jackknife.

Tom Casselman was no less determined in the courtroom.

◆   ◆   ◆

The bullet occupied the remainder of Day Two, from Dan Castle's marble-slinging discovery to Det. Lt. Ray Kenny's identification of possible rifles to Connie Swander's analysis of what the bullet had carried.

Castle's story of persistence in searching for the bullet did not prove anything other than that a bullet had been found in the woods along Cherry Lane. However, it was good theater for the court groupies who gathered each day on the right side of the room. It was a tale they had not previously heard in their coffee klatches. Castle had been sworn to secrecy that a bullet had been discovered.

"By whom?" Casselman asked.

"Det. Ball told me not to say anything to anybody."

Casselman never missed an opportunity to portray Ball as control-ling and obsessive when it came to the investigation of his client.

In another effort to impeach the investigation's thoroughness, Cas-selman quizzed Castle about why he did not continue to seek the shell casing after the bullet had been found.

"Well," Casselman asked with seeming impatience, "when did find-ing the shell casing not become important? Once you found the bul-let?"

"That's not up to me to decide."

Castle eventually testified that, at Ball's request, he made another trip to the scene just after Labor Day, 1993, to look for the shell casing.

"Did you say, gees, Bob, why didn't we look for this thing in June?" Casselman asked. "You know, we're looking while the leaves are falling here in September. Why aren't we looking for it when the leaves aren't falling and it's spring?"

He hadn't, of course. Casselman knew that. The "question" was his way of making a point and maybe scoring a point.

Kenny, the microscopist from the Marquette State Police labora-tory, testified that he had gone to the Cane Funeral Home in Onton-agon with Bob Ball and Dr. Castilla the day before the services for Judy. Their purpose was to remove bullet fragments from the body, realizing they could well be of no help but also realizing that fragments may be all they would get. The fragments were really of no help, but Castle later eliminated that dilemma.

What Paczesny wanted most from Kenny was his identification of rifles that could potentially have shot that bullet. She drew him through a meticulous description of how he was able to isolate a rela-tively short list of possibilities, a list that included a Savage 110.

Casselman brought the fragments into play when he asked how much they weighed, then asked the weight of the bullet. The com-bined weight was 19.3 grams lower than that of a bullet made by Rem-ington, which Kenny had testified was the likely brand. The defense attorney's implication was that maybe it was a smaller caliber bullet and, consequently, a different caliber gun.

In his opening remarks, Casselman had said the prosecution had little with which to work when the opposite was really the case. He was the one who had to nit-pick at the littlest of things, such as bullet fragments.

"Can you account for the 19.3-gram difference in weight?" Paczesny asked.

"It doesn't really mean very much," Kenny said. "It just means a small portion of the core was missing from the bullet. The important part for me in my examination for firearms investigation is the metal jacketed surface."

Paczesny had gotten testimony back on track toward the acceptance of the Savage 110 as the weapon that killed Judy Moilanen. It was a subtle but significant point.

Connie Swander, a forensic scientist with the Grayling Post in Lower Michigan, had gotten the bullet from Kenny. She specialized in trace evidence, linking the microscopic bits and pieces Kenny found on the bullet with the clothes Judy was wearing as well as the tree it hit after it passed through Judy's body.

"The fiber fragments, pinkish purple," she said, "were microscopically similar in several characteristics with swatches of the shirt worn by the victim."

In her words, the fiber was a "probable" match with Judy's fuchsia shirt and the feather was a "possible" match with the down in Judy's jacket. The wood and moss were consistent with samples from the tree.

Casselman was condescending, to say the least, in his cross-examination of Swander. He frequently addressed her as "Scientist" rather than "Ms. Swander."

"Scientist," he would say, "can you tell me..."

◆   ◆   ◆

Beth Paczesny was unsettled by Friday's testimony. Not all of it, just part of it. Just Dr. Hugo Castilla, the medical examiner.

"I don't like leaving it like that," she told Ball.

The jury had gotten a contradictory report on entrance and exit wounds and a totally confusing estimate of the time of death. These issues, particularly the latter, were vital to the prosecution.

"Don't worry, Beth," Ball said. "We'll clean it up when Dr. Cohle gets here."

"I know," Paczesny said, "but I don't like leaving something like that for the jury to think about over a weekend."

Regardless of whether jurors dwelt on Castilla's testimony over the weekend, the prosecutor spent a long weekend wondering if they were.

◆   ◆   ◆

The Casselmans had another burden on their minds. The attorney had received a very thinly veiled death threat in the Ontonagon Court-house hallway, ironically from an individual on the list of defense witnesses. Deputies were aware of it and they would tighten already vigilant security.

It might seem such a threat incongruous in such a typically passive community, but hunting—deer, bear, moose, birds, rabbits—was such a way of life that virtually every household had firearms of some nature. It's just that they were so rarely used on humans.

This was not the first time the Casselmans had dealt with the dark cloud of such a threat. A few years earlier in another area of the U.P., he had defended an Indian accused of murdering five family members. Vincent Loonsfoot had led law enforcement officers on an 11-day chase through the woods, barefoot and armed only with a knife. When he was arrested, he confessed. Casselman was hired as his attorney and his wife did the defense investigation.

"We get the ones where there's no hope in hell," Casselman said later.

Casselman battled and drew the wrath of those who preferred that the defendant be strung up from the nearest tree. Death threats came and deputies scanned spectators with metal detectors. The Casselmans, however, were concerned with weapons the metal detectors might not pick up, such as crossbows.

In the Moilanen trial as with the Loonsfoot trial, they took personal protection a step further. Rhonda Casselman, being a licensed private investigator, was also licensed to carry a concealed weapon. And she could shoot, on one occasion downing an antelope at 1,500 yards.

For the duration of the proceedings, Rhonda Casselman had a handgun in her purse. And Tom Casselman never used a public restroom. In fact, he never used any facility without being accompanied by a sheriff's deputy.

◆   ◆   ◆

Roy Gotham was constantly impressing upon the jury the importance of avoiding outside influences, such as the media, when away from the courtroom. His vigilance had intensified on the second day of jury selection when the *Ontonagon Herald* carried a story that stated in part:

> *Police arrested Moilanen April 24 for the murder and that same weekend he confessed to the murder.*

Indeed, a prospective juror incurred Gotham's wrath when she admitted she had read the *Herald* story.

"I thought I told you not to," Gotham said.

"It was on the front page…"

"You're excused ma'am."

After she left, he said: "A juror must be excused if I can't be confident that they will abide by the instructions of the court. I've likened this situation…to an operating room where we must maintain a sanitary, germ-free environment."

The trial led Marquette's Channel 6 news each night and both daily papers in the area, Houghton and Ironwood, carried it at the top of their front pages. Jurors had to virtually crawl into a hole to avoid news reports or conversation about the trial, because the topic was hot enough to thaw the icebergs forming at the edge of Lake Superior.

Indeed, at one point in the trial, Gotham mandated that jurors and spectators would not mingle in the Ontonagon County Courthouse's narrow hallways. On departure, for example, jurors would clear the building before spectators could leave the courtroom.

Gotham was particularly stern as Day Three was about to begin, because it was Monday and jurors had been away for the weekend. The 14 jurors shook their heads when he asked if anyone had heard anything about the case.

What the jurors were about to hear about was money, because Beth Paczesny had a succession of bank employees and insurance representatives to parade to the stand. First, however, Dr. Stephen Cohle, the forensic pathologist from Grand Rapids, was called upon. The prosecution needed to fortify its position on entrance and exit wounds in light of its disagreement with Castilla's autopsy report. Cohle had probably examined more gunshot wounds than all of the medical examiners in the Upper Peninsula combined.

Cohle, when originally consulted, had been asked only about entrance and exit wounds, but Castilla's testimony was gnawing at the prosecution. At dinner the previous night, Paczesny and Ball had discussed with him time of death. They gave him parameters based on what the investigation had uncovered.

Paczesny established his qualifications and launched into a discussion of how time of death could be established.

"Well," Cohle said, "there is no precise way to tell time of death unless there's a reliable witness that saw it. So what I do is take the window of time...during which the person might have died. And this is defined by when the person was last seen alive and when the person was found dead."

The time of death, the window in this case, was between approximately 1:15 and 5. The onset of *rigor mortis* having been noted at 5:30 or 6, Cohle said the time of death was likely between the opening of the window at 1:15 and 3. Further, the 30-degree temperature would inhibit the onset of *rigor mortis* and likely make the time of death earlier than 3.

The jury, to Paczesny's relief, now had heard an experienced forensic pathologist meticulously place the time of death and, likely, erase the confusion created by Castilla's testimony. That accomplished, the prosecutor could move on to the wounds themselves.

Cohle went through a detailed explanation of the characteristics of entrance and exit wounds, describing their affect on clothing as well as body tissues. Paczesny asked Cohle about the protruding tissue from the entrance wound. If she didn't, Casselman would. It was Cohle's understanding that the tissue had been pulled out when clothing was removed. There was no question in his mind that entrance was from the front.

The prosecution had gotten an almost professorial buttressing of its stance on the wounds and time of death. Cohle even ruled out the possibility the bullet was a ricochet.

Casselman came out smoking, asking about a wide variety of manners in which time of death could be ascertained. He was hauling around Werner Spitz's book, "Medical-Legal Investigation of Death," and he had done his homework. He asked about the examination of stomach contents, tests on body temperature, chemical analysis, conjunctiva of the eyes. None of these methods had been employed, partially because such sophisticated techniques were not available in a rural county and partially because the death was being considered a hunting accident at the time of the autopsy.

Since none of these more sophisticated tests had been performed, dialogue involving what they may or may not prove was almost moot. However, Casselman took the opportunity to attempt to discredit the prosecution's version of when the death had occurred. He had to create reasonable doubt that it had happened in the 2 to 2:15 time span.

Taking a different tack, he elicited testimony that Cohle had had dinner the previous night with Paczesny and Ball. He colored it as a suggestion of intimacy between the prosecution and witness…and a chance maybe to rehearse.

"Prior to last night," the attorney said, "you've not been asked to discuss time of death, have you?"

"No sir," Cohle said. "I had not."

Casselman hammered at this dinner conversation, suggesting, not in so many words, that it was testimony of convenience, concocted some-where between the salad and the entrée, to support the prosecution's version of what happened Nov. 29, 1992…and when.

"Do you have an estimate of your fees?" Casselman asked later.

"It will probably be around $700," Cohle said.

"Transportation?"

"That's been paid for."

This, of course, is a commonplace defense tactic, making an expert witness look like a hired gun. What's more, through all of the tedious and technical questioning of Cohle, Casselman had a letter in front of him. It was the one Cohle had written to Ball in August rendering his opinions as to entrance and exit wounds.

"Please be aware," the letter said, "that if you need a consultation on a case and money is not available for a consultation fee, I will do it gratis. You're on my good list."

Casselman looked down at the letter and then up at Cohle. He wanted to plant the notion in the jurors' minds that this was a buddy-

buddy type of thing, Cohle willing to testify to whatever Ball suggested would work for the prosecution…for free.

"Why are you willing to do consultations for him free?" Casselman asked.

"Because what I was asked to do," Cohle responded, "was look at some photographs and give an opinion as to which was the entry and which was the exit. It did not take much time, and I don't have a problem doing that for individuals, especially if I know them and know that they won't waste my time."

"You would do consultation for him if there was no money available for free because you're on my good list, right?"

"That's right."

◆   ◆   ◆

In spite of Casselman's lengthy and technical cross-examination, Paczesny felt she had reinforced the pathological side of the case. She was ready to go to bankers and insurance agents for financial motives.

Robin Bartanen, benefits manager from Marquette General Hospital, testified to $20,000 in life insurance with an additional $20,000 for accidental death. She also told of Judy's tax-deferred annuity, which had been at $18,000 before the withdrawal was made to pay for the van the Moilanens drove to Ontonagon that Thanksgiving weekend.

Bruce Moilanen, she said, came by her office to fill out the paperwork to make the claim on the life insurance not long after Judy's death. Bartanen testified that Moilanen had completed the paperwork on Dec. 18.

"Dec. 18?" Casselman said.

"Correct," Bartanen said.

"Would you say that he had rushed in?" Casselman said with a trace of sarcasm.

"No."

Cheryl Houle, the assistant manager at Marquette First Bank, testi-fied that Moilanen had come into the bank on Dec. 15, 1992 to pay off a loan. He also inquired about $1,000 in life insurance Judy had because of her membership in the credit union through Marquette General. That policy represented the "odd" $1,000 in the $321,000 total investigators had settled on.

Ogden Johnson told of how Moilanen beefed up Judy's insurance with Lutheran Brotherhood from $40,000 to $80,000 in 1991, then lowered it back to $60,000 in March of 1992.

"He said he couldn't afford it," Johnson said, "because money was too tight."

Moilanen saved all of $54 in annual premium cost, lowering it from $870 to $816.

John Evans had a tale to tell about how Moilanen saved money on insurance premiums with the Northwestern Mutual. He detailed the two $75,000 policies and the two $70,000 policies through Big Creek Kennels, in each case one on each of the Moilanens. All were put in place just before the chimney block incident, but the jury had not heard anything about that…and might not.

"Did anything happen to the defendant's policies before his wife's death?" Paczesny asked.

"Yes, the policies lapsed for nonpayment of premium."

"What about his wife's policies?" Paczesny continued. "I assume they lapsed at the same time."

"They did not."

"They continued to be paid?"

It was Paczesny's turn to look at the jury with a look of disbelief on her face.

"That's correct," Evans said. "I called on several occasions and left messages on his answering machine. Mr. Moilanen finally sent in a check, but the check was dishonored."

"So the check bounced?"

"Correct."

20

The Pest

Roy Gotham advised the jurors that they could sleep late the next morning…Day Four, Dec. 7. They did not have to be there until 10 a.m. Gotham offered no further explanation. Proceedings would begin at 9, as usual, when the attorneys would argue the admissibility of Jon Lyle's identification of Bruce Moilanen.

Bob Ball took the stand and told of Det. Lt. Goad's diligence in scanning months and months of Action Shoppers in search of classified advertisements for 30 caliber rifles…the right 30 caliber rifle. The Savage 110 on Moilanen's list of assets had to come from somewhere and someone, and Moilanen himself had revealed that he had answered an ad in the Action Shopper.

Bruce Moilanen and Richard Goad both responded to Jon Lyle's ad, Goad, of course, long after the paper had started to turn yellow.

Matter-of-factly, Ball explained that Jon Lyle had identified Moilanen, tentatively from pictures and positively in person when Moilanen was brought to the court to be arraigned on new charges stemming from his July 31 escape.

"Lyle was so positive," Ball told Gotham, "that he said he was very uneasy just being in the same room with him."

Paczesny had orchestrated a melodious version of the identification of Jon Lyle. Casselman was ready to rock 'n' roll with his cross-examination.

Jon Lyle had been shown pictures of how many subjects?
Just Bruce Moilanen?
Casselman's voice took on an edge of incredulity.

Bruce Moilanen was not in a lineup with other subjects for this in person identification? He was in a courtroom where he was obviously a subject in custody? And this identification was being made without any discussion with me?

Casselman's voice was almost cracking with disbelief.

And this man knew he was being asked to identify a man accused of homicide?

"I believe it's only common courtesy," Ball explained. "Number one, I do share some information with people when they're assisting me. Number two, I wanted him to realize the importance of this so he didn't shove this thing off as something that was insignificant."

Through both his tone of voice and a succession of questions suggesting he did not believe what he was hearing, Casselman underscored his contention that the identification had been established in an underhanded and illegal manner.

"Through my training and my past knowledge," Ball said, "this situation we had here, having Mr. Lyle just identify a party that he made a transaction with, is quite different than having Mr. Lyle identify an individual he saw committing a crime. If I'm wrong, then I'll be corrected by the court, I'm sure. But I felt okay at the time."

Jon Lyle took the stand after Ball. He was an account executive for Action Shopper advertising and somewhat of an Exhibit A for the effectiveness of the product he was selling. He was a sincere young man who could not have known *his* Savage 110 would become a pivotal issue in a murder case.

Lyle's version of the transactions was different from Moilanen's in terms of location. He said the gun had been sold at his apartment, because the party making the purchase commented on his bear skin rug. He explained that he was discounting the price because of the damage the bear had done to the gun's stock.

"Lt. Goad pulled pictures out of a photo envelope," Lyle said, "and showed me a whole bunch."

Later, Casselman would gain the concession that every picture in the envelope was of his client.

"I told him I'd be more comfortable if I could see him," Lyle explained.

And that was arranged.

"I came to Ontonagon to the courthouse," he said, "and he came walking through the door and right away the hair on the back of my neck stood up. I recognized him as soon as he walked through the door."

Casselman again went through a litany of questions designed to reinforce his point that the identification had been illegally obtained. For his purposes, that was much more important than whether the transaction had taken place between his client and Jon Lyle.

"What was it Det. Ball told you about this case?" he asked.

"He explained it was a murder case, not an accident," Lyle said. "He said a man's wife had been shot and killed and they had reason to believe he may have bought the weapon from me. He was trying to find out by questioning me whether or not it may have been this person."

When Ball and Lyle were finished testifying, not a person in the room doubted that Bruce Moilanen had purchased a Savage 110 from Jon Lyle. Of course, the jury box was empty. Jurors had heard none of this and Judge Roy Gotham was to decide if they ever would.

When the jury returned, Jon Lyle was called to the witness stand. His testimony was brief. He had run an advertisement to sell a Savage 110 in the Action Shopper. A person had answered that ad and bought the gun. Jon Lyle was excused.

Jurors looked bewildered.

Had they missed something? This guy had driven over from Marquette to sit in a Circuit Courtroom and testify that he had sold a gun? Why had questioning been so brief? Was that really all there was?

Judge Roy Gotham had ruled that the one-man photo identification and one-man courtroom identification were "impermissibly suggestive," also noting that Casselman should have been present on behalf of his client. The jury would not hear Jon Lyle's identification of Bruce Moilanen.

"That was a hard-fought contest," Casselman said to his wife. "If we lose that, the ballgame's over."

♦   ♦   ♦

Mike Fedrizzi and Kim Hall, both with First National Bank of Marquette, delivered very matter-of-fact testimony about the Moilanens' financial status, which seemed relatively untroubled entering 1992. There had been delinquencies, many apparently, but the Moilanens had obtained and, eventually, paid off 15 loans with their institution.

The key to their appearances was not what was said, but what was admitted into evidence. When Bruce Moilanen was attempting to refinance the house in spring of 1992, he had submitted that typewritten list of assets to go with the loan package. He had listed a Savage 110, valued at $300, as part of $20,700 in assets.

All of the papers associated with that loan application were submitted as evidence. The list of assets was mentioned in testimony, but not specifically as to its contents. That would come later.

♦   ♦   ♦

Lee Anne Daniels Wysocki stepped to the witness stand. Her voice was soft, difficult to hear beyond the front of the courtroom. During her testimony, she purposefully looked from the witness stand toward Moilanen. He never looked in her direction, as though ignoring her presence in the room.

Lee Anne was Judy's friend, her neighbor when they were preschoolers and her chum until college took them separate ways. Judy had gotten them back together by getting Lee Anne a job at Marquette General Hospital.

The jury heard how Judy had always been such a friend for Lee Anne and it also heard how Bruce had always made her so uncomfortable, sarcastically cutting her down. She had ignored his taunts in the interest of sustaining her friendship with Judy.

Bruce changed.

"After Judy's funeral," Lee Anne said softly, "Bruce started calling and coming over to my home to visit, and coming over and visiting and talking, shoveling my driveway, sending me flowers."

Bruce shoveled her walk and took her for pizza and sat and talked…and used her telephone. Her daughter had lost her key so Lee Anne was leaving the apartment unlocked, which is not that uncommon anyway in the U.P.

"Bruce started walking in like he owned the place," Wysocki said.

And less than a month after Judy's death?

"He asked me if we could ever be more than just friends," Lee Anne said, a distasteful look on her face. "I told him, 'No, our lifestyles are too different.'"

It had been a gentle putdown. As obnoxious as he might have been, he was still her best friend's husband and she felt sympathy toward him. And he played very well with sympathy.

Lee Anne talked about the conversation they had at the Pizza Hut, where Moilanen was describing, essentially, how random the shot had to be because it would have taken such a perfect marksman to shoot Judy where she had been shot. This was the time when he drew a chart and stood up to imitate the arm-swing of a person taking a walk.

Paczesny was doing her direct examination and this woman had had direct and candid conversations with the defendant. He had been more guarded with Judy's family, but he wasn't trying to impress Judy's family.

"Did he talk about life insurance?" Paczesny asked.

"He talked about being a single parent living on one income," Wysocki said. "He talked about his policies. He hadn't gotten them yet, but he talked about what they had. I don't remember the numbers, but I do remember I couldn't imagine anyone having that much life insurance."

The family had been hearing all along about how modestly Judy was insured, but Moilanen would use the "wealth" he had coming when he was trying to buy friendship...and love. He never actually said the word "sex," but the "more than friends" question rather strongly implied what he had in mind.

Casselman stood to cross-examine.

"Was it unreasonable," Casselman asked, "for his knowing your relationship to his wife as good friends to try to console you?"

"Bruce? No."

"It was not reasonable?"

"Not Bruce."

"Did you encourage Mr. Moilanen?" he asked at one point.

"To be friends, yes," she said, "but not more than friends. When he was visiting and he tried to put his arm around me, I *did not* like that."

"You didn't like the flowers?"

"No."

The same question would come back in a different form. Casselman had to find a way to portray *her* as a woman with designs on his client. It would be tough sledding because Wysocki was very firm in her recollections and steadfast in where her feelings had been.

"I did not encourage him," she said. "I wanted to be there for Elise...because of Judy."

And it had struck her as odd that Judy was somehow missing from this friendship.

"I had to bring up Judy's name," she said, "or it never came up."

Casselman, surprisingly, brought up the issue of sex.

"More than just friends," she said, "could mean that."

And now the defense attorney would switch directions. He asked about Det. Ball. If he could not portray her as a designing woman, maybe he could weaken her testimony by making her look like a conniving woman who became a pawn for the State Police.

"He wanted you to get information for him, true?" Casselman said.

"I didn't do it at the request of the police," she said. "There were things I myself wanted to know. Right from the beginning, I had doubts. Right from the beginning, I kept a notebook because I didn't trust him."

Wysocki explained that she made copies of her notes and turned the originals over to Det. Ball.

"Have you reviewed your notes?"

"I got past the first page," she said, "and then it was just too painful to keep reading."

Casselman recalled the conversations between Wysocki and Moilanen about the financial travails inherent with single parenthood and touched upon earlier testimony. Wysocki had told Paczesny that Bruce had proposed that she and her daughter move in with he and Elise. The defense attorney suggested that this was simply a thoughtful and kind gesture.

"I had never known Bruce Moilanen to be kind," Lee Anne Wysocki said. "Right from the beginning, I thought he was trying to buy friendship."

She was looking directly at the defendant. He was writing on a legal pad, as if disinterested in what had been said.

◆　　　◆　　　◆

Gayle Lampinen's face was unfamiliar in Ontonagon and even her name might go unrecognized. However, The Sweater Letter and its contents had been conversational grist for months. Court groupies would get their first look at this woman who had received the letter that triggered the ultimate downfall of Bruce Moilanen. It was as though all of Ontonagon would see her through their eyes.

Obviously, this 36-year-old woman was no vamp. She had a demure, almost pixyish, look. Her frosted blond hair was trimmed functionally short, as if she was much too busy to worry about fussing with gadgets such as curling irons. It would have been easy to imagine a mischievous twinkle in her eyes on any occasion other than this, when her eyes were wary and her jaw firmly set.

At one point in her testimony, Casselman would call her Stony Face.

Paczesny, of course, examined her first and quickly worked her way into Lampinen's relationship with Moilanen.

"He was more…my husband I considered him…"

She seemed to be looking for the right word.

"…basically a pest."

Her testimony was vague as to dates but specific as to conversations during the early months, when Bruce was calling her at work and stopping in her office and calling her at home. She remembered what he was telling her about Judy leaving him and running up credit cards and running off with money, but not exactly when he was saying it.

"Did he ever talk to you about his marital situation?"

"That first summer, I believe it was in '91," Gayle said, "he told myself and the girls in my office that he was getting a divorce."

Beginning with early December of 1992, Lampinen became very specific as to dates. Det. Ball had visited her and her husband Paul and they had begun noting times and dates and places. Bruce helped them, to be sure, by corresponding so openly, though none of the letters or notes were addressed to Paul.

Gayle recalled reading in the newspaper about a Judy Moilanen being shot in a hunting accident, but being unsure if she was related to Bruce.

"I didn't know until I read the full article. I didn't know if that was his wife or not, because I had met her only on one occasion."

Paczesny let this statement lead her to The Sweater Letter, formally Exhibit No. 30, the one "Judes" had purportedly written to Gayle back in June. Gayle testified to her surprise at receiving both the letter and the clothes. She had met Judy so briefly she could hardly be considered as much as an acquaintance.

Gayle's first name was spelled G-A-Y-L-E rather than the more common G-A-I-L.

"I didn't feel Judy would know how to spell my name correctly," Gayle said.

Paczesny was now going letter-by-letter and card-by-card, Gayle would verify their authenticity and Paczesny would submit them as evidence. Everything she received, she said, including the boxes of clothes, had gone to Det. Ball. All but the Teddy bears. She returned them to Moilanen along with the only letter she ever wrote him.

The Good-Bye Letter.

Strangely, the prosecution did not press Lampinen to testify as to the contents of the letters. They lay there on the clerk's desk like unopened mail.

When Casselman stood to cross-examine, he would attack Lampinen as he attacked Wysocki. Her complicity with the police, he would maintain, was a betrayal of a friend.

"You've told us," Casselman said, "that for four months, regularly, repeatedly, daily, this man was either calling there or delivering something to you, gestures or gifts. And each time he did so, you told him in effect to take a hike?"

"No," she said, "I was nice to him."

"Was that because you were friends?"

"No, it was because I'm a nice person."

Casselman gained Gayle's admission that she had not told Bruce she was forwarding his correspondence to the police, a continuing suggestion of complicity…and secrecy.

"You were hiding from your friend a secret?" Casselman said.

"Keep in mind," Gayle corrected, "he was not my friend."

"There's a distinct difference between your being friendly and considering him a friend?"

"Yes, there is."

"You did not discourage him?"

"I listened to him."

Lampinen had testified that Moilanen was down in the dumps when he talked to her on the telephone after his wife's death. That call was followed shortly thereafter by lunch in Chassell, after which Bruce delivered five boxes of clothes…and The Sweater Letter.

"He was different than I expected at lunch from the phone call that I had the night before," Lampinen said. "He was happy, in a good mood. He was talking and joking and saying he was going to retiring June 1."

"He said he was retiring? What were his words?"

"He said he was retiring from Marquette General June 1."

"Did you ask why?"

"No."

Casselman too would take Lampinen through each meeting, each telephone conversation. He would attempt to twist what was said to a more favorable light. He had to change the characterization of what Moilanen sought from the relationship.

However, during Gayle Lampinen's testimony, Bruce Moilanen himself betrayed what *his* feelings really were.

Moilanen had been so unemotional during the proceedings that it was almost as though he wasn't there or wasn't hearing what was being said. As Lampinen testified, his jaw noticeably tightened. He was suddenly fighting emotion. Soon, he was sobbing uncontrollably. The whole courtroom watched as his shoulders quivered and he looked to a deputy for tissue.

If Gayle Lampinen noticed, she did not let on. Unlike Lee Anne, she seemed to be avoiding looking at the defendant.

Tom Casselman also noticed. And he was not happy with what he was seeing.

When Gotham called for a recess, Casselman and Moilanen retreated to the law library. He had an annoyed look on his face as the door shut.

"What the hell are you doing?" he demanded.

Moilanen said nothing.

"Are you're crying because your wife is dead or are you crying because you love this woman?" he said, his voice rising. "I'll tell you, if you're crying for your wife, forget it. She's dead and she ain't coming back. If you're crying for this woman, forget that too because she's trying to bury you. I'm trying to pound the crap out of this *girlfriend* who isn't a girlfriend and you're making a liar out of me."

Moilanen glowered.

"Understand?"

Moilanen nodded.

"I want to see no more emotion. *None.*"

Day Four ended with The Sweater Lady on the witness stand.

◆   ◆   ◆

Day Five, Dec. 8, began with The Sweater Lady on the witness stand.

Tom Casselman had copies of the letters and cards Bruce had sent Gayle. He knew there were things written that would cast his client in a better light. He would focus on the warmth and love he had expressed for Judy.

The Jan. 20 letter—the "I Love You" letter—had made her uneasy.

"The contents of the letter bothered me," she said.

Casselman scoffed at the notion that the letter represented a romantic overture. His interpretation was that Bruce was expressing value for the friendship, apologies for being a nuisance and generally offering to be there for her—and Paul—should they ever need him. If it was warm, he was saying, it was warm in a most platonic way.

"That's what the letter says," Gayle said, glaring, "according to your words."

Gayle had a copy of the nine-page letter written Feb. 28, 1993 and Casselman was directing her to what he wanted read. He would read a little bit and look up, waiting for her to pick up on the next words.

"Even while I sit here," Casselman read, *"I just can't believe how much…"*

He looked up.

"I loved her," Gayle read.

Casselman continued: *"It's like a big piece of me was removed & the door has been slammed shut."*

Casselman was smart. This nine-page letter, written in the wee hours of the morning, rambled so much that it represented a veritable buffet. The prosecution could nibble what it chose to nibble and the defense could do the same.

Ms. Lampinen was asked to read from Page Three…

"Even though I came from a basic broken home, my Dad kind of taught me all women should be treated like ladies, no matter what. Maybe that is why I do some of the things I do. A card here, flowers there, a touch of a hand, a hug. Nothing too costly or emotionally expensive."

Casselman went through a touching segment where Moilanen was writing about how he would get up an hour before either he or Judy had to leave for work, put the coffee on and then return to bed to snuggle. He hit repeatedly at points where Moilanen was warm and fuzzy toward Judy, using Gayle to underscore that he had expressed all these feelings toward his late wife in correspondence with a woman portrayed by the prosecution as an obsession to him and, thus, a motive for murder.

A "different" Bruce Moilanen was emerging as Casselman continued the most lengthy cross-examination of the trial, at least until Bob Ball was on the stand.

At one point in that Feb. 28 letter, Moilanen had written: *"Well, Sassy* [one of the dogs] *just jumped up on the couch. She has been a good partner through all this, but that's animals' unconditional love. You feed me and I love you."*

The gaunt man at the defense table, who had broken down so inconsolably the previous day, was suddenly looking like a man who had loved his wife so very deeply, treated women in general as treasures, valued the reciprocal love of animals and appreciated Gayle Lampinen…as a friend.

Casselman came to the end of that letter. He had already taken Lampinen through Moilanen's description of his perfect woman, which happened to fit her perfectly, and submitted that this could be taken as innocently flattering as opposed to suggestively predatory. Gayle had the last page in hand and was, as usual, warily eyeing the defense attorney.

"*Gayle,*" she read, "*sometimes I feel wrong about talking to you about my problems, but right now you're kind of the only thing I have in someone to trust. So maybe the wrong thing is better than nothing. Sometimes I feel as though I'm clinging to you and that's not right. But if you let me hold on for a little while, 'Till I get through this,' I promise not to hold too tight. If at any time this is or becomes uncomfortable to you, just say so & I won't bother you again.*"

Casselman was hammering on his point that Moilanen's intentions were innocent. He asked Gayle to read from a card she received with flowers on Valentine's Day.

"Nothing more than friends…Thanks…I hope you enjoy these."

Casselman wanted to make Gayle Lampinen look like an unfeeling accomplice to the investigation. He expressed disbelief that she had allowed the unwanted attention to continue, then nodded his head as if to acknowledge that he understood that Det. Ball was at the root of this "encouragement."

"We didn't encourage him," Lampinen said firmly. "We never invited him. He just came or called. We never made him welcome."

Tom Casselman did not choose to deeply pursue The Sweater Letter, wary perhaps of its potential to be a minefield. He had asked Lampinen what she thought Moilanen had meant by what was said in other letters, but not this one. He got to it out of sequence, near the end of his cross-examination, and pulled up short of the post-script. The impression he conveyed was that "Judes" could well have been the writer, not Bruce.

Beth Paczesny went right to The Sweater Letter's P.S. in her re-direct of Gayle Lampinen, who had become a pivotal witness as to both Moilanen's romantic intentions as well as impending wealth. Ironically, Casselman had elicited testimony on the exact figures contained in the letter of Feb. 28. Her testimony had struck at two emotions…greed and lust.

"There is a part of this exhibit that Mr. Casselman didn't question you about?" Paczesny asked.

"Yes."

"What part is that?"

"The P.S. on the bottom of the letter."

"What does it say?"

"P.S., "Lampinen said, reading from The Sweater Letter's postscript, *"don't tell the prospects, but believe it or not he's incredible in the sack."*

"Did that give you a sexual connotation?"

"It would. Yes."

Intending to erase any possible doubts about The Sweater Letter's author, Paczesny had Gayle note the salutations on Moilanen's correspondence. In each case, the word "Gayle" was followed by a colon. She might also have noted that Moilanen never spelled out the word "and" in any of his letters, using an ampersand instead. The Sweater Letter was consistent with this quirk as well.

Paczesny also went back to the Feb. 28 letter, in which Moilanen had written about his wealth. She wanted to make the point that Moilanen had gone from his "bragging" about assets into his description of his idea of the perfect woman, establishing through Gayle's answers to a succession of questions that she fit Moilanen's description of his perfect woman.

By the time prosecutor and defense attorney were finished with Gayle Lampinen, the jury was left to decide exactly what this man was all about. Jurors could come away with the impression that this was a perfect and loving husband who appreciated his friendship with Gayle Lampinen. Or they could come away with the impression that this was a conniving man who attempted to represent himself as a perfect and loving husband to entice this woman into becoming more than just a friend…and using his "wealth" as part of that strategy.

Was this man innocent in his friendship and maybe, just maybe, equally innocent of the charges against him? Or was he a predator who had murdered one woman, his wife, while stalking another?

Gayle Lampinen was on the stand for four hours and 47 minutes.

◆   ◆   ◆

Paul Lampinen followed his wife to the stand. He was a comfortable witness, open-faced and affable. He was Smiley Face to his wife's Stony Face, though Casselman never bestowed him with a nickname. In contrast to Gayle's wariness, Paul seemed eager and willing to help.

Lampinen talked of how he had met Moilanen and remembered that he had hired him a few years ago to appraise a car. And he talked about visits, such as the time in the summer of 1992 when Moilanen invited him on an upcoming hunting trip—all expenses paid—and left him an itinerary. Paczesny had Lampinen describe three pages of North Country Claims Service stationery Moilanen left with him in the summer of 1992.

"Some of it is an itinerary," Paul said. "The first page is a description of how to mix a certain product that he told me eliminates the scent of a person while he's deer hunting. He was going to try to market it."

This was a meaningful aside, because the prosecution did not know what the defense had in mind in terms of exactly what the five dogs had been doing when Moilanen purportedly pulled the trigger in the woods along Cherry Lane. This planted the possibility that he was wearing this "product" to eliminate his scent and raised the possibility that they were unaware of his presence. Little things can build up in a circumstantial case.

Moilanen visited Lampinen at his bank in Baraga in mid-October in search of a loan.

"He told me he'd been turned down by GMAC," Lampinen said, "because his wife had run the credit cards to the max and she was late with loan payments, and he was turned down for that reason. I told him he was out of our lending area."

How did Lampinen handle these visits to his office?

"There were times where I had to put him off," he said. "He would call and I would instruct the girls that I am busy, that I did not have time to talk. He would call again. He was awful annoying and pesty."

Paczesny eventually worked her way to The Sweater Letter. Paul had taken the letter as well as the five boxes of clothing to his office, where he turned them over to Bob Ball.

"What did you think about that P.S.?" Paczesny asked. "About him being incredible in the sack?"

"He's good," Paul Lampinen smiled.

The room twittered with amusement for one of the very rare times in this trial, probably for the first time since Marie Lyons described how she was hitchhiking to the Candlelight to hear Russell Reid play his violin.

It was a measure of Paul Lampinen's security in his relationship with Gayle that he could make light of such a suggestive postscript.

◆   ◆   ◆

The Sweater Letter was about to hit the jury in the face. Paczesny put it on a screen and called to the stand Lt. James Steggell, a document examiner from the Bridgeport State Police Crime Laboratory. Steggell was an expert in handwriting analysis as well as indented writing, the science of reading what had been written on the sheet *above* a piece of paper he was examining.

Det. Sgt. Ball had sent Steggell samples of the known writing of both Bruce and Judy…and also The Sweater Letter. The authorship of The Sweater Letter was indicated to Steggell as unknown.

"Did you find matches with Judy's known writing?" Paczesny asked.

"I found no handwriting habits to match," Steggell said, nodding at The Sweater Letter behind him and to the right on the screen. "It's my opinion that she did not author the letter."

"Did you find matches with Bruce's known?"

"It's my opinion that the name 'Judes' on the bottom was in fact written by Bruce Moilanen," Steggell said. "I found many, many similarities in the body of the letter which indicate he could have written it. I found nothing to indicate he did not write the letter. There were one or two letters I could not resolve with his known writing."

"Why would that be?"

"The individual could be attempting to disguise the questioned writing."

Paczesny led him into a discussion of indented writing and he pointed to The Sweater Letter's beginning: *"Gayle: These are for you..."*

The sheet above, Steggell testified, began: *"Gayle: These sweaters..."* And stopped right there, obviously to be discarded as a false start of sorts.

"Did Judy write that?" Paczesny asked.

"It's my opinion Judy did not write those impressions."

"Did Bruce?"

"The impression of 'Gayle' and 'these sweaters' was consistent with the writing on this letter," Steggell said.

Casselman would attack the credibility of Steggell's analysis.

"We're talking art, true?" he asked.

"Art based on scientific guidelines," Steggell said.

"Art requiring interpretation, true?"

He was pounding away at reasonable doubt and his clear intention was to create an impression that Lt. Steggell's testimony was subjective rather than objective. His client might have written The Sweater Letter, but then again maybe he didn't.

The biggest problem for the defense was that Lt. James Steggell was steadfast about one conclusion, that being that Bruce Moilanen had written the word "Judes" at the bottom of the letter.

◆   ◆   ◆

"Amateur" witnesses such as Mary Ann Blake, Jerry Schoch and Gayle Lampinen testified as though in conversation with either Paczesny or Casselman. They looked at the attorney asking them the question and looked at the attorney as they delivered their responses, only occasionally letting their eyes look elsewhere. It was usually a case of their eyes wandering elsewhere rather than focusing elsewhere.

Expert witnesses took their questions from the attorneys and then turned to the jurors. These were, to be sure, the people they were addressing.

The next expert witness was Lt. Chuck Allen, who had come from downstate to administer the polygraph test on April 23, 1993. The jury, of course, would not know that this was a polygraphist in front of them. To them, he was another cop interviewing Bruce Moilanen.

Beth Paczesny knew there was no way she could introduce the fact that the defendant had flunked a polygraph test, unless Casselman made a monstrous mistake on his cross-examination. She also knew there was no way an attorney of Casselman's skill and experience would make such a mistake.

Allen detailed the basic background of the early stages of his interview with Moilanen and got to the point where he was laying out information uncovered by the investigation. He could not say Moilanen's responses were being charted and so it might have come as a surprise to the jury when he divulged the conclusion he reached.

"I told him I thought he had shot his wife," Allen told Paczesny.

Allen told of asking Moilanen whether it had been deliberate and sparring back and forth over whether an attorney should be present. He said he offered a chance to call an attorney, but Moilanen eventually declined.

"He said, 'I'll go ahead, it wasn't deliberate,'" Allen said.

Allen had not revealed that the bullet had been found, so he tested Moilanen's knowledge of The Marble Man's discovery.

"I asked him if he knew that they had a bullet," Allen said, "and he told me, 'No, just fragments.' And he chuckled about that."

The jury had now heard testimony from a witness who said Moilanen told him he had shot his wife, but not deliberately. It was somewhat of an admission as well as a denial. However, it also heard about this "chuckle" over the perceived absence of the bullet, a wordlessly incongruous reaction in the midst of a seeming insistence that Judy Moilanen's death had been accidental…albeit at her husband's hands.

Tom Casselman had to tiptoe through the minefield of procedure without letting the jury get a hint that this was a polygraph test rather than a mere interview.

"Was this interview recorded?" he asked.

"State Police policy would not allow recording," Allen said.

"So Det. Ball sat in a separate room and took notes off a television monitor?"

"That's correct, sir."

"But you *could* record Det. Ball when he took over?"

"I had to find a tape-recorder," Allen said, "but, yes, I could record Det. Ball's interview."

In different circumstances, Casselman might have had fun with Allen's recording of Ball's interview with Moilanen. Allen had to admit that he had trouble with dead batteries and pushed wrong buttons and came up with a rather disjointed tape of Ball talking with his client. Casselman was sternly portraying both interviews as exercises in incompetence, hardly worthy of consideration when it came time to consider the merits of the prosecution's case.

If the jury could be persuaded that the events of April 23, 1993 were one nightmarish boondoggle for his client, Tom Casselman just might be able to set his client free to hunt again.

21

Forgiveness…and Accountability

Det. Sgt. Bob Ball had nothing but respect for Tom Casselman, though they had never met head-to-head in the course of a trial. Ball had had one previous case in which Casselman was defending a marijuana grower who had been arrested with 3,000 plants on his farm. Casselman pled him guilty.

"I know where's he's going to be coming from," Ball said. "He has a history of attacking the police in the courtroom. He'll do what he has to do to try and do his job."

Ball stepped to the witness stand at 3:14 p.m. on Dec. 8…Day Five. Courtroom groupies expected fireworks, but they were not likely to get them. The detective was too experienced to let the attorney rattle him.

In the preliminary hearing, which served as sort of a dress rehearsal, Casselman had questioned his presence in the morgue the night of the killing. Paczesny set Ball up with an opportunity to pre-empt such a query.

"I had a 35 millimeter camera," Ball said, "and I took it into the morgue with me."

"Why did you do that?" Paczesny asked.

"I was not familiar with Deputy Cousineau's abilities with a camera," Ball said, "and I felt confident that if I took some photographs I would have some pretty good evidence preserved. And I knew I couldn't be at the autopsy the next day. I knew Dr. Castilla did not take pictures. I've never seen him take photos."

What's more, Ball advised that Cousineau had not taken pictures that included miniature rulers to give reference to the size of things such as entry and exit wounds. He described these as "textbook" entrance and exit wounds.

"Did you prod or poke the wounds?"

"The only thing I did that would have caused any alteration of the wound whatsoever was when we moved the shirt to take a picture of the entrance wound," Ball said. "That caused a piece of tissue to come out onto the chest area. That is depicted in the photograph."

Ball detailed the testing done on the maple tree's graze mark to establish that it had been freshly struck by a bullet, Paczesny again letting that conclusion lead to another.

"Could this have been a ricochet that hit Judy?"

"The bullet passed through the body before it hit the tree," Ball said, almost yawningly matter-of-fact. "If it had hit the tree first, it would have been badly damaged on impact. It was in good condition when it entered the body."

Ball conceded that his first query in this or any other situation like it would be about the spouse.

"Standard operation procedure," he said. "The husband, you might say, is first on our list for elimination purposes. If we find out the husband was nowhere near and the woman has no known enemies, we know we have a scenario that's probably an accident."

That first meeting with the family that Sunday night, at least the men in the family, did not raise any red flags, although Ball testified that Moilanen appeared smug. However, he came away with the impression that all of the men, Bruce included, had been hunting together.

"At that point," Ball said, "we didn't have much reason to think it was anything other than an accident. I started receiving information the next day that caused me concern. I learned about Gayle Lampinen."

In these early stages of investigation, Ball explained that the focus was undergoing subtle changes. It was not so much that Moilanen was being isolated as a suspect, but rather that it was appearing less and less likely to be an accident.

"The height of the wounds, with the exit higher, indicated the bullet was possibly rising when it struck the victim," he explained, "as opposed to a long-range shot that would come lobbing in from out of the area."

Paczesny moved forward in tedious detail. She was presenting Exhibit A in the drudgery involved in police work. There were points, in fact, when eyelids drooped and heads nodded in the courtroom, including a bailiff behind Gotham's peripheral vision as the judge twisted in his chair to listen to the witness.

Ball was droning onward about the guns Moilanen had disclosed, the alibis he had provided, insurance policies he claimed not to have and the first search of his residence. Not even Ball's recounting of Dan Castle's method of finding the bullet seemed to renew interest. Ball had taken the witness stand late in what had been a long day of testimony. When the jurors too became noticeably lethargic, Gotham called it quits. It may have seemed that he was acknowledging their drowsiness, because he told them they could sleep late the next morning.

In truth, the court had other matters scheduled for first thing in the morning of Day Six. The admissibility of The Chimney Block Incident was on the docket.

◆   ◆   ◆

Tom Casselman was under the weather the morning of Dec. 9. This was understandable. Not only was the trial an emotional burden, but he and Rhonda were spending between four and five hours a day on the highway between Marquette and Ontonagon. They had chosen to commute rather than stay in the Ontonagon area.

During these drives, Rhonda updated her husband on the upcoming witnesses and what they might be expected to say. She prompted him with questions based on what her investigations had uncovered. No attorney likes surprises and Casselman's wife covered his backside figuratively as well as literally.

The Casselmans were lucky with the weather, encountering only two or three blizzards during the course of the trial. They were unlucky with what Casselman called suicidal deer, which are all over the roads in the U.P., especially after dark. The days were quite short in December and all of the Casselmans' driving was done in the dark. On one occasion, on the way to Ontonagon, Casselman clipped the third of three deer he was trying to avoid as they darted in front of him.

When he arrived in Ontonagon, he called the county and informed them of the deer's whereabouts. The meat would go to the needy.

Rhonda had been at her husband's side throughout the trial, sitting between him and the defendant. She fed him questions and passed him notes from Moilanen. During breaks, she often tied up the only pay telephone at the end of the hall on the second floor of the courthouse.

Mrs. Casselman's presence fascinated courtroom groupies, who were unaware of the significant role she played on the defense team. Each morning, they whispered among themselves about what Rhonda Casselman would be wearing until the law library door opened and she came out with maybe a clinging knit dress or short, pleated skirt.

One thing about Ms. Casselman became apparent as the trial wore on. She never smiled. Not once, at least in the courtroom. She was as rigid as a strict schoolmarm.

On the morning of Day Six, Rhonda Casselman's husband was equally unsmiling. His lower lip had a way of protruding in the manner of a pouting child. It would have supported a bald eagle's nest on this day as he took his place at the defense table.

◆   ◆   ◆

The jury box was empty and a television set, attached to a VCR, was in front of the courtroom. The bust of Oliver Wendell Holmes was looking down at it. The clock said 2:32, as always.

Det. Sgt. Bob Ball was called to the witness stand to begin the hearing. His recitation would be limited to the chimney block incident and would be heard without the jury present. This testimony was for the ears—and eyes—of Judge Roy Gotham alone.

Ball described how detectives and troopers had gone to Moilanen's house, with a search warrant, to conduct the chimney block experiment as well as look for a scaffold. Moilanen had at one point claimed the block fell off a collapsing scaffold and Casselman argued that such a scaffold existed near a shed behind the house.

Paczesny had been there at the time of the experiment, but Ball, the witness, would have to set up the specifics of what was being sought.

"We basically wanted to determine if, in fact, an 85-pound chimney block would slide from the roof or slip off or accidentally fall off the roof," Ball explained. "I did a number of things to try to determine this."

Casselman protested that the whole process had been clandestine in nature and violated his client's right to due process.

Nevertheless, the room was darkened and the television set turned on. The methodical description of what the deputies were doing was punctuated by the thump, thump, thump of Trooper Don Brown and, later, Ball himself jumping up and down on the roof next to the chimney blocks, proving conclusively that white man *can* jump. They noted that the vibrations could not budge the chimney blocks, but Gotham could see that for himself.

Nearing the end of the tape, Casselman abruptly got to his feet and went out the back door of the courtroom. Spectators were startled by this seeming brash exit, but Gotham knew the attorney was feeling ill. He declared a recess.

When the hearing reconvened, Gotham looked over the top of his glasses at Casselman.

"I trust your illness caused you to have to leave abruptly?" Gotham said.

"Well, I'd like to say it was the film content," the attorney said dryly. "But it wasn't."

The experimental portion of the videotape ended and the camera zoomed in on a scaffold, presumably *the* scaffold, near the shed. Ball pointed out that a leg was missing, but there were no nail holes to indicate it ever existed. They zoomed in with a 35mm camera and took color close-ups.

"Construction was never completed," he said. "Had it been completed, it could have been used. But it wasn't."

Casselman cross-examined Ball for 15 minutes and then objected again to the whole proceedings.

"Are we now going to have a second trial?" he asked.

Was this, in fact, a trial within a trial? There had been no charges filed at the time of the incident and no charges had been filed since, but Moilanen's role in the "falling" of the chimney block was certainly under scrutiny.

"This would require the defendant to give up either his right to speak or his right remain silent," Casselman said to Gotham. "So the accused, should you admit this material, is now confronted with which right do I give up."

The problem was that Bruce Moilanen could not be put on the witness stand to defend and explain his version of what happened on Sept. 23, 1991 without being exposed to Paczesny's questions relating to all that had happened since. Obviously, Casselman did not want his client on the witness stand.

Gotham was in a difficult position. If he was not careful, the prosecution could successfully portray Moilanen as a bad man in 1991 who, therefore, must have been a bad man in 1992. This, of course, was exactly what the prosecution believed and wished to convey.

The judge issued a carefully worded ruling that said, in essence, that the incident was admissible only in its most objective form. The prosecution could present the fact that it had happened and show the videotape of the experiment without elaboration. The jury would have to absorb what it heard and use what it concluded *only* if and when it got to the point where it was considering premeditation and intent. The chimney block incident could not be a consideration in the determination of guilt.

Casselman was baffled by the prosecution's insistence on introducing the chimney block incident and Gotham's decision to let it be introduced, albeit in a watered-down matter.

"I don't understand it," he muttered to his wife. "This case is so prosecutorially-sided, why take the risk of letting the brick incident be ammunition for appeal?"

◆   ◆   ◆

At 11:37 a.m., the jury was back and Bob Ball was talking about the investigation. The subject was the Dec. 11, 1992 interview with Moilanen.

"Bruce brought up an incident involving a chimney block," Ball said, "which he stated in September of the prior year had fallen off the roof and struck his wife on the head."

Ball did not go into much detail on the incident, relating it more to the Dec. 11 interview than to anything more ominous. He continued through that interview, explaining how Moilanen had been asked to disclose weapons that were or had been in his possession.

Ball had a screen over his right shoulder and Paczesny dimmed the lights and hit a switch. The list of assets submitted to First National Bank with a loan application was on the screen.

A Savage 110, Model 30 was highlighted.

"Why is that highlighted?" Paczesny asked.

"That was a gun which was not disclosed to me in the Dec. 11 interview," Ball said, "nor in any of the subsequent interviews prior to the confession."

This was the first time the jury had heard the word "confession" from a witness and Ball delivered it in such a routine fashion it was as if the existence of such a thing was understood.

"I gave that information to Lt. Kenny to see if that firearm could be consistent with the fired bullet recovered at the crime scene and he said that was a possibility."

It was not until April 23, C-Day for Confession-Day, that Moilanen admitted to owning a Savage.

"How did he disclose it?" Paczesny asked.

"He stated that that was the weapon he had used to shoot his wife," Ball said, "and gave me more details on that particular weapon."

Ball was now into his interview with Moilanen at the Marquette Crime Lab. He had taken over following Lt. Allen's interview and he was offering Moilanen varying scenarios of what had happened.

"Bruce," he had said to Moilanen, "you shot your wife, didn't you?" Silence.

"Bruce, you did it, didn't you?"

"I did," he quoted Moilanen as saying, "but it wasn't for Gayle."

"We had previously talked about Gayle," Ball told the jury, "and I had brought in several things...including what I call The Sweater Letter. I asked him who wrote that letter and then I said, 'You wrote that letter, didn't you?' And I put it right in front of him. He didn't give me a verbal response, but he gave me a head nod."

If not for Gayle, why?

"He said his wife was a tyrant at work and a tyrant at home," Ball said. "He gave a whole list of reasons."

Ball went through a list, as recited by the defendant, which included a threatened divorce, the loss of Elise, poor cooking, preoccupation with her job and even a perceived affair with an architect from Texas.

The jury was now absorbing the fact of a confession along with a succession of reasons that did not add up to justification of murder. Paczesny led Ball through the damning interview of April 23, from the purchase of the gun to the pulling of the trigger to the flight from the scene and the disposition of the weapon.

Tom Casselman was about to get his long-awaited shot at Det. Sgt. Bob Ball. This was strictly business, of course. Onlookers who would watch as he picked at the investigation, sarcastically at times, would hardly believe he had a soft side. Det. Sgt. Don Poupore, Ball's partner, was missing from the trial because he had undergone back surgery in mid-November. Casselman visited him at his home after the surgery to inquire as to his health and comfort.

As Casselman rose to cross-examine, Bob Ball's comfort would not be a consideration.

Through his questions, Casselman was able to portray Bill Burgess as a gofer for the medical examiner, criticize Ball for examining the body the night of the death, call into question whether Judy had been stripped or clothed and review Dr. Castilla's testimony that he could not remember police unilaterally examining a body in his 25 years of doing autopsies.

"Perhaps Dr. Castilla saw it many times and didn't remember it," Ball said.

"So you would say Dr. Castilla doesn't have a very good memory?"

"I would have to go along with that," Ball nodded. "Plus, he doesn't make many notes, nor does he tape-record like many pathologists do."

"So you were fearful about Dr. Castilla's handling of this matter?"

"I had some concerns," Ball said. "Yes, I did."

And, yes, he had concerns about Deputy Cousineau's camera work.

"Many of my own people have problems with a 35mm camera," Ball said. "It's not a cut on the deputy."

"So you were going to get there and…"

"I did it my way," Ball interjected.

Casselman hit at the failure to find tracks near the scene and proceeded to query Ball on why Moilanen's footgear was not examined. This should have been a moot point, since tracks had not been found, but this was another play to the jury casting aspersions about the police work in the immediate aftermath of the death.

Ball was a battler, but a quiet battler. He admitted that he came away from the Blake house the night of the incident with the impression that Moilanen had been elsewhere, but described the scene in the kitchen and dining room where he had talked with Dale and David Blake and Bruce Moilanen.

"The answers," he said, "more or less came from Dale and David."

"Then they were the lying persons?" Casselman said.

"I wouldn't call it a lie," Ball said. "Their faces were drawn and their color was poor. They looked like they were in shock. They had lost a daughter and sister. Bruce looked much different."

"He looked much different...and *they* were the ones lying?"

"He let it pass," Ball said, "because it was to his benefit."

"Isn't there just as likely a conclusion that this guy is in a state of shock?"

"He did not appear to be in a state of shock," Ball said. "In fact, he criticized his wife to me. A flag went up. He brought it to my attention she was not wearing orange that day. This man was criticizing his wife who was just killed. That I thought was unusual."

This investigative process, Casselman suggested, seemed to focus rather quickly on his client.

"Mr. Moilanen was a suspect within how much time?" Casselman asked.

"In the first 24 hours, you have to look at the husband," Ball said. "After 48 hours, I had received the Gayle information, if you want to call it that. Probably within 72 hours we were starting to get rumblings that the defendant was not at the hunting camp with the family. By Dec. 15, when I had the bank record in my hand with the gun record, having done the Dec. 11 interview and having learned about the life insurance policies, I would say the defendant was a strong suspect from that point forward."

"How soon do you say we're done here in River City? There ain't nobody else?"

"That would have been within three weeks of the shooting, that he was the only real suspect."

Ball emphasized *real* suspect, maintaining that investigators did not close doors on other leads. The detective detailed investigations into tracks in Turpeinen's Clear-Cut, Schoch's guests and the juvenile who might have been hunting in the Christmas tree farm across M-38. Police were not, he said, investigating the husband to the exclusion of other possibilities.

And about this Gayle Lampinen? Where did you get this Gayle information?

"Sheriff Jim Ruotsala of the Houghton County Sheriff's Department," Ball said. "The information was that Moilanen had a woman at Portage View Hospital that he was stalking. That's the way it came to me."

"Stalking?"

"It bordered on stalking," Ball said, "but that's much too strong a term for it. Some people just have a hard time confronting other people and saying 'Don't bother me anymore.' Gayle was one of those persons. She was just a nice person who couldn't hurt his feelings."

◆   ◆   ◆

Court watchers by now had come up with their own characterization of Casselman. Each day's activities during the trial were reported and spread by word of mouth throughout Ontonagon almost faster than the five minutes it took to get from the courthouse to the main street. And Casselman was perceived as a Dick Cavett lookalike with the demeanor of Attila the Hun, a description he would likely find more amusing than denigrating.

One of the hottest stories in the streets was, in truth, an unspoken moment. Casselman was doing his "lookabout," gazing randomly around the room while addressing a witness, when he inadvertently caught Mary Ann Blake's eye. She gave him one of those looks that could kill and then mouthed words for Casselman's eyes only. He was startled, taken aback, then looked at the witness to regain his train of thought.

For his part, Casselman's task at hand was his portrayal of Det. Ball and, by extension, the investigation. He was depicting Ball as a dictatorial state cop who rode into town and usurped local authorities, sending, for example, Deputy Cousineau to do, by implication, meaningless busy work at the ski hill. The detective would launch a veritable vendetta against the husband, building on illusion rather than reality. The attorney implied more than once that others had changed their stories to fit the needs of the investigation.

Day Seven, Dec. 10, was a Friday and it began with Det. Sgt. Ball on the witness stand and defense attorney Casselman at the podium, leaning on one elbow. He started by pounding once again on Moilanen's footwear, then abruptly switched to Marsha LaFernier and the two men she and her children had seen down Cherry Lane.

"Can I stand corrected on one thing, Mr. Casselman?" Ball asked.

"Sure."

"I received a request from Marsha LaFernier yesterday to stop and see her at the restaurant," Ball explained.

Ironically, LaFernier worked at Syl's, a main street Ontonagon restaurant that was responsible for feeding Moilanen and all of the other prisoners, few though there usually were, in the Ontonagon County Jail.

"Did she give you any news?" Casselman asked.

"No, just that she was a little bit concerned about testifying."

LaFernier was on the list of defense witnesses and she was far from thrilled that she might be called to testify.

"You mean she lives in this community and being called by the defense was a problem?" Casselman said wryly.

"She was just concerned."

"Am I right?"

"She felt bad she was being called by the defense."

Regardless of whether he would ultimately call the reluctant LaFernier as a defense witness, Casselman chose to use her to cast doubt through the detective. He entered into a dialogue about Schoch's guests who were supposedly walking along Cherry Lane the morning of the shooting and the men LaFernier originally said she had seen in the afternoon.

"Then two total strangers were down there in that community at 2:45, sir, relatively close in time to when you say these particular events occurred, two persons you've never interviewed. Correct?"

His voice was running up and down a scale, but it did not sound musical to Ball. Casselman used vocal inflection to accent "total strangers" and "you say" and "you've never interviewed." He was trying to put other shooters in an area where the prosecution could not put Moilanen.

Ball had to concede it was a possibility, but only if LaFernier had not become confused about what she saw on which occasion she was leaving her driveway that day. He was convinced she had mixed up what she saw and when. Casselman, however, used this occasion to once again suggest Ball was gerrymandering facts to sit his needs, believing what he wanted to believe.

The defense attorney abruptly changed to money as a motive.

"Bankruptcy relieves debt, doesn't it?" he said. "And they were consolidating loans to lower their payments?"

Again, these were statements as much as questions. Ball, at one point, was sarcastically addressed as "Mr. Detective," just as Connie Swander had been called "Scientist." Casselman was on the subject of money as a motive and now he suggested to Ball that the defendant did not know what life insurance monies were available.

"You're trying to insinuate he didn't know," Ball said with outer calm, "and there's no way he could not have known, not when he was orchestrating all this stuff with the agents himself."

"That's your opinion."

"We have physical evidence."

Casselman continued with questions that essentially answered themselves, Ball as often as not disagreeing. Impatiently, the detective listened to a convoluted statement disguised as a question and leaned forward.

"What *is* the question now?" he asked.

They continued to spar and Casselman moved to the asset list that included the Savage 110.

"Did you have that listed examined," he asked, "to determine on whose or which or what typewriter, sir?"

Maybe Bruce Moilanen had *not* typed that list. The attorney had to blow some smoke into the jury room. He drew an admission that a typed list was "somewhat inconclusive," but Ball illustrated how far-fetched he considered that notion by suggesting Casselman could have typed it.

"Now," Casselman said, "it's more likely, in our hypothesis, that you would have done it, isn't it?"

Ball had gone to an extreme with his illustration and Casselman had come back in his face with an equally extreme idea, that police had planted evidence.

"If you're going to suggest to this jury, Mr. Casselman, that I made up a document and inserted it into the file, then I think maybe you should come up with some sort of factual basis to throw out that type of red herring here today."

"Whose idea," Casselman asked, "was this that *I* might have typed this, mine or yours?"

"You brought up the point that anybody could have typed it."

The entire exchange, while ludicrous, underscored the concept that anybody could, in fact, have typed the list. Casselman, for his part, had made that point. However, Ball, as the person answering questions, had successfully raised the question of exactly who would have planted such a list in a bank asset package...and why.

Casselman's approach had become very peripatetic. He attacked the confession and the fact that Ball had chosen to believe some of what Moilanen had said, specifically incriminating statements, but not all that he had said.

"He says Judy was a bad person," Casselman said, "but you don't believe that."

Mary Ann Blake got up and walked out of the courtroom.

"I didn't believe all of the reasons," Ball said, "but I did believe the confession."

"The reasons are all baloney?" Casselman said.

It definitely was not a question. Ball did not respond.

Considerable time was spent on the various alibi lists, but the gap between 11 a.m. and 2:45 to 3 p.m. simply would not go away. Wade Johnson's original, and vague, acknowledgment to Moilanen that their near-collision near Tank Creek could have been between 2:15 and 2:30 had been debunked by Lori Johnson's more specific recollection based on the time she had to be at work. The defense *might* have had a rather insurmountable alibi if Lori Johnson had the day off that Sunday.

Casselman eventually worked his way to the confession...and then back *from* the confession. He needed to plant reasons why the confession should not be believed, the principal reason being that Moilanen was so beleaguered by the investigation that he admitted to something he didn't do.

Everywhere Moilanen turned, Casselman suggested, he encountered people who had been interviewed, some repeatedly, about his possible involvement. Family. Employees at Marquette General. Insurance agents. Bankers. Neighbors. Baby sitters. Friends.

"Friends?" Ball said. "I don't believe I found anybody like that."

Casselman had made his point that investigators were hounding Moilanen to a breaking point. And Ball had retorted with a subtle, though unrelated, point about people's feelings for the defendant. These subtleties, both knew, would play at jurors' minds.

The absence of a weapon was a point Casselman could underscore. He did it by relating that Moilanen said he threw the gun into the Ford River on the way to Green Bay on Dec. 17.

"You would have found it when you searched on the 11th, true?" Casselman said.

Ball had been insisting all along that he did not believe Moilanen's story about the disposal of the gun. He could insist until he was blue in the face, but Casselman would use that insistence to suggest the confession, thus, was not to be believed.

"He's throwing it away six days after you searched? It doesn't fit. It's a crock. It's not true. Moilanen got caught with his own bull." Casselman continued as though he were Moilanen. "I can't have thrown the gun away, because I never had it. I couldn't have done it."

Ball twisted his neatly trimmed moustache and looked quizzically at the attorney.

"What *is* the question?" he asked.

"Isn't all that true? It doesn't fit. None of it."

"He could have discarded the gun prior to the 11th and was just not willing to cough up all the evidence or, as I would say, completely throw in the towel here."

Casselman, the bulldog, was snarling.

"Where's the scope?…Where's the shell?"

Neither had been found. Casselman pressed forward on the notion that they were not found because they did not exist. Ball steadfastly insisted either would be easy to hide, noting that a killer could have thrown the shell almost anywhere. The largest fresh-water lake in the world was a few hundred yards away, for example.

The Casselmans had one more area they wanted to explore and maybe exploit. They had noted that the forensic report from Connie

Swander, the scientist, had noted the presence of a blue fiber on the bullet, which was inconsistent with the victim's black jacket and fuchsia shirt. The attorney had chosen not to address this issue with Swander herself, which may have surprised the prosecution. He determined that it might be tactically more effective to take it up at the end of his cross-examination of Ball, giving the detective a few more anxious moments and maybe raising doubt at a point where the jury would remember it more distinctly.

"And last, sir, the bullet," Casselman said. "How do you reconcile the blue cotton fiber?"

"It could have been a blue cotton fiber from Mr. Moilanen's blue jeans," Ball said. "It could have been something off my clothing at the time that I picked up the bullet. Highly unlikely, but it's a foreign fiber that has not been identified. I cannot really reconcile it."

"Are you suggesting you were clumsy? Or that it isn't particularly the bullet?"

"You can call it clumsy," Ball said, "but I will never believe that that is not the bullet."

Tom Casselman was finished with Ball at 3:30 on Day Seven. He had used statements disguised as questions as well as a tone of voice that bordered at times on the incredulous to try to weaken Ball's testimony and, in turn, the prosecution's case. Ball had never wavered in either his conclusions or how he reached them and tossed in jabs of his own for the jury's benefit. It had been like a heavyweight title fight, but the decision was far from determined.

Paczesny's re-direct was swift. She did not want to lose the jury's attention with another lengthy series of questions. Ball, she thought, had fared well in his battle with the defense attorney. She limited her questions to areas where she thought Casselman might have created a bit of uncertainty and closed with a series of questions about confessions.

"Detective Ball," she asked, "how many confessions have you taken in your lifetime?"

"I would have to say several hundred," Ball said. "Not everything in all of them was true, but Bruce Moilanen had to be there when Judy was killed to know what he knew."

◆   ◆   ◆

Beth Paczesny returned after a recess and Bob Ball followed her pushing a two-wheeled cart. It contained a chimney block and onlookers gasped when they saw the block's size and contemplated its weight. People's Exhibit 48 was an effective visual tool, but Paczesny had to create the impression that it could not have fallen accidentally without saying as much.

Elise had told family members on one occasion and a stranger on another that she had seen her father drop the block on her mother's head, but neither Paczesny nor Ball thought it wise to put her on the witness stand. She was, after all, four years old and she had been two years younger when the incident occurred. Elise was so young and so innocent she would hardly be traumatized by such an experience, but they just did not want the youngster exposed to such a scenario.

Instead, Paczesny called Trooper Don Brown and EMTs Tom Flynn and Brad Wyman. They were the three at the scene on Sept. 23, 1991 and they testified to what they saw on arrival and what they did not see. They had heard, from Moilanen, that the block had accidentally fallen from the roof while Judy was cutting flashing on the patio. They had not seen a scaffold, collapsed or otherwise.

"Is this block similar to the one you found next to Judy?" Paczesny asked Brown.

"It's the same size, shape and form," he said.

"Did you talk with Judy?"

"She was in and out of consciousness," Brown recalled. "She couldn't remember what had happened."

Paczesny worked her way to the experiment.

"Don Poupore said we were going to do an experiment of the incident," Brown said. "He said it may or may not be helpful to the current case."

Jurors looked at the block and they looked at Brown and they looked at Paczesny in anticipation of an explanation. They also looked at a television set in front of them.

Beth Paczesny turned on the television and jurors watched and listened as the State of Michigan's finest jumped up and down on the roof of Bruce Moilanen's house in Harvey. They too could see that these blocks don't slide around like wet bars of soap.

Tom Casselman had no cross-examination for any of the witnesses from the scene of the chimney block incident.

"I have a continuing objection," he said crossly. "Other than that, I have no comment."

He was adamantly against the inclusion of any testimony relating to an event that occurred more than a year before Judy's death. Only one person could testify as to precisely what happened that day and Casselman was not about to put him on the stand.

◆　　　◆　　　◆

Another weekend intervened between Day Seven and Day Eight. The prosecution had two witnesses remaining. Casselman and his partner, Roger Kangas, meanwhile, had gone to Moilanen's house and retrieved a scaffold.

"Where is it?" Casselman had asked Moilanen.

"Beside the house."

Casselman and Kangas went to the Harvey home in field boots and mucked around in a few feet of snow looking for the scaffold and found the parts they needed to put it back together.

"Roger," Casselman frowned, "I don't see any nail holes."

He threw the wood into the back of a truck.

Casselman virtually stormed into the law library on Monday.

"Bruce, Ball's right," he snapped. "There aren't any nail holes. It's a lie."

"There *are* holes," Moilanen insisted. "You can't rely on what Ball told you. I'll show you."

Casselman, who had the scaffold with him, looked closely, almost squinting, and saw what looked like nail holes. Maybe they had been squeezed shut as moisture caused the wood to expand.

When Casselman hauled the scaffold into the courtroom, it had nail holes where a second leg might have been attached. The two legs on one side and no legs on the other side would create a flat surface on which to work with material on a slanting roof. The experimental videotape, plus the 35mm photographs, showed a scaffold with no nail holes.

Bob Ball was back on the witness stand and, for the first time, he was visibly perturbed. Inside, he was more than perturbed. He was seething with anger. Casselman had surprised the prosecution by bring the scaffold into the courtroom, entering it as Exhibit No. 502.

"All indications are that this is the platform," Ball said, after stepping from the stand for a closer inspection. "One thing is different. There are two small nail holes that were not there when I last looked at this platform."

"Are you able, Detective, to tell us that that is the platform?"

"Being that this thing has been altered," Ball said, "I would like to look it over a little bit closer."

Casselman had previously objected to the entire issue of The Chimney Block Incident as irrelevant to what happened Nov. 29, 1992, but he himself spent virtually all of the morning of Dec. 13, 1993 in vigorous debate with Ball over the existence of nail holes in the scaffold. The man was obviously quick on his feet, because he had come to the courtroom that morning convinced that those very holes did not exist.

Ball, subjected to another morning of critical interrogation, was very unhappy with the implications thrown in the direction of the investigation.

"We examined that scaffolding very carefully in good sunlight," he told Paczesny during the lunch break, "and the holes were not there. If they had been, it would have been functional at one time."

Ball had held his temper inside, though he knew Casselman himself was above altering evidence. However, he was convinced that the defendant's family had tampered with the scaffold and that Casselman himself had been duped. These were things he could not have said on the witness stand.

Casselman's point was that the cops had made a mistake and nothing could make Ball more irate…and there was nothing he could do but tersely relay what he had seen.

All of this had to be confusing to the jury, because Moilanen himself had offered versions of the incident where a scaffold was not mentioned, Trooper Brown had seen no scaffold the day of the incident and Casselman was objecting to the whole concept of the inclusion of that incident anyway.

◆   ◆   ◆

David Blake and Mike Niemi were the last prosecution witnesses, taking the stand after the lunch recess on Monday, Dec. 13.

Niemi, actually the last witness, was asked about Moilanen's skills with a rifle.

"He was steady," Niemi said. "A good shot. He killed several big bucks he had mounted. The furthest shot I saw was maybe 200 yards, but he used to brag he shot a power pole out by Gardner Tower and that it was four poles out. He said it was 100 yards between them."

Niemi testified about the day of the killing, taking time off to be with Moilanen in the aftermath and trips he made with the defendant. Niemi had not been included in the very tight inner-circle who knew why the investigation was focusing on Bruce Moilanen, whom he considered to be a friend as well as cousin-in-law.

The jury heard Niemi testify about his jailhouse conversations with the defendant.

"I asked him how the situation happened and he told me he just snapped," Niemi said. "He told me he must be crazy because only a crazy man could do what he did. I asked, 'Why not divorce? We could all have lived with divorce and still be here as friends.' He said that his friend Gayle talked him out of divorce."

That was Niemi's first jailhouse visit. Paczesny wanted him to describe an apparent change of heart, or at least a change of story, Niemi encountered when next he visited.

"At that time," Niemi recalled, "he asked me if I thought he was nuts. At that time, he told me he didn't do it…he didn't kill Judy. He was trying to make people think he was nuts."

Niemi testified that Moilanen told him he might get away with 18 months in a "nuthouse" if he could mount an insanity defense.

"He said that's what his lawyer told him," Niemi said.

Niemi testified that he excused himself and asked John Gravier, the undersheriff, not to allow Moilanen to call him again. The one person who had fervently stood by him was gone.

David Blake had preceded his cousin. He was an impressive witness, straightforward and honest. He had suspected Bruce Moilanen from the moment he heard what had happened, but kept it to himself.

Paczesny worked him matter-of-factly through events leading up to and following his sister's death. She was headed toward the telephone calls *he* got from his sister's widower from the Ontonagon County Jail. David Blake was a touching witness as he talked about forgiveness, in spite of what Moilanen admitted to him he had done to Judy Blake Moilanen.

"Bruce called me at home April 26," David testified, "and told me, 'I don't think I'll ever be able to explain why it happened.' He told me he tried to hang himself, but they got there too early. I'm assuming the police."

"What did you say?"

"I told him the hell he's going through now is nothing compared to the next. Then we went into what I consider spiritual things. I told him I can forgive him, but what he needs was to seek the forgiveness of God."

David told the jury of the painful things the defendant had said about his sister, even as he was extending forgiveness. Moilanen had told him how two-sided Judy had been and about her threats to leave him.

David's voice was steady. He showed none of the emotion he was surely feeling.

Casselman could not do much with David Blake, though he did take a stab at portraying the young man as a person who figured to benefit from the insurance money due Elise. Blake, after all, was Elise's guardian.

"Who gets the money connected with the child?" Casselman asked.

"On the one policy," David said, "I'm the beneficiary…with the understanding that it was for the child."

"If there's no trust set up, how is it that the child gets the money?"

"You have to trust me," Blake said simply.

Jurors may not have known David Blake, but they could not help but seeing him as a most trustworthy individual. With utmost sincerity, he explained that nothing had been done to access any of the life insurance money that might be available. This was not a person who seemed interested in the material side of life.

Casselman tried to poke holes in David Blake's willingness to forgive, but David was adamant.

"I did offer my forgiveness," he said, "but he still has to be accountable."

◆   ◆   ◆

The prosecution rested its case at 3:22 p.m. on Day Eight. The defense had subpoenaed 29 witnesses, accounting for many of the strange faces in the courtroom. Word had spread that Moilanen's mother was also in the courthouse, ready to testify on his behalf.

Beth Paczesny settled back into her chair. She and Ball were ready to go to the notes they had gathered from interviews with witnesses on Casselman's list, most of whom were names from Moilanen's assorted alibi lists.

Gotham was organizing papers on his desk. He had sat through all these days and all these witnesses, but he felt the last two—David Blake and Mike Niemi—had been the most effective for the prosecution. Moilanen's jailhouse admissions to David and Mike carried more weight than a confession made to police detectives. These thoughts he had to keep to himself.

It was time for the defense to take its shots.

"Mr. Casselman?" Gotham said, looking up with a countenance that blended the curious and the serious.

Court watchers looked with anticipation at the defense table, where Casselman was slowly getting to his feet, gazing downward as if to check his notes.

Prosecutor and detective were prepared for anything but what they heard.

"Thank you, Your Honor," Tom Casselman said. "The defense rests."

"Excuse me?" Gotham said.

"The defense rests."

◆　　　◆　　　◆

Ontonagon was stunned by the abrupt conclusion of testimony. Another week of defense witnesses had been anticipated. Paczesny, who had not even begun to outline her closing argument, was headed for a sleepless night. Only Casselman had known that testimony would end when the prosecution rested its case.

Gotham had expressed the surprise of the whole community with two words.

"Excuse me?"

Conversational wildfires came to the conclusion that Casselman had rested because none of the defense witnesses could account for Moilanen's whereabouts at the time of the shooting. It would take such a witness to punch a hole in the prosecution's case.

Casselman had two such witnesses…for awhile. He had Wade Johnson, who had conceded to Moilanen that 2:15 could have been when they crossed paths, and he had Marcia LaFernier, who had seen the strangers down Cherry Lane. Neither Johnson nor LaFernier were precise in their recollections and that left them vulnerable.

"LaFernier didn't want to testify," Casselman said later. "She was calling Ball asking how she could be excused."

"Who knows what she might have said," Mrs. Casselman added. "You don't put a witness on the stand when you don't know what the answers are going to be."

Significantly, Paczesny had not called LaFernier either. She likely had the same concerns. Ball essentially testified on her behalf through recollections of his interviews with her.

"When Ball screwed up Wade Johnson," Casselman continued, "there was no alibi witness for the exact moment."

In truth, Johnson's memory was not altered by Ball as much as it was jogged by his wife Lori's certainty of the time she had to be at work. Neither Johnson testified either, again Ball detailing interviews with them.

"Ball," Rhonda Casselman said, "went through all the testimony of any value."

Casselman could only play with the concept of time of death, arguing through his questioning of assorted witnesses that 2:15 was hardly cast in stone. He had created confusion, particularly with Dr. Hugo Castilla, and there was no one further he could call to debate this critical issue.

One "potential" witness was sitting two seats away from him... Bruce Moilanen. The gossip around town was that Moilanen's ego was such that he would insist on taking the stand.

"I didn't think he'd be able to handle it," Casselman said later. "Peggy Sue (Paczesny) would have been in his face, whacking him around. He would have been up there for days under cross-examination. I couldn't put him up there and have him trying to explain what he said in his confession. I'm his lawyer and I'd be sitting there with no idea what he might say."

Casselman's concern as the defense team filed out of the courtroom was the last two witnesses. Gotham, from his perch, had come to the same conclusion. David Blake and Mike Niemi were tough witnesses, testifying to Moilanen's jailhouse admissions.

"Before them," Casselman said, "we had the police form of a confession. They believed what they wanted to believe out of *that* confession."

"The other two," Mrs. Casselman said, "those were the nails."

Tom Casselman had used the prosecution's witnesses to create uncertainty and confusion in many areas with many witnesses, but only jurors knew if he had significantly damaged the prosecution's case.

◆　　　◆　　　◆

The day of closing arguments, Dec. 14, began on a bizarre note. Two jurors were called into Gotham's chambers. They were called individually...and dismissed.

Shortly thereafter, word spread that radio station WUPY had reported that one of the jurors was dismissed because she had had an affair with one of the witnesses. Gotham was incensed, labeling the report indiscriminate and incorrect. Ultimately, he met with the reporter and his superiors and banned him from further involvement in coverage of his court.

Skip Schulz, WUPY's general manager, wrote a letter of apology that ran in the next week's *Ontonagon Herald*. The same edition covered the verdict on Bruce Moilanen as well as the fact that Jerry Schoch, who had testified as to the time he heard a shot, had been sentenced to 12 months in the Ontonagon County Jail after pleading guilty to the use and manufacture of methcathinone.

In this atmosphere of turmoil and controversy, Beth Paczesny presented her closing remarks. She went for 26 minutes, essentially outlining the case as it had been presented.

"The Sweater Letter," she said, "set the tone for this case. Hey, don't tell the other prospects, but he's great in the sack. What kind of a letter is that?"

Until then, bits and pieces had caused detectives to be suspicious of the defendant, but this letter had shocked them into narrowing the focus of their investigation. A man who wrote such a letter, attributing it to his late wife, could do…almost anything?

Paczesny's recitation touched on motives, insurance, admissions, The Chimney Block Incident and that time gap that would not go away. She had to get the confession characterized as more than an unbelievably rambling oratory by a stressed suspect and she had to do it through the testimony of Dets. Ball and Allen.

"We were on the defendant's own terms on April 23, 1993," she said. "The defendant tells us about how he murdered his wife. He knew the caliber of the bullet used. He knew the type of gun was that undisclosed Savage that happened to have a damaged stock. He knew the direction of travel of the bullet. He knew where he was standing. You know why he knew those things, ladies and gentlemen? Because he was there."

She was nearing her conclusion.

"There's evidence to show you, ladies and gentlemen, that the defendant in this case is nothing but a cold-blooded assassin of a woman that he promised to love and cherish."

She sat down to reserve time to rebut Casselman's closing.

As Casselman got to his feet, there was a minor stir two rows behind the prosecution table. Mary Ann and Dale Blake were leaving. They were not going to listen to closing remarks on behalf of the defendant.

Tom Casselman once again characterized Judy Moilanen's death as a hunting accident, disputing the time of death and attacking investigators for what they had not done. He noted again that detectives made no attempt to link Moilanen's boots with tracks along Cherry Lane. He said tests to determine a more specific time of death, such as stomach contents, were not done. He debunked the concept of a time gap being meaningful as well as the concept that Moilanen needed to provide an alibi.

"The law," he said, "says that the defendant need not prove he was elsewhere."

The burden of proof was on the prosecution to prove where he was, not where he wasn't, and Casselman said this had not been accomplished.

It figured he would come back to the entrance-exit wounds and he did, sarcastically detailing one episode after another from Dr. Gervae telling Bill Burgess not to allow the body to be touched to Det. Sgt. Ball advising Dr. Cohle that he had pulled the protruding tissue from the wound as he disregarded Gervae's instructions.

The suspected weapon itself, Casselman said, was on a list of "possibles." Period. There was no certainty, he argued, that a Savage 110 had been the weapon which killed Judy Moilanen.

And then there was Mrs. LaFernier, whose first recollection of when she saw strangers down Cherry Lane raised the potentially threatening question of someone other than Moilanen being in the area near the time of the shooting.

"You have Mrs. LaFernier," Casselman said, "saying, 'I live here. I'm nervous. It would be tough to be called for the defense.'"

Casselman was depicting the investigation to be an exercise in which intimidation was used to cover gaps and blunders. Witnesses were bullied, he suggested, and so was the defendant. He painted a forlorn picture of a Moilanen who could turn nowhere to find someone to trust, not even Gayle Lampinen.

"And then at the end of all that," Casselman said, "he gets dumped by the only person he thought was his listening friend…The last straw, she's an informant. All those things of your inner-most being that you told her are being used."

The attorney was shaking his head.

"All stress is not physical," he said. "We all reach a point when we've all had it. And we've all said, 'I've had it.' Or we've heard our parents say, 'I've had it. You've pushed me over the edge. I've reached it with you.'"

This, he argued, was the point Moilanen had reached with the investigators, the point that culminated with the confession of April 23.

"The prosecutor's argument this morning is that this guy never tells it the way it is," Casselman said, "except…when he makes some blithering idiot confession."

Tom Casselman argued the case for 63 minutes and concluded that the prosecution's burden was to prove its case beyond reasonable doubt. That, he said, had not been done. He sat down. He had done all he could do.

Beth Paczesny took 21 minutes with her rebuttal, but one sentence encompassed the sentiment she wanted to leave with the jury.

"Bruce Moilanen was hunting that day," she said, "but he was hunting his wife."

◆   ◆   ◆

Judge Roy Gotham instructed the jury in the criteria to be considered in assessing various verdicts: first degree premeditated murder, second degree murder or, of course, not guilty. He warned once again that the chimney block incident was not to be a factor in the deliberation of guilt vs. innocence, only premeditation and intent should guilt be determined.

The jury now had Bruce Moilanen's fate in its hands.

◆   ◆   ◆

The morning of Dec. 15, 1993, one year and 16 days after the murder, was relatively mild. The temperature was in the mid-30s, but a cloud cover shrouded Ontonagon in darkness until 8:30. Jurors returning to the courthouse pulled into the parking lot with their lights on.

The second floor was eerily quiet after the jury began its first full day of deliberation. Deputy Terry Dove sat in front of the door to the jury room, Sheriff Jerry Kitzman sat in the back and Undersheriff John Gravier stood in the aisle. Reporter Sonja Chrisman from Marquette's Channel 6 sat where Ball had sat at the prosecution table and played solitaire.

Conversation was idle, but anxious. Paczesny walked in.

"I think we presented a solid case," Kitzman said. "I feel good about it."

"I dreamed about this all night," Paczesny said, "and it came out guilty every time."

The hallway outside the courtroom was empty, but voices came from outside the prosecutor's office behind the elevator. The Blake family and friends had formed a private sitting area of their own and they were talking quietly. No one intruded on their anxiety. David Blake, for one, was confident because of eye contact he had made with a couple of jurors as they filed into the courtroom.

Life was at a standstill, yet life was going on. Judge Roy Gotham advised bailiffs at 10:15 that he would be out for maybe 30 minutes. He had to run downtown to pick up a table.

At 11:12, the 22-year-old from Bruce Crossing opened the door from the jury room and handed a note to the bailiff. He folded it without a glance and went across the room to the judge's chambers. Adrenaline pumped each time one of these notes had come from jurors to judge.

One note, early the previous afternoon, had contained a juror's complaint that a soft drink had not been delivered with his lunch as well as, more significantly, a request for a review of Jon Lyle's testimony of Dec. 7. Lyle was the Action Shopper account executive who testified to selling a Savage 110, but stopped short of saying he had sold it to the defendant. Jurors wondered if they had missed something. They had not, of course, because Gotham had ruled that detectives used inappropriate procedures in making the identification.

Another note had been a request for Rolaids. All eyes were on Gotham's door, deputies wondering if they were going to be sent on another shopping trip or...

The verdict was in after six hours and 39 minutes of deliberation.

Suddenly, it was as if a hush settled over all of Ontonagon. Wordlessly, the Blake entourage filed into the courtroom. The previously empty hallway was filled with people who seemingly popped out of the woodwork. The courtroom was filled with people and tension. Paczesny and Ball were in place when the door on the right side opened and the Casselmans and Moilanen came in.

All eyes watched the 12 jurors as they took their places. Maybe their eyes or their body language would give them away. They sat stone-faced, staring straight ahead. The young man who had been at the end of the second row was now in front. Jeffrey Vlahos had been the foreperson, not merely a gofer.

The verdict slip went from Vlahos' hand to the bailiff's hand to clerk Julienne Takala's hand. *Her* hands were shaking. She was almost afraid of what she might read. She took a deep breath and looked down.

"As to Count One," she said, her voice breaking, "the jury finds Bruce Robert Moilanen guilty of first degree premeditated murder."

The courtroom itself seemed to gasp. Dale Blake's strong arms surrounded his wife as she broke into tears. Paczesny turned and hugged

Ball. Eyes were awash with tears throughout the room. Takala, fighting emotion herself, read the guilty verdict on the felony firearm count, but it was so anticlimactic it went almost unheard.

Only one person in the room seemed stoic and untouched by the emotion of the moment.

Bruce Robert Moilanen.

Epilogue

Bruce Robert Moilanen was sentenced to life without parole on Jan. 21, 1994. He was sent initially to Marquette Branch Prison, where he was visited a few days later.

"I was tried and convicted by the media before I ever got into court," he said.

He has exhausted his appeals and lost a legal battle for parental rights.

◆　　　◆　　　◆

Tom Casselman no longer represents Bruce Moilanen. He had done what he could do with what little he had.

"I felt we'd earned a moral victory when the jury didn't come back in 10 minutes," he said. "I knew we'd done a good job, but I didn't have any doubt they would convict."

◆　　　◆　　　◆

Bob Ball and Don Poupore were both commended by the Michigan State Police for their work on the Moilanen case, as were Gayle Lampinen and Lee Anne Wysocki for their cooperation.

Ball also received another "award," this one from the Casselmans. At one point in the proceedings, the attorney had inadvertently referred to the detective as Dr. Ball. When the Casselmans went to one of Dr. Werner Spitz's seminars on investigative pathology, they obtained an updated copy of his book, *Medical-Legal Investigation of Death*, and had Spitz autograph it.

"To Dr. Ball…"

◆   ◆   ◆

Beth Paczesny has moved from Ontonagon County to Escanaba, where she is now Delta County's chief assistant prosecutor.

The last murder in Ontonagon County was Nov. 29, 1992.

◆   ◆   ◆

David and Yvonne Blake have adopted Elise Moilanen.

0-595-65446-0

Printed in the United States
62697LVS00004B/107